Evictionism

Walter E. Block

Evictionism

The compromise solution to the pro-life pro-choice debate controversy

Springer

Walter E. Block
Miller Hall 318, Box 15
Loyola University New Orleans
New Orleans, LA, USA

ISBN 978-981-16-5016-1 ISBN 978-981-16-5014-7 (eBook)
https://doi.org/10.1007/978-981-16-5014-7

This Springer imprint is published by the registered company Springer Nature Singapore Pte Ltd.
The registered company address is: 152 Beach Road, #21-01/04 Gateway East, Singapore 189721, Singapore

Acknowledgements

I am greatly in the debt of David Gordon for substantive comments on previous versions of several of the essays in this book. I would also like to thank Antón Chamberlin, Leith Edgar, and Anthony J. Cesario for putting this material together and their valuable editing contributions. In addition, Michael R. Edelstein and Matthew A. Block have made helpful comments. I am inspired by John Locke, Murray N. Rothbard, Hans-Hermann Hoppe, and Stephan Kinsella who have brilliantly made the case for private property rights and stressed their application to pretty much all that matters in political economy. Here, I apply these insights to yet another area of contention.

Contents

The original version of this book was revised: The book was inadvertently published with a typo error in the title which has been corrected now. The correction to this book is available at https://doi.org/10.1007/978-981-16-5014-7_13

Part I
Introduction

Chapter 1
Introduction

The present book is a presentation of how a libertarian, me, analyzes the controversial issue of abortion. Not only is this a contentious issue on the part of members of the general public, this applies to libertarians as well. Libertarians are a particularly contentious lot on many issues; on this one, even more so. Our opinions on this vital issue ranges all the way from Murray Rothbard, on the "left" who favors the pro-choice position, to Ron Paul on the "right" who is an ardent pro-lifer. Nor are these two gentlemen fringe members of this movement. Rothbard has been rightly characterized as "Mr. Libertarian" and Ron Paul's libertarian credentials would be difficult to equal.

Why is this? Why is it that so much heat, and not as much light, has been spent on this issue, both within the libertarian community and in the general public? Why is this, perhaps, an issue upon which our nation may fracture?[1] Why is it that this is perhaps the most divisive issue threatening to rend our social fabric since the unpleasantness of 1861?

I suggest it is due to the fact that we, all of us, scholars and the man in the street, have been talking past one another. It is as if an automobile in an accident were painted red on one side and blue on the other[2] and the witnesses were vociferous in contradicting one another.

It is also as if two people were arguing about the proper legal status of a labor strike, and one thought it consisted of employees laying down their tools and

[1] The Supreme Court hearings on Brett Kavanaugh were in one sense concerned about his fitness as a judge. But, lurking in the undergrowth, it cannot be denied, were fears and hopes that he would cast the deciding vote in some upcoming case concerning Roe v. Wade.

[2] These illustrative colors were not chosen purposefully, but now that I mention them, it is beyond me why red states are categorized as the preserve of the Republicans and blue is reserved for the Democrats. Should it not be the other way around? Who started this color scheme anyway?

W. E. Block, *Evictionism*, https://doi.org/10.1007/978-981-16-5014-7_1

engaging in a mass quit, while the other opined it also encompassed engaging in physical violence against "scabs."[3]

What are the specifics in the abortion case? This appellation, too, akin to a labor "strike" commonly refers to two very, very different acts. On the one hand, it signifies a woman expelling, emitting, evicting or in some other way ridding herself of the fetus – in which case it is unclear as to whether the embryo will live or not.[4] On the other hand, there is an entirely different act, also seen as an aspect of this act: killing, murdering, the pre-born child, as in the case of partial birth abortion. Here, the youngster's brains are sucked out of him while still in the womb, and he is pulled out, dead.

The present book will make, hopefully, two contributions. For one thing, it will offer a libertarian analysis of the matter based on private property rights. For another, it will tirelessly, endlessly, boringly, repetitively, insist upon the distinction between transferring the baby out of the mother's body, and outright murder of the infant.[5] I will strongly defend the right of the woman to engage in the former act, even if the young child dies[6] but bitterly oppose the latter, except when it is medically necessary to save the mother's life or health. This book makes the case for evictionism, and refutes numerous objections to it, emanating from both sides of this dispute.

The evictionist position advanced based on these libertarian premises constitutes a compromise between the pro-life and pro-choice philosophy. The former allows neither eviction nor killing; the latter justifies both. The position defended herein allows eviction, but not abortion (eviction plus murder). Hopefully, this compromise will be accepted by both sides of this controversy, and thus lead in the direction of a resolution of this highly contentious issue.

So, before advancing to the case in point, a few words about this philosophy may not be out of order.[7] Libertarianism is a theory of just law. It is predicated upon two pillars. One is the non-aggression principle (NAP): people may act in any manner they wish, except they may not initiate, or threaten, violence against anyone else, or their legitimately owned property. And how do we determine the latter? This is

[3] I think I know why this word is not considered an example of "hate speech" as is the "N" word for blacks, the "K" word for Jews or the "C" or "P" words for women. The powers that be who rule on these sorts of things take the position that African-Americans and females (matters seem to be changing for members of the Jewish faith) are victim groups, alongside unionized workers, but not those, mainly black and Puerto Rican, who compete for these jobs as replacement workers. Go figure.

[4] He will survive, given present medical technology, in the last trimester but not the first two.

[5] The unwanted baby is seen as a trespasser. If an abortion is needed in both these senses, eviction plus killing, in order to save the mother's life, this can be interpreted as an act of self-defense on her part.

[6] As he will in the first two trimesters but not the third.

[7] Organizing libertarians is akin to herding cats. Most supporters of this viewpoint are wildly individualistic. If there are 10 libertarians who are asked a question, there are likely to be 11 or more responses. Thus, I cannot speak for all libertarians; only one; viz., your present author.

based upon the other foundation: homesteading of virgin territory, and any licit title transfer, such as barter, sale, lending, renting, etc.[8]

Pretty much everyone has a strong opinion on this issue, but I must concede, the minds of most people are irrevocably made up, and will not even consider an alternative opinion, even one they have never heard of before, evictionism. Hopefully, there will be at least some individuals with an open mind on this matter; they are the target for this book.

This publication is a real "man bites dog" operation. No one, apart from a few libertarians (most of whom have rejected its thesis) have so much as even heard of the possibility of a third option in this debate. Once this becomes publicized, there is an outside chance that this will break through and become a non-fiction best seller.

One last word in this introduction; I am a male; the overwhelming proportion of the scholars mentioned in this book, and others who have written on this subject, share the same type of chromosomes. And yet, obviously, the subject of this discussion, abortion, disproportionately affects members of the female persuasion. This has led some critics to cry "foul," and even to insist that the analysis of this issue should be left to members of the distaff side. Stuff and nonsense. This objection is part and parcel of what Mises (1998) has called "polylogism": the doctrine that there are separate logics for men and women, and that never the two shall overlap. I reject this notion in its entirety.

References

Mises, Ludwig von. [1949] 1998. *Human Action, Scholars' Edition*. Auburn: Mises Institute. www.mises.org/humanaction/pdf/HumanActionScholars.pdf

Rothbard, Murray N. 1973a. Free Market, Police, Courts, and Law. *Reason*, March, 5–19.

———. 1973b. *For a New Liberty*. New York: Macmillan. http://mises.org/rothbard/newliberty-whole.asp

———. 1998a. *The Ethics of Liberty*. New York: New York University Press. Retrieved from http://www.mises.org/rothbard/ethics/ethics.asp

———. 1998b [1982]. *The Ethics of Liberty*, 40–41, 135–136. Atlantic Highlands: Humanities Press. http://www.mises.org/rothbard/ethics/ethics.asp

[8] For further elaboration, see Rothbard 1973a, b, 1998a, b.

Part II
What Is Evictionism? The Background

Chapter 2
What Is Evictionism?

The abortion controversy is tearing our society apart. Some people are pro-choice, others are pro-life, and never the twain, seemingly, will meet, let alone calmly discuss this issue with each other. This is perhaps the most important controversy to beset our society since the one taking place until 1865. And, it is far less philosophically clear, with cogent arguments made by both sides, unlike that earlier debate.

I offer a compromise position between the pro-life and pro-choice positions, called evictionism. Philosophically, this is a principled compromise. (If A says that 2 + 2 = 4, and B opines that 2 + 2 = 6, then 2 + 2 = 5 is a compromise, but not a principled one, since there is no case to be made in behalf of that assertion other than it splits the other two claims down the middle). The pro-life view will not permit the woman to kill the fetus, nor evict it (before its nine month term);[1] the pro-choice perspective allows both. Evictionism cuts "this baby in half" so to speak, allowing the latter, but not the former. That is, the mother may legally evict her baby at any time, but may not kill the infant, ever.[2] Of course, given present medical technology, the pre-born child is viable outside the womb only in the third trimester. If evicted before that time, the baby will perish.

How is this principled? I rely on the John Lockean homesteading theory of private property rights. The fetus, we posit, is a human being, beginning from the fertilized egg stage; but the mother owns the womb. Therefore, as in the case of any other private property owner, she has the right to evict an unwanted trespasser (think of the case where this young human being is the product of rape), but not to kill him, since that would be murder as he is entirely innocent of any crime, in contrast to his evil rapist father. The pro-life side protects the fetus for nine months; it is illegal for him to be put to death at any time. The pro-life position does not protect the infant at any time during pregnancy; he may legally be killed for the entire gestation

[1] Ideally, I should not refer to the fetus as an "it." More properly, the preborn child should be referred to as a person. However, this appellation is so heavily ingrained in our language that I have not made efforts to avoid such usage. Perhaps I should have.

[2] Except when she does so out of defense: when her life or health are at stake.

W. E. Block, *Evictionism*, https://doi.org/10.1007/978-981-16-5014-7_2

period. Evictionism safeguards the baby for the last trimester, but not the first six months, given present medical technology.

Most people are totally and completely familiar with both the pro-life and pro-choice positions. Virtually no one is cognizant of evictionism. Thus, I risk repetition in saying that the pro-choice philosophy maintains, in effect, that the pregnant woman may evict the fetus, and, also, kill that young person. The pro-life viewpoint takes the position that she may do neither. Evictionism is a compromise perspective. Here, this woman may evict her baby from her "premises" but may not kill him.

This insight constitutes the application of libertarian property rights theory to a vexing controversy, abortion. This compromise solution will not fully please either of the two sides of this debate, but is the only possible reconciliation between the two. Nor are its benefits limited to the fact that the opposing forces in this debate may be brought together. Evictionism, also, is the only philosophical position fully compatible with human rights – our ownership of our own bodies; neither of the other two can make this claim.

There are many, many books and learned articles supporting the pro-life position. There are numerous other publications defending the pro-choice viewpoint. Evictionism is the *only* one that offers a perspective on abortion that is radically different than both. This book is the only one to apply the private property rights theories we all agree upon when referred to issues such as real estate, crime, torts, etc., to abortion. The underlying philosophical contribution of evictionism is that these basic legal premises can be utilized in this controversial case as well as practically everywhere else in law.

With Brett Kavanaugh replacing retiring Justice Anthony Kennedy – who was the main bulwark against the repeal of Roe v. Wade – that Supreme Court ruling will now become an important focus of attention. It might thus be timely at present to consider a compromise between the pro-life and the pro-choice philosophies. Evictionism constitutes a principled compromise, not merely adding up the two positions and dividing by two.

"Abortion" really is a misnomer. It consists of two separate acts, not just one. First, evicting the fetus from the womb. Second, killing the pre-born baby. The two are conceptually distinct, since even with present medical technology, it is entirely possible to evict the fetus without killing him, in the third trimester. (This is similar to "labor strike;" it too consists of two separate acts: downing tools, on the one hand, and preventing "scabs" from taking over the jobs, temporarily abandoned).

When does human life begin? I posit, arguendo, it is with the fertilized egg. (In the Jewish tradition, it is when the fetus graduates from medical school!) Why? Two reasons. First, the baby one hour before birth, and one hour afterwards, looks as much alike as all of us reading this book, two hours apart. Birth is merely a change of address. Second, so as to avoid a strawman argument. Evictionism calls for the killing of innocent human beings (e.g. fertilized eggs), and I want to make the case for this conclusion as difficult as possible for me.

So, what is evictionism? The pro-life side maintains that the pregnant woman may not evict the baby (of course until the nine-month period has elapsed) and certainly not kill it, while the pro-choicers take the position that she may both evict the young child at any moment of her choosing, and, she may also kill it, even if it is viable outside of the womb (partial birth abortion in the third trimester). The evictionist compromise is that she may evict the pre-birth infant whenever she wishes, but may never kill it. That would be murder. Yes, the fetus will die if evicted in the first six months, but she will not be guilty of killing it, only of expelling it from her body and allowing it to die, a completely distinct matter.

Consider, first, the case of rape. The woman now has, inside her body, a small human being. A very much unwanted one. This youngster is akin to an innocent stowaway on an airplane. If we adhere to strict private property rights, this rape victim has the right to evict, but not kill, the fetus. Now, it might well be nice, and moral, for the woman to keep this tiny trespasser in her body, and for the airplane owner to land the innocent stowaway, but the doctrine of strict private property rights does not require it.

Now, take the case of voluntary sexual intercourse. One objection to evictionism is that the woman, in effect, agreed to carry the baby to term; she, in effect, signed a contract with the preborn infant. In the case of the host mother, she did indeed legally obligate herself to a nine-month stint; no eviction would be allowed in that scenario, let alone, abortion, which consists of ejection plus killing. Set aside the possibility of making binding contracts with under-aged persons. At the time of voluntary sexual intercourse, there was not even a fertilized egg with whom to make a contract of any sort. This is because it takes a period of time for the sperm to reach the egg. It does so only several long minutes after ejaculation. Even if we posit that "contracts" can be made with such an entity, voluntary sexual intercourse will still not qualify.

If Roe v. Wade is overturned, this will not constitute the death knell for the pro-choice position. Rather, one possibility is that each state will have to decide this matter for itself. Presumably, those on either coast will tend in the direction of pro-choice, the ones in flyover country, pro-life. Some states might hit upon yet another compromise: abortions up to the 20-week mark, but not afterward. This time period roughly demarcates when the fetus is viable outside of the womb – at present. However, as medical technology improves, this dividing line will come earlier and earlier. Better to adopt evictionism, which is philosophically sound, than to choose a time demarcation which will have to change with every alteration in medical technology. The point is, that would not be a principled compromise. It is not based upon the ownership rights women have over their own bodies, as is evictionism.

The "states' rights compromise" cuts the cake somewhere near the middle, and, on a pragmatic basis, it might well satisfy both sides more than the present situation. But as a reconciliation based upon philosophical principle, it is a non-starter. Only evictionism attains that goal. It is important to attain deontological clarity, since there are reasonable arguments on both sides of this debate. It is perhaps the most vexing, and complicated issue our society now faces.

Part III
Response to Libertarian Critics of Evictionism

Chapter 3
Responses to Three Leading Libertarians: Rothbard, Paul and Rand

In this chapter we critically consider the views of three leading libertarians on the topic of this book. Their comments appear below. They are interspersed with my responses.

The first up in the batter's box is Rothbard (1973a, b, pp. 131–132) who states:

> "This brings us to the more complex case of abortion. For the libertarian, the 'Catholic' case against abortion, even if finally rejected as invalid, cannot be dismissed out of hand. For the essence of that case – not really 'Catholic' at all in a theological sense – is that abortion destroys a human life and is therefore murder, and hence cannot be condoned. More than that, if abortion is truly murder, then the Catholic – or any other person who shares this view – cannot just shrug his shoulders and say that 'Catholic' views should not be imposed upon non-Catholics. Murder is not an expression of religious preference; no sect, in the name of 'freedom of religion,' can or should get away with committing murder with the plea that its religion so commands. The vital question then becomes: Should abortion be considered as murder? Most discussion of the issue bogs down in minutiae about when human life begins, when or if the fetus can be considered to be alive, etc. All this is really irrelevant to the issue of the legality (again, not necessarily the morality) of abortion. The Catholic antiabortionist, for example, declares that all that he wants for the fetus is the rights of any human being – i.e., the right not to be murdered. But there is more involved here, and this is the crucial consideration. If we are to treat the fetus as having the same rights as humans, then let us ask: What human has the right to remain, unbidden, as an unwanted parasite within some other human being's body? This is the nub of the issue: the absolute right of every person and hence every woman, to the ownership of her own body. What the mother is doing in an abortion is causing an unwanted entity within her body to be ejected from it: If the fetus dies, this does not rebut the point that no being has a right to live, unbidden, as a parasite within or upon some person's body. The common retort that the mother either originally wanted or at least was responsible for placing the fetus within her body is, again, beside the point. Even in the stronger case where the mother originally wanted the child, the mother, as the property owner in her own body, has the right to change her mind and to eject it."

Rothbard (1973a, b) avers: "What human has the right to remain, unbidden, as an unwanted parasite within some other human being's body?"

He correctly labels this the "nub" of the issue. But he fails to incorporate the undeniable fact that an abortion really consists of two entirely separate acts: killing

W. E. Block, *Evictionism*, https://doi.org/10.1007/978-981-16-5014-7_3

and evicting. This father of libertarianism almost achieves a correct analysis when he mentions "ejection" but does not quite attain it. Consider the fetus aged eight months. He is perfectly viable outside of the womb. And, yet, Rothbard's support of abortion would entitle the woman to in effect murder this young person. Had this world-famous economist and philosopher plumbed the depths of his own mention of "ejected," I contend he would have arrived at my position: the woman has the right to "evict" or "eject" the unwanted fetus from her private property, her body, but not to kill the baby.

My friend and mentor (Block 2012) also maintains: "The vital question then becomes: Should abortion be considered as murder?"

My response is, of course abortion is murder. For, the woman is only entitled to eject the fetus, not to kill him. Abortion allows both. Suppose an unconscious stowaway is hidden on your boat. May you shoot him? No. He is innocent. However, he is occupying space on your property, so you are entitled to remove him from your ship. If he can live when disposed, well, then, more power to him. If not, it is not your fault. Blame rests with the person who placed him there in the first place. The latter is the real murderer. You are only defending your property rights. Now, it would be nice if you carried this person to port, to safety. But there are no positive obligations in the libertarian philosophy.

Next in the line-up is Ron Paul. He, too, along with Rothbard, must be counted as among the leading lights of the libertarian movement. And yet, he takes a position 180 degrees removed from that of this fellow libertarian groundbreaker of his. It is unfortunate that the two of them never subjected the other's analysis to constructive criticism. Had they done so, they both might well have adopted the intermediate position of the author of this present book, namely, evictionism, or ejectionism, a compromise between their two extreme, and erroneous, positions.

Here are Dr. Paul's views on the matter.

1. Morning-after pill is the same as birth control pill; not immoral.

> "Q: Sen. Santorum said he would talk about what no president has talked about before – the dangers of contraception. Your thoughts?"
>
> "PAUL: As an OB doctor, I've dealt with birth control pills and contraception for a long time. This is a consequence of government control of medical insurance. The problem is the government is getting involved in things they shouldn't be involved in, especially at the federal level. But along the line of the pills creating immorality, I don't see it that way. I think the immorality creates the problem of wanting to use the pills. So you don't blame the pills. The pills can't be blamed for the immorality of our society."
>
> "GINGRICH: When government provides a morning-after abortion pill [under ObamaCare], you inevitably move towards tyranny."

> "PAUL: Actually, the morning-after pill is nothing more than a birth control pill, so if you legalize birth control pills, you really can't separate the two. They're all basically the same, hormonally."[1]

I think Congressman Paul is in error on a basic medical fact. As far as I am concerned, human life starts with the fertilized egg. Therefore, a condom amounts to birth control, as does the intrauterine device, and, also birth control pills (the pill). All three prevent the sperm from entering the egg in the first place.

With no human being in existence at this point, there can be no question of abortion, or, even, of eviction. However, the morning-after pill is not nothing more than a birth control pill, for it operates after the sperm and the egg have interacted. Well, that is not quite right either. It takes anywhere from 30 minutes to 48–72 hours for the sperm to travel through the fallopian tube so as to impregnate the woman. If the morning after pill is taken before the egg is fertilized, then, it also amounts to birth control. However, if it occurs afterward, abortion has occurred.

2. Right to privacy is explicit, but not for contraception

> "Q: [to Paul] Sen. Santorum believes that the Supreme Court was wrong when it decided that a right to privacy was embedded in the Constitution. And following from that, he believes that states have the right to ban contraception, although he's not recommending that states do that."

> "SANTORUM: The Supreme Court created through a penumbra of rights a new right to privacy that was not in the Constitution."

> "PAUL: No, I think the 4th Amendment is very clear. It is explicit in our privacy. You can't go into anybody's house without a search warrant. This is why the Patriot Act is wrong, because you have a right of privacy by the 4th Amendment. As far as selling contraceptives, the Interstate Commerce Clause protects this; it was originally written not to impede trade between the states, but it was written to facilitate trade between the states. So if it's not illegal to import birth control pills from one state to the next, it would be legal to sell birth control pills in that state."[2]

Again, I must part company with my friend and mentor (Block 2012), Ron Paul. As far as my understanding of libertarian theory is concerned, there simply is no right to privacy. If there were, then the detective profession would have to be banned. Looking at each other would also have to be declared illegal, for, when we do so, we, strictly speaking, violate each other's privacy. Does this mean the libertarian must support the Patriot Act? Heaven forbid. While there is no right to privacy, per se, government is entirely a different matter. The Constitution does indeed prevent government from invading our privacy, as Mr. Constitution, Ron Paul, would have it. But that is an entirely separate matter from any so-called "right-to-privacy." Privacy, vis-a-vis each other, amounts to an aspect of wealth. Those who can afford it, may avail themselves of gated communities, private jet planes, secluded island

---

[1] Source: CNN's 2012 GOP Debate on eve of Arizona Primary, Feb 22, 2012.

[2] Source: WMUR 2012 GOP New Hampshire debate, Jan 7, 2012.

retreats, etc., where they may increase the level of privacy they enjoy. Others of us will just have to close our blinds, wear sunglasses, hoodies, etc.

3. More laws don't solve problems on abortion

> "Q: You have said that you believe that life begins at conception and that abortion ends an innocent life. If you believe that, how can you support a rape exception to abortion bans, and how can you support the morning-after pill? Aren't those lives just as innocent?"
>
> "PAUL: They may be, but the way this is taken care of in our country, it is not a national issue. This is a state issue. And there are circumstances where doctors in the past have used certain day-after pills for somebody with rape. And, quite frankly, if somebody is treated, you don't even know if a person is pregnant; if it's 24 hours after rape, I don't know how you're going to police it. We have too many laws already. Now, how are you going to police the day-after pill? Nobody can out-do me on respect for life. I've spent a lifetime dealing with life. But I still think there is a time where the law doesn't solve the problems. Only the moral character of the people will eventually solve this problem, not the law."[3]

There are problems here, too. Dr. Paul is quite correct in saying that at present levels of technology we have no way of knowing that a woman is pregnant or not after intercourse, within one day. However, the correct way of addressing the "rape exception to abortion bans," is to say that all abortions should be banned by law, and, if we need an additional law for this, so be it. Yes, we have all too many laws; but this should not mitigate against an additional one, provided, only, that it is compatible with the libertarian non-aggression principle (NAP). Nor is the utilitarian concern about the difficulty of policing a justification for jettisoning such a law, or not placing it on the books in the first place. It is exceedingly difficult to determine guilt in rape cases. Almost always, there are only two persons present when it occurs: "he" and "she." Does this mean we should not have laws prohibiting this type of assault and battery? Of course not. But the same applies to morning after pills.

4. Efforts to fund abortion ranks among stupidest policies

> "PAUL: One thing I believe for certain is that the federal government should never tax pro-life citizens to pay for abortions. The constant effort by the pro-choice crowd to fund abortion must rank among the stupidest policies ever, even from their viewpoint. All they accomplish is to give valiant motivation for all pro-life forces as well as the antitax supporters of abortion to fight against them."[4]

On this matter Dr. Paul and I are on the same page, fully and enthusiastically. I would only add that forcing some people to finance the abortions of others is not only "stupid" but, even more so, "evil." Abortion in and of itself is murder. It only adds insult to injury to compel innocent people opposed to such procedures to fund such activities on the part of others.

5. Deregulate the adoption market

[3] Source: 2011 GOP Google debate in Orlando FL, Sep 22, 2011.

[4] Source: Liberty Defined, by Rep. Ron Paul, p. 6, Apr 19, 2011.

> "Deregulating the adoption market would also make a margin of difference in reducing abortion. This would make it easier for nonprofit groups to arrange for adoptive parents and for them to compensate the mother enough to absorb the expenses and opportunity costs associated with carrying the child to term. Small changes could make a large difference here."[5],[6]

Once again the congressman and I are in full accord. This is not an elegant solution, such as banning abortions altogether, but it would indeed reduce their incidence. And that is greatly to be desired. Further, adoption markets would be a God-send on other, completely separate, grounds.

6. Abortion laws should be a state-level choice

> "It is now widely accepted that there's a constitutional right to abort a human fetus. Of course, the Constitution says nothing about abortion, murder, manslaughter, or any other acts of violence. Criminal and civil laws were deliberately left to the states.
>
> "I consider it a state-level responsibility to restrain violence against any human being. I disagree with the nationalization of the issue and reject the Roe v. Wade decision that legalized abortion in all 50 states. Legislation that I have proposed would limit federal court jurisdiction of abortion, and allow state prohibition of abortion on demand as well as in all trimesters. It will not stop all abortions. Only a truly moral society can do that.
>
> "The pro-life opponents to my approach are less respectful of the rule of law and the Constitution. Instead of admitting that my position allows the states to minimize or ban abortions, they claim that my position supports the legalization of abortion by the states. This is twisted logic."[7]

This is a brilliant initiative of Rep. Paul's. Given that abortion is an abomination, if we cannot ban it entirely, then, as a second best solution, let us at least minimize it. If placed on the state level, then, presumably, some of these jurisdictions would allow it, others not. True, women seeking one can visit a state more in keeping with their beliefs, but it is a staple of economics that demand curves slope in a downward direction. Increase the (travel, hotel, etc.) costs of something, and less of it will be demanded.

7. Abortion causes inconsistent moral basis for value of life

> "In the 1960s when abortion was still illegal, I witnessed, as an OB/GYN resident, the abortion of a fetus that weighed approximately 2 pounds. It was placed in a bucket, crying and struggling to breathe, and the medical personnel pretended not to notice. Soon the crying stopped. This harrowing event forced me to think more seriously about this important issue. That same day in the OB suite, an early delivery occurred and the infant boy was only slightly larger than the one that was just aborted. But in this room everybody did everything conceivable to save this child's life. My conclusion that day was that we were overstepping the bounds of morality by picking and choosing who should live and who should die. There was no consistent moral basis to the value of life under these circumstances. Some people believe that being pro-choice is being on the side of freedom. I've never understood how

---

[5] When not otherwise indicated, the source of all quotes in this section is Dr. Ron Paul

[6] Source: Liberty Defined, by Rep. Ron Paul, p. 8, Apr 19, 2011.

[7] Source: Liberty Defined, by Rep. Ron Paul, p. 2&6–7, Apr 19, 2011.

> killing a human being, albeit a small one in a special place, is portrayed as a precious right."[8]

Who has such a hard heart that he cannot be shocked, dismayed and yes, outraged that a precious human being was placed in a bucket and allowed to die while struggling to breathe. The people responsible for this abomination deserve a low level in hell for this despicable act. Back on earth, they merit at least a jail sentence. But what Dr. Paul describes was not an abortion; rather, it was an eviction. The baby exited the womb while still alive. He (not "it") could have been saved without in the least dis-accommodating the mother in any manner, shape or form. If she does not wish to be the guardian over this child, she has an obligation[9] to see to it that he is brought to a hospital that will take care of him, or an orphanage that will bring him up.

8. Day-after pill allows individual moral choice

> "My argument is that the abortion problem is more of a social and moral issue than it is a legal one. If we are ever to have fewer abortions, society must change. The law will not accomplish that. However, that does not mean that the states shouldn't be allowed to write laws dealing with abortion. Very early pregnancies and victims of rape can be treated with the day after pill, which is nothing more than using birth control pills in a special manner. These very early pregnancies could never be policed, regardless. Such circumstances would be dealt with by each individual making his or her moral choice."[10]

Here, Representative Paul and I once again diverge. In my view, abortion most certainly is a legal issue. It ought to be against the law, since it is a violation of the NAP. Moreover, the day after pill, is quite a bit more than using birth control pills in a special manner; *au contraire*, based on the timing of the sperm reaching the egg, it constitutes abortion. And, again, whether or not something can be "policed" is a mere pragmatic consideration. Deontologically, if an act constitutes an unjustified border crossing, a NAP violation (Block 2003), it should be prohibited by law, and damn the utilitarian difficulties thereof.

9. Abortion is murder

> "A popular academic argument for abortion demands that we think of the child in the womb as a parasite. but the same argument justifies infanticide, since it applies just as well to an infant outside the womb. newborns require even more attention and care. People ask an expectant mother how her baby is doing. They do not ask how her fetus is doing, or her blob of tissue, or her parasite. But that is what her baby becomes as soon as the child is declared to be unwanted."[11]

---

[8] Source: Liberty Defined, by Rep. Ron Paul, p. 1, Apr 19, 2011.

[9] This, of course, is not a positive obligation, anathema to libertarians. Rather, it is an obligation people have if they wish to avoid being a negative rights violator. How so. This is due to the fact that a woman who wishes not to care for her newborn, and does not see to it that the baby has another care giver is guilty of the crime of precluding; she is no longer the child's guardian, but is preventing others who wish to take on this role from doing so. For an explanation, see Block 2016

[10] Source: Liberty Defined, by Rep. Ron Paul, p. 5, Apr 19, 2011.

[11] Source: The Revolution: A Manifesto, by Ron Paul, p. 59–60, Apr 1, 2008.

I must part company here. First, the unwanted fetus most certainly is a parasite (McDonagh 1996), a trespasser. Nor does this argument at all justify infanticide. It cannot be denied that newborns require a lot of care, but they are no longer invaders of private property rights of other people. As Rothbard (1973a, b) trenchantly observes: "If we are to treat the fetus as having the same rights as humans, then let us ask: What human has the right to remain, unbidden, as an unwanted parasite within some other human being's body? This is the nub of the issue: the absolute right of every person and hence every woman, to the ownership of her own body." And, contrary to Doctor Paul whether something is "unwanted" or not is absolutely crucial for the libertarian. A socks B in the nose. If they are in a boxing ring by consent, then this is "wanted" in the sense of agreed upon in advance. C has sexual intercourse with D. If both parties "want" this, such an act is licit. If either does not, then it is illicit. So, yes, there is nothing philosophically unexceptionable with a fetus, or a blob of tissue becoming a parasite, upon his becoming "unwanted."

10. Roe v. Wade decision was harmful to the Constitution

> "The federal government should not play any role in the abortion issue, according to the Constitution. Apart from waiting forever for Supreme Court justices who rule in accordance with the Constitution, Americans do have some legislative recourse. Article III, Section 2 of the Constitution gives Congress the power to strip the federal courts of jurisdiction over a broad categories of cases."[12]

There are several ways in which we can incorporate constitutionality into the libertarian nexus. One possibility is to note that this document was concocted by dead white males who owned slaves; it left out not only blacks, but also women, and even poor non-property owning whites. If we do this, we should pretty much deduce that the very opposite of whatever this manuscript avers, for it can be interpreted as in the interest, only, of a relatively small sliver of our population. This, indeed, would seem to be the position of those who see this document as a "living one" constantly in need of revision based upon more modern considerations. I reject this interpretation. For one thing, even though watered down, it gave rise to one of the most successful nations on the planet. For another, it was based to a large degree upon the thought of John Locke, one of the wisest and most humane philosophers in the history of that discipline. There is a third reason for great respect for the constitution: yes, it was a document written to bring about justice and prosperity for wealthy white men; but it can be extrapolated to all human beings, given that its basic premises were to a great degree in accord with libertarianism.

There is another reason to turn the entire controversy between the pro-life and the pro-choice advocates over to the states. There are fifty of them. They thus constitute living laboratories that do not require our society to place all of its eggs in one federal basket. If twenty five of them rule in one direction, and an equal number in the other, each side will obtain half a loaf. That is far better, in terms of not rending the social fabric, than if one side takes home all the marbles. And, crucially important, with fifty possibilities, there is at least some small chance that one state will

[12] Source: The Revolution: A Manifesto, by Ron Paul, p. 60, Apr 1, 2008.

reject both the pro-life and the pro-choice positions, and, instead, embrace the one true stance on this matter, evictionism!

11. Define life at conception in law, as scientific statement

> "On the right-to-life issue, I believe, I'm a real stickler for civil liberties. It's academic to talk about civil liberties if you don't talk about the true protection of all life. So if you are going to protect liberty, you have to protect the life of the unborn just as well.
>
> "I have a Bill in congress I certainly would promote and push as president, called the Sanctity of Life Amendment. We establish the principle that life begins at conception. And someone says, 'oh why are you saying that?' and I say, 'well, that's not a political statement – that's a scientific statement that I'm making!..."[13]

All rights imply obligations. If I have a right not to be murdered, you have an obligation not to murder me. If I have a right not to be raped, you are obliged to refrain from violating me in this way. If I have a right not to be stolen from, you must desist from robbing me. These are all negative rights, and libertarians support them fully, and fulsomely. However, we do not support positive rights. For example, there is no right to food, clothing and shelter, since short of any contractual obligation, no one else should be obliged to supply these goods to anyone else. Moreover, rights are timeless. The cave man had just as much right not to be molested as the modern man, and the latter is the equal in this regard of the space-man in the future. In contrast it would have been impossible to provide modern dentistry, air-conditioners, clothing, food, to people 10,000 years ago. But rights imply possibility; if it is downright impossible to supply someone with something, it cannot have been his right to have it, let alone the obligation of anyone else to supply him with it.

The right to life, in sharp contrast, is a positive right, and this is incompatible with the liberty philosophy. Were there any such right, we would all be guilty of murder, since, right now, there are people dying of starvation in some parts of the world. We all know this, and, yet, do not fulfill our supposed requirements to call a halt to it through violence, if need be. Suppose, moreover, that the last man on earth perishes due to starvation. According to positive right to life doctrine, his rights will have been violated. And, yet, by stipulation, there will be no other person left on the planet who could have violated his rights. Similarly, storms, earthquakes, floods, etc., do not violate rights, but they would, were this viewpoint correct. If there are no rights to life, then the unborn do not have them, either. I fully support the contention that human life starts at conception. But this cannot establish that these very young human beings have any right to life.

12. Protecting the life of the unborn is protecting liberty

> "Liberty is the most important thing, because if we have our liberties, we have our freedoms, we can have our lives. But it's academic to talk about civil liberties if you don't talk about the true protection of all life. So if you're going to protect liberty, you have to protect the life of the unborn just as well...."[14]

[13] Source: Speeches to 2008 Conservative Political Action Conference, Feb 7, 2008.

[14] Source: Speeches to 2008 Conservative Political Action Conference, Feb 7, 2008.

Here, Dr. Paul and I are fully aligned. Neither of us wants to allow any human being, no matter how young, whether born or preborn, to be murdered. There is no right to life, but there most certainly is a right not to be murdered. However, this is totally consistent with evictionist theory. For, there, the trespassing fetus may only be ejected, not murdered. If this doctrine were ensconced in law, that would spell the end of partial birth abortion in the third trimester, during which time the fetus is viable outside of the womb. True, it would not protect life from eviction in the first two trimesters, but that is not murder, merely killing in self-defense of the private property rights of the pregnant woman.

13. Get the federal government out of abortion decision

> "Q: If abortion becomes illegal and a woman obtains an abortion anyway, what should she be charged with? What about the doctor who performs the abortion?"

> "PAUL: The first thing we have to do is get the federal government out of it. We don't need a federal abortion police. That's the last thing that we need. There has to be a criminal penalty for the person that's committing that crime. And I think that is the abortionist. As for the punishment, I don't think that should be up to the president to decide."[15]

Yes, the abortionist is guilty of murder, since he not only evicts, but purposefully kills the unborn human being. But so is the mother guilty of this crime, unless she is unconscious, and/or otherwise unaware of the offense being perpetrated upon her child. Yes, it is cruel and heartless to consider the distraught woman in this manner. But that is the ineluctable conclusion that must be drawn regarding her decision in this matter.

14. Delivered 4000 babies; & assuredly life begins at conception

> "Q: What will you do to restore legal protection to the unborn?"

> "PAUL: As an O.B. doctor of thirty years, and having delivered 4000 babies, I can assure you life begins at conception. I am legally responsible for the unborn, no matter what I do, so there's a legal life there. The unborn has inheritance rights, and if there's an injury or a killing, there is a legal entity. There is no doubt about it."[16]

There are no inheritance rights. The child has no right to receive wealth or anything else from his parents. That would be a positive right. However, the parent has a right to offer a gift to his children, whether while alive or posthumously. This stems from the right of private property. It consists of using that which is owned in any way desired, as long as it does not violate the equal rights of others. This includes preventing others from using it, selling it, lending it, giving it away, etc.

Strictly speaking, Mr. Paul is here engaging in the logical fallacy of *ad hominem*. The question of when life begins cannot be based on how many babies have been delivered. As it happens, I agree with this conclusion. I have delivered no babies at all. My reasoning is that if the fertilized egg is placed in the proper environment, it

---

[15] Source: 2007 GOP YouTube debate in St. Petersburg, Florida, Nov 28, 2007.

[16] Source: 2007 GOP Values Voter Presidential Debate, Sep 17, 2007.

will become a baby, when it changes its address, and then later an adult, after a while. Indeed, there is not a one of us who has not started out precisely in that manner. Moreover, we all need the correct environment in order to survive. If any of us were plunked down on the moon or Mars, without a space suit, we should perish within a matter of seconds. Even with a space suit, our lives could be measured in minutes. So there is no difference in this regard between the preborn child and the rest of us human beings.

15. Save "snowflake babies": no experiments on frozen embryos

> "Q: Our children were adopted as embryos. They were snowflake babies, which means that for the first part of their lives, they were frozen embryos. Can you look at them now and honestly tell me that it would be OK with you if someone used them in medical experiments and snuffed out their little lives? Is that your position?"
>
> "HUCKABEE: No.
> "TANCREDO: No.
> "COX: No.
> "BROWNBACK: No.
> "PAUL: No.
> "HUNTER: No.
> "KEYES: No."[17]

A strong "No" also emanates from the present writer. Well, with one possible exception: only if there is no one on the entire planet willing to take on the responsibility for keeping these unborn baby humans alive. Then and only then would it be permissible to "snuff out their little lives" for medical research, or, indeed, for any other purpose. And the same applies, horrifyingly, to completely unwanted post birth babies (Singer 1979). I realize this is very inhumane, but I feel obligated to follow the logical argument wherever it leads me, and, here, it leads me in a very uncomfortable direction. If they are going to die in any case, it would be better for them to have a quick painless death, then a long slow one through starvation and dehydration. In any case, embryos cannot feel pain. However, even regarding unwanted infants, if they were tortured to death, as opposed to being painlessly removed from life, then the perpetrator would be considered a despicable murderer.

16. No tax funding for organizations that promote abortion

> "Q: The Mexico City Policy states that as a condition for a foreign organization to receive federal funds, they will neither 'perform nor actively promote abortion.' Would you work to apply this Mexico City policy to organizations within the US?"
>
> "HUCKABEE: Are we being asked to apply a Mexican law to the US?"
>
> "Q: It's the principle of not giving our tax dollars to organizations within our country that actively promote or provide abortions. It's an American law."

[17] Source: 2007 GOP Values Voter Presidential Debate, Sep 17, 2007.

"BROWNBACK: This is Ronald Reagan' policy that we wouldn't use federal funds to support organizations that promote abortions overseas."

"HUNTER: It's actually a UN policy."

"KEYES: Actually, it was a policy of the Mexico City Population Conference. I was the deputy chairman. I actually negotiated the language into the final resolution at that conference."

Q: I want to know, will you defund Planned Parenthood?

"HUCKABEE: Yes.
TANCREDO: Yes.
COX: Yes.
BROWNBACK: Yes.
PAUL: Yes.
HUNTER: Yes.
KEYES: Yes."[18]

As an anarcho-capitalist libertarian, I oppose all taxes. So the issue would never arise under this situation. Since I regard abortion as murder, I would imprison all abortionists and all women who hired them to perform this operation. Promoting abortions, or, outright murder for adults, is a different matter. On this issue I am indebted to Rothbard (1973a, b), who maintains that mere incitement should not be a crime.[19] We all have free will. That being the case, the guilty parties are those who are influenced by the inciter, not the latter himself.

"Embryonic stem cell programs not constitutionally authorized."

"Q: Would you expand federal funding of embryonic stem cell research?"

"A: Programs like this are not authorized under the Constitution. The trouble with issues like this is, in Washington we either prohibit it or subsidize it. And the market should deal with it, and the states should deal with it."[20]

No, no, no, the "market" should not be allowed to "deal" with this. Embryonic stem cell research, subject to the exceptions mentioned above, constitutes outright murder. The market should no more deal with this than it should include Murder Incorporated. The free market should include only acts compatible with the NAP, and these activities do not pass muster in this regard in any way, manner, shape or form.[21]

"Voted NO on expanding research to more embryonic stem cell lines."

---

[18] Source: [Xref Keyes] 2007 GOP Values Voter Presidential Debate, Sep 17, 2007.

[19] See, also Block 2011.

[20] Source: 2007 GOP primary debate, at Reagan library, hosted by MSNBC, May 3, 2007.

[21] Source: No Taxpayer Funding for Abortion Act; Bill H.3; vote number 11-HV292 on May 4, 2011.

"Allows federal funding for research that utilizes human embryonic stem cells, regardless of the date on which the stem cells were derived from a human embryo, provided such embryos:

"have been donated from in vitro fertilization clinics;

"were created for the purposes of fertility treatment;

"were in excess of the needs of the individuals seeking such treatment and would otherwise be discarded; and

"were donated by such individuals with written informed consent and without any financial or other inducements."

17. Proponents support voting YES because:

"Since 2 years ago, the last Stem Cell bill, public support has surged for stem cells. Research is proceeding unfettered and, in some cases, without ethical standards in other countries. And even when these countries have ethical standards, our failures are allowing them to gain the scientific edge over the US. Some suggest that it is Congress' role to tell researchers what kinds of cells to use. I suggest we are not the arbiters of research. Instead, we should foster all of these methods, and we should adequately fund and have ethical oversight over all ethical stem cell research."

"Opponents support voting NO because: A good deal has changed in the world of science. Amniotic fluid stem cells are now available to open a broad new area of research. I think the American people would welcome us having a hearing to understand more about this promising new area of science. As it stands today, we will simply have to debate the bill on the merits of information that is well over 2 years old, and I think that is unfortunate.

"The recent findings of the pluripotent epithelial cells demonstrates how quickly the world has changed. Wouldn't it be nice to have the researcher before our committee and be able to ask those questions so we may make the best possible judgment for the American people?"[22]

Amniotic fluid stem cells are not human beings. They will not develop into members of our species. They are not akin to fertilized eggs. Therefore there can be no objection to research on this material emanating from the libertarian philosophy. Here, Ron Paul and I once again converge.

18. Voted NO on allowing human embryonic stem cell research.

"To provide for human embryonic stem cell research. A YES vote would:

"Call for stem cells to be taken from human embryos that were donated from in vitro fertilization clinics;

"Require that before the embryos are donated, that it be established that they were created for fertility treatment and in excess of clinical need and otherwise would be discarded;

"Stipulate that those donating the embryos give written consent and do not receive any compensation for the donation."[23]

This is entirely appropriate from the perspective of my libertarian evictionist approach. The argument in favor of such research is that it can help find cures for all

[22] Reference: Stem Cell Research Enhancement Act; Bill HR 3 ("First 100 hours"); vote number 2007-020 on Jan 11, 2007.

[23] Reference: Stem Cell Research Enhancement Act; Bill HR 810; vote number 2005-204 on May 24, 2005.

sorts of dreaded diseases such as diabetes, stroke, Alzheimer's, spinal cord injuries, birth defects, etc. Posit that this is true. Would it then be justified to seize adult human beings, murder them, use their bodies as material for research, so as to eliminate these ailments? Of course not. Even mentioning this as a theoretical possibility fairly turns even the strongest stomach. But yet these stem cells are simply very young human beings. We would not subject new born babies to such indignities. Why single out the unborn for such a diabolical fate? There is simply no justification for such "ageism." All human beings have the same rights, no matter how old they are.

19. Voted NO on making it a crime to harm a fetus during another crime.

> "Vote to pass a bill that would make it a criminal offense to harm or kill a fetus during the commission of a violent crime. The measure would set criminal penalties, the same as those that would apply if harm or death happened to the pregnant woman, for those who harm a fetus. It is not required that the individual have prior knowledge of the pregnancy or intent to harm the fetus. This bill prohibits the death penalty from being imposed for such an offense. The bill states that its provisions should not be interpreted to apply a woman's actions with respect to her pregnancy."[24]

A fetus inside the womb is akin to a baby riding piggy-back on the mother. Suppose a criminal engages in assault and battery upon such a parent, and, as a result, the piggy-back riding baby is also hurt. Certainly, this would constitute a crime against the mother. But would the perpetrator also be guilty of a crime against the baby? It is difficult to see why this would not be the case. According to one basic aphorism of the criminal code, the malefactor takes his victim as he finds him. If someone softly pushes an old man to the ground, and he dies from that slight attack, the lawless individual is still guilty of murder, even though death was no part of his intention. In a similar manner, the evil-doer is responsible for the harm not only to the mother, but to the unborn child as well. On the other hand, we read as follows: "This bill prohibits the death penalty from being imposed for such an offense." This is unjustified. Why, ever, should not the death penalty be imposed upon the offender, if in his attack on the mother, the baby dies? "Dr. No" has long held the position that if any clause in a bill violates the libertarian code, he opposes it in its entirety. Therefore, he was eminently justified in rejecting this bill.

20. Voted YES on banning partial-birth abortion except to save mother's life.

> "Partial-Birth Abortion Ban Act of 2003: Vote to pass a bill banning a medical procedure, which is commonly known as "partial-birth" abortion. The procedure would be allowed only in cases in which a woman's life is in danger, not for cases where a woman's health is in danger. Those who performed this procedure, would face fines and up to two years in prison, the women to whom this procedure is performed on are not held criminally liable."[25]

---

[24] Reference: Unborn Victims of Violence Act; Bill HR 1997; vote number 2004-31 on Feb 26, 2004.

[25] Reference: Bill sponsored by Santorum, R-PA; Bill S.3; vote number 2003-530 on Oct 2, 2003.

Here, I go part way with my mentor, Dr. Paul. I agree with him that abortion, not merely eviction, would be justified if that was the only way to save the mother's life. How do I reconcile this with my claim that only eviction, not abortion, is justified? In this case I borrow a leaf from Thompson (1971a, b, c). Consider the following case. You are in a room with no egress. There are doors, but they are all locked. You own the room. However, there is an innocent trespasser who is also in the room with you. The problem is, this small person is getting bigger. Bigger and bigger. So big that he will soon squash you to death. You simply cannot evict this child from the room. You have a hat pin. If you stick that into this young human being, he will explode, but your life will be spared. Then, the doors will open, and you will be safe. Are you justified in using this hatpin? You most certainly are. For, in this scenario, the baby is not merely trespassing, a "crime" for which you may properly evict him. No, in addition, he is also (innocently, through no malice on his part) threatening your life. Not only threatening it, but actually in the process of killing you; nay, murdering you, since this is an unjustified killing.

But I go further. This fetus in the room is still growing, alright, but will not kill you. Instead, he will only get so big as to break your arm, or your leg, or your neck, or the pinky on your right hand. Eviction is again precluded by the terms of this mental experiment. You still have that hat pin. May you use it? Yes, according to libertarian theory, at least as I understand it. The baby is in the process not merely of trespassing, but of engaging, innocently to be sure, in assault and battery upon your person. Now, I have no idea of whether or not an abortion, as opposed to an eviction, is ever necessary to save a mother's life, let alone preserve her health. I am now positing that this is true, nevertheless, *arguendo*. I do so in order to confront this important philosophical case. It is legitimate to use violence in self-defense, no matter what the age of the perpetrator, no matter what his status is insofar as mens rea is concerned. So, yes, abortion is justified, to save the mother's life, and, also, to defend herself against physical attack of lesser moment.

I must also part company with Dr. Paul when he states: "Those who performed this procedure, would face fines and up to two years in prison, the women on whom this procedure is performed are not held criminally liable." If the woman is comatose, then, of course, she is innocent of any crime. However, if she agrees to any such procedure it is difficult to see why she should not bear any responsibility for it. Without meaning to insult the medical profession, doctors are merely servants, similar to carpenters and plumbers. If I pay such a workman to build something illegal, and one of them does it, then, of course, he is a criminal. But so am I.

21. Voted NO on forbidding human cloning for reproduction & medical research.

> "Vote to pass a bill that would forbid human cloning and punish violators with up to 10 years in prison and fines of at least $1 million. The bill would ban human cloning, and any attempts at human cloning, for both reproductive purposes and medical research. Also forbidden is the importing of cloned embryos or products made from them."[26]

[26]Reference: Human Cloning Prohibition Act; Bill HR 534; vote number 2003-39 on Feb 27, 2003.

I cannot see my way clear to reconciling this vote with libertarian theory. Human cloning consists of taking a nucleus from a cell in the body and implanting it into an enucleated egg cell, in order to create an embryo. Why should the only legitimate way to create a fetus be the natural way, via a sperm and an egg? Remember, libertarianism forbids one and only one act: the initiation of violence against an innocent person or the threat thereof. Creating a zygote in an altogether different manner is simply not a *per se* violation of the NAP. Perhaps, one day, babies will be created by magic, or delivered by the stork, or produced by playing chess. We must look at all such acts through the prism of the NAP, and, all will pass, as long as they do not violate that foundation of this philosophy.

What are the arguments against human cloning? There are several, and none of them fall to the level which would mandate that they must be banned by law. In the usual process, many, many clones are created. In case of the most famous sheep on the planet, Dolly, "From 277 cell fusions, 29 early embryos developed and were implanted into 13 surrogate mothers. But only one pregnancy went to full term…,"

But what about the other 276 cell fusions, and the additional 28 embryos. They were discarded. Posit that these numbers applied to an attempt to clone a human being. Would not these redundant young people have been murdered? Even if they were, still, there could be no case against cloning the one person who did survive. Nor were these castoffs aborted. No, they were merely in effect evicted.

Another objection is that family relationships would be thrown into confusion. Suppose a 25 year-old woman creates a clone. Is the resulting person her twin sister, 25 years younger than she, or her daughter? Our language, our institutions, our laws, are not really ready to incorporate such challenges. But, still, there are no NAP violations. Our language, our institutions, our laws, will just have to change when and if these sorts of births occur. These things should adjust to the NAP, not the other way around.

An additional difficulty is that this process is dangerous. "In many animals, only one in 100 cloned embryos ever leads to a live birth. Some embryos expire in the IVF dish. Others wither in the womb. Of those that are born, a few suffer from abnormalities and quickly die". But much of life contains hazards. There is hang-gliding, car racing, space travel, etc. Just because a behavior is perilous gives no warrant for its prohibition, at least not under libertarian law.

Then there is this claim: "On the level of morality, reproductive cloning is also wrong because it tells God 'move over, you're in my seat'. It takes out of His hands, the act of creating life. Human cloning does so by violating natural laws which God Himself has set in place."[27] The less said about this objection, the better. For the bible prohibits all sorts of acts between consenting adults which are compatible with the NAP of libertarianism.

22. Voted YES on funding for health providers who don't provide abortion information.

[27] https://www.campaignlifecoalition.com/human-cloning

> "Abortion Non-Discrimination Act of 2002: Vote to pass a bill that would prohibit the federal, state and local governments that receive federal funding from discriminating against health care providers, health insurers, health maintenance organizations, and any other kind of health care facility, organization or plan, that decline to refer patients for, pay for or provide abortion services. In addition the bill would expand an existing law 'conscience clause' that protects physician training programs that refuse to provide training for abortion procedures."[28]

This is unexpected. Perhaps there is a typographical error here? Of course, Dr. Paul would be likely to oppose those who discriminate against those who "pay for or provide abortion services." But to provide government "funding for health providers" who do not engage in such discrimination? One must be excused for thinking that the Congressman would not want to financially support them, even though they refrain from such discrimination. Where in the U.S. Constitution is there warrant for such government expenditures?

23. Voted YES on banning Family Planning funding in US aid abroad.

> "Vote to adopt an amendment that would remove language reversing President Bush's restrictions on funding to family planning groups that provide abortion services, counseling or advocacy."[29]

We are once again back in the realm of the predictable. There are not one but two reasons to oppose this initiative on libertarian grounds. First, "family planning" is code for abortion, and the proper philosophical position is to favor eviction, not murder of the fetus. Second, even if this foreign "aid" were for a good purpose, it is simply not the business of the government to compel its citizenry to give up their hard earned money to anyone else, and this certainly includes foreigners.

Third in the batting order is Ayn Rand (1963, pp. 58–59).[30] Her views on this subject are as follows:

> "An embryo has no rights. Rights do not pertain to a potential, only to an actual being. A child cannot acquire any rights until it is born. The living take precedence over the not-yet-living (or the unborn)."

An embryo is not living? If it is not living, it is either dead, or undead. The latter refers to a corpse which acts as if it is alive, animated by the supernatural. Examples include ghosts, vampires and zombies. I think for present purposes we may safely ignore this latter possibility. This leaves only the second option: the fetus is dead. But if this is the case, there can be no dispute about its "rights." Does Rand seriously believe that all zygotes, without exception, are not alive, are never to be counted amongst the living? This is a preposterous alternative. We are left with the only

---

[28] Reference: Bill sponsored by Bilirakis, R-FL; Bill HR 4691; vote number 2002-412 on Sep 25, 2002.

[29] Reference: Amendment sponsored by Hyde, R-IL; Bill HR 1646; vote number 2001-115 on May 16, 2001.

[30] She characterized herself not as a libertarian, but, as an "Objectivist." Why, then, do I categorize her in this manner? It is due to the fact that she supported very limited government and private property rights.

remaining possibility: this philosopher-novelist is greatly mistaken in thinking that human beings are not alive until they are born. Given that they are indeed alive, they most certainly do have rights: negative rights to be sure, not positive ones, but rights nevertheless. That is, it would not be legally required to keep them alive, they may be evicted from their present home in the womb, but they may not be murdered, that is, aborted.

And what is this "take precedence" business? It reeks of a conflict in rights. If A must "take precedence" over B, the logical implication is that the rights of the former are greater than those of the latter. However, Rand (1963) is correctly on record as maintaining that rights can never clash. If they seem to be at variance with one another, then one (or both) is mis-specified. The Rand of 1963, is spot on; the one of 1990 is in error, in thinking there could be any "precedence" in rights. The point is, A is correct, and B mistaken, or the other way around, if there seems to be an incompatibility in the rights they aver. Nor is there any conflict between the rights of the mother and that of her unborn baby. The latter is occupying the private property of the former, and only remains there on sufferance: for as long as the host, well, hostess, agrees to this occupancy.

> "Abortion is a moral right – which should be left to the sole discretion of the woman involved; morally, nothing other than her wish in the matter is to be considered. Who can conceivably have the right to dictate to her what disposition she is to make of the functions of her own body?"

"Her own body"; that is it? That is all that is involved? Not at all. Rather, there is a stowaway inside of "her own body." Yes, her bodily functions affect this trespasser, but they are conceptually and biologically distinct. Rand, too, fails to distinguish between abortion and eviction. Yes, the latter, but only the latter, "should be left to the sole discretion of the woman involved; morally, nothing other than her wish in the matter is to be considered." But the former is a bit much. Why should the woman be allowed to engage in first degree murder against an innocent refugee? It is not enough that she should be able to rid herself of this unwanted passenger? Rand's response: blank out.

> "Never mind the vicious nonsense of claiming that an embryo has a 'right to life.' A piece of protoplasm has no rights – and no life in the human sense of the term. One may argue about the later stages of a pregnancy, but the essential issue concerns only the first three months. To equate a potential with an actual, is vicious; to advocate the sacrifice of the latter to the former, is unspeakable.... Observe that by ascribing rights to the unborn, i.e., the nonliving, the anti-abortionists obliterate the rights of the living: the right of young people to set the course of their own lives. The task of raising a child is a tremendous, lifelong responsibility, which no one should undertake unwittingly or unwillingly. Procreation is not a duty: human beings are not stock-farm animals. For conscientious persons, an unwanted pregnancy is a disaster; to oppose its termination is to advocate sacrifice, not for the sake of anyone's benefit, but for the sake of misery *qua* misery, for the sake of forbidding happiness and fulfillment to living human beings."

There is more wrong here than you can shake a stick at. To be sure, the embryo does not have a "right to life." No one has any such right. That would constitute a positive right, something *verboten* in the libertarian philosophy. But this young human being certainly, along with everyone else of whatever age, has a right not to be murdered.

"A piece of protoplasm?" You mean, Miss Rand, sort of like a kidney, or an elbow, or a cyst, or a wart, or a bunion or a toe? Maybe akin to a fingernail, all of which may fairly described as "A piece of protoplasm." And this applies to the fetus when he is a mere hour or two away from being born?

Wait. What's this: "One may argue about the later stages of a pregnancy"? Why should anyone "argue" about anything of the sort? A piece of protoplasm is a piece of protoplasm is a piece of protoplasm. Yes the baby is quite a bit more mature in the eighth than in the second month, but nothing else, nothing at all else, has changed. In both cases, the unwanted baby is a burden to the mother. In both cases, he is, sooner or later, likely to become a real live adult human being. In both cases, he has equal rights. You say no rights for the former and that with regard to the rights of the latter, "One may argue about" them. But where oh where, Miss Logic, is the relevant difference between the unborn baby two and eight months old? I suggest there is none whatsoever.

Then we have the claim that "To equate a potential with an actual, is vicious." "Vicious" seems a bit strong. Maybe "mistaken" might be more accurate. But if we take this sentiment to its logical conclusion, a sleeping person, or an unconscious one, is only potentially awake, or conscious. Only an awake person, or a conscious one, is actually awake or conscious. Extrapolating, may we say that the latter has rights, while it is "vicious" to think that the former does too? It would appear that we must, were we to employ the "logic" of Objectivism. Two week old babies are not self-aware. They are only potentially cognizant of their surroundings, or themselves, of their hopes, fears, ambitions. It would appear then, that their rights, too, are on the chopping block.

Nor is it at all true "that by ascribing rights to the unborn, i.e., the nonliving, the anti-abortionists obliterate the rights of the living." The only "right" of the mother that is being obliterated is the "right" to murder the pre-born infant. In this view, she retains the right to evict the baby trespasser from her property at any time. Young people may still set the course of their own lives without any diminution of them whatsoever. If they do not wish to take on the obligations of parenthood, evictionism will not in any manner, shape or form compel them to do so.

Yes, "for conscientious persons, an unwanted pregnancy is a disaster;" but the evictionist theory does not at all "oppose its termination." The only "sacrifice" implied by this viewpoint is that the parent may not murder the baby. Is that really too much to ask?

References

Block, Walter E. 2003. *The Non-aggression Axiom of Libertarianism*, February 17. http://archive.lewrockwell.com/block/block26.html

———. 2011. Rejoinder to Kinsella and Tinsley on Incitement, Causation, Aggression and Praxeology. *Journal of Libertarian Studies* 22: 641–664.

———. 2012. *Yes to Ron Paul and Liberty*. New York: Ishi Press.

———. 2016. Forestalling, Positive Obligations and the Lockean and Blockian Provisos: Rejoinder to Stephan Kinsella. *Ekonomia Wroclaw Economic Review*. https://repozytorium.uni.wroc.pl/Content/94352/03_Block_W_E_Butt_J_A_Forestalling_Positive_Obligations_and_the_Lockean_and_Blockian_Provisos_Rejoinder_to_Stephan_Kinsella.pdf

McDonagh, E.L. 1996. *Breaking the Abortion Deadlock: From Choice to Consent*. New York: Oxford University Press.

Paul, Ron. 2008. *The Revolution: A Manifesto*. New York: Grand Central.

———. 2011. *Testimony on Feminists' Inconsistency on Pro-choice*. Retrieved from http://blog.mises.org/15982/who-is-the-friend-of-the-consumer/

Rand, Ayn. 1963. *Collectivized 'Rights'*, June. www.aynrand.org/site/PageServer?pagename=arc_ayn_rand_collectivized_rights

Rothbard, Murray N. 1973a. Free Market, Police, Courts, and Law. *Reason*, March, 5–19.

———. 1973b. *For a New Liberty*. New York: Macmillan. http://mises.org/rothbard/newliberty-whole.asp

Singer, P. 1979. Not for Humans Only: The Place of Non humans in Environmental Issues. In *Ethics and Problems of the 21st Century*, ed. K.E. Goodpaster and K.M. Sayre. South Bend: Notre Dame University Press.

Thomson, Judith Jarvis. 1971a. A Defense of Abortion. *Philosophy and Public Affairs* I: 47–66.

———. 1971b. *A Defense of Abortion*. University of Colorado at Boulder, Fall, 2007, March 4. http://spot.colorado.edu/~heathwoo/Phil160,Fall02/thomson.htm

———. 1971c. A Defense of Abortion. *Philosophy & Public Affairs* 1 (1, Fall); Reprinted in Intervention and Reflection: Basic Issues in Medical Ethics, 5th ed., ed. Ronald Munson (Belmont; Wadsworth 1996), 69–80.

Chapter 4
Rejoinder to Doris Gordon on Abortion

Gordon (Doris 1999) starts off her essay on a strong note:

> "The unalienable right not to be unjustly killed applies equally to all human beings. Day One in a human being's life occurs at fertilization – that is high school biology. If pregnant women are human beings, why not when they themselves were zygotes? A two-tiered legal policy on human offspring that defines a superior class with rights, and an inferior class without rights, is not libertarian."

This is an important opening on many grounds. First, an "omission": she speaks not of a so-called "right to life" which is really a positive right, a demand for the property of others to care for and feed someone else. Rather, she couches rights, properly, in the negative: the "right not to be unjustly killed," e.g., murdered. Then, she incisively maintains that this right "applies equally to all human beings." How could it not? We are not all equal in terms of opportunity. Some of us have way more "opportunity" to become physicists, or pharmacists, or musicians than others. We are certainly not all equal insofar as (legitimate) results are concerned. Bill Gates and LeBron James have much more wealth than the rest of us. But there is one thing that Gates, James, Gordon and all the readers of this book have, and equally so, and that is the right not to be murdered. The murderers of anyone on the planet are equally guilty of this frightful act. But more. Also in this short passage Gordon correctly notes that life, human life, starts with the fertilized egg. Given the right environment, and which of us does not need the right environment, the egg and sperm combined together are every much as human as anyone else. And last but not least, she insightfully proclaims that libertarianism does not recognize superiors and inferiors with regard to this right not to be unjustly put to death.

She also accurately avers that many people maintain

> "…that unwanted pregnancy must be an insoluble clash between the unalienable rights of two people: the child's right not to be killed and the (pregnant) woman's right to liberty."

So far, so good.

But then, unhappily, Gordon goes downhill. She then supports Branden's (1962, 55) assertion

W. E. Block, *Evictionism*, https://doi.org/10.1007/978-981-16-5014-7_4

"… that 'the basic necessities of food, clothing, etc.,' are the child's 'by right.'"

Gordon continues (footnotes deleted):

"Given this right of children, then the 'insoluble' clash is solved, and unwanted pregnancy is neither slavery nor involuntary servitude. There may be a clash of needs between parent and child – but not a clash of rights. Given personhood, a human fetus has the same right as every innocent person not to be attacked and killed."

There are grave difficulties here. First of all to say that anything, "basic necessities" or not, is a "right" of anyone, can only be deduced from a contractual obligation. If A sells a car to B for $10,000, a contractual agreement to which they both voluntarily consent, then, yes, B has a "right" to the car, and A to that amount of money. But this is very far removed from the situation of a child, let alone a fetus. The difficulty is that Gordon first quite properly renounces positive rights, in my first quote from her essay, and, now, in the follow-up, she takes it all back, and embraces this mischievous doctrine. No, the infant, the zygote, has no "rights" other than not to be murdered, not to be stolen from, not to be victimized by assault and battery, etc.

Second, there is no "clash." Rights do not, cannot, be incompatible with one another. If they seem to be at variance with each other, then one or both are misspecified. The clash is not "insoluble" since it cannot exist in the first place. At least in the libertarian philosophy, there is no need to "balance" one right against another. All true rights are inviolate.

But then Gordon commits a far more gargantuan error. She declares that

"… since her parents owe her support and protection from harm, she (the preborn child) has the right to reside in her mother's womb and take nourishment there"

Our authoress moves entirely too quickly here. Note how fast we have arrived at the pro-life position that the mother is compelled, on libertarian grounds no less, to feed, support, house, the zygote, even against her will, if necessary. None of this follows from the premises Gordon first builds. In the libertarian philosophy, no one owes anyone else anything of the positive variety apart from those things that emanate from freely made contractual obligations. There was no contract between mother and preborn infant. Moreover, the fetus is a trespasser onto, inside of, the mother's womb. She has private property right to that bit of "real estate." Consider the case of pregnancy which results from rape. Can there be any doubt that the fetus is a(n innocent) trespasser? How, then, can the proposition be defended that the mother is obliged not to evict this intruder from her body?

But Gordon is not without a response to this sally. She maintains:

"… no one has a right to negligently or intentionally endanger the innocent and then allow the harm to happen. If we endanger others without their consent, we incur a positive obligation to prevent the harm. This might be called the non-endangerment principle: you endanger them – you protect them from the harm."

She is relying on the claim that the pregnant woman worsened the plight of the fetus, and thus is legally obliged to care for him. The difficulties with this position are two. First, creating life does not worsen the zygote. Rather, it was an improvement. Surely, existence is preferable to non-existence. Before the mother gave him life, the preborn baby did not exist at all. Afterward, he does. An enhancement in welfare has occurred, not a diminution. Second, again consider the fetus who is a result of rape. It seems to be a stretch, a gigantic one, to assert that the woman has endangered the baby, even assuming the foregoing point to be false. Rather, it was the rapist, not his victim, who is guilty of "endangerment." Moreover, all fetuses have equal rights. No matter how they were conceived, voluntarily or not, none of them are second class citizens in this regard. And, yet, the ones who resulted from a rape were certainly not endangered by the mother. So, on that ground, given Gordon's premises, they are not entitled to being protected from harm, at least not by the mother. But if they are not, then neither is any other pre-born infant so entitled.

Gordon, very properly, very eloquently and very powerfully, makes the case that life begins not with birth, but with conception; she states:

> "Why do people say, "Children come into the world at birth," sounding as if storks bring them? Obstetricians know that at conception the woman has already reproduced, that they now have not one but two patients to consider: mother and child. Since a pregnant woman is in the world, her womb is in the world, and so is the fetus in her womb; she has been in the world since Day One – conception."

And again:

> "Fertilized ova, zygotes, have the power to mature into adults. Still, it is difficult to think that the zygote inside one's mother was "me." But by playing one's life in reverse, as if in a movie, getting younger day by day until we reach Day One, we find no way to identify any day when we were essentially different from the day before – until conception. The moment before, there was no "me." If a different sperm of my father had fused with my mother's ovum, it would not have been me but someone else, a boy perhaps."

This must be definitive vis-a-vis the pro-choice, that is pro-abortion position. However, it is not telling against my own perspective, evictionism. For, I entirely agree with her that human life starts with the fertilized egg, not a moment sooner, and, also, not a moment later. What then is the issue of disagreement I have with Gordon? The dispute is, should it be legal for the pregnant woman to expel, evict, separate from, eject, dislodge, oust, this tiny human being from her premises, but not kill him, as in an abortion, even though, outside of the womb, present medical technology will not allow him to survive? Gordon, unhappily, never wrestles with this issue, so intent is she, and, again, quite properly so, to refute the abortionist viewpoint.

Next, consider this statement of Gordon's (footnote deleted):

> "Since human beings do not mature until adulthood, why not permit infanticide? Apparently seeking a time to start applying the brakes, Blackmun wrote, 'With respect to the State's important and legitimate interest in potential life, the "compelling" point is at viability. This is so because the fetus then presumably has the capability of meaningful life outside the mother's womb.' But what is meaningful? By whose standard? In ordinary language, 'viable' means 'capable of living or developing in normal or favorable situations.' To abortionists, 'viable' requires survivability under hostile conditions. Either way, what does viability have to do with what an entity is, or with the right not to be killed? The principle the Court

advanced here is that if you need help, you can be killed, but if you can manage, you cannot be touched. Under viability, the more a child needs the womb, the less right she has to stay there."

She offers a very powerful indictment of Blackmun. He is indeed vulnerable to the reductio ad absurdum of infanticide. However, her last statement is problematic. "Stay there?" Stay where? Where? In the mother's womb, obviously. But the first question that should be asked by a libertarian is, Who, exactly who, is the owner of the premises in which Gordon is suggesting that the pre-born baby has a right to "stay." And the answer is that it is the mother's womb and she, not the zygote is the owner of it. Therefore, the unwanted fetus is in effect a(n innocent) trespasser, and, the mother has the right to remove, but of course not, kill him. This basic building block of libertarianism – private property rights – completely eluded our otherwise staunch libertarian in this one case.

Can there be any question of who is the proper owner of the pregnant woman's body, her or her zygote? No. She was there first. She in effect "homesteaded" the premises. She is, let us say, twenty-five years old. The fertilized egg is now 25 minutes "old," having been conceived of less than one half hour ago. According to libertarian homesteading theory, it is "first-come, first-served." The first person to mix her labor with the property under dispute is the proper owner of it. Well, the pregnant woman has been doing so for 25 years. She has clear title to the "premises," not her baby, the interloper. This sounds harsh, but consider the pre-born infant who now "resides" in her body as the result of rape. If that young person is not a trespasser, there is no such thing as trespassing. According to the evictionist theory I am articulating, the mother has a right to expel the fetus from her body, but not kill him. If the baby is in the last trimester, he is viable when ejected; the mother must acquiesce in someone else raising the baby, if she does not wish to do so. She may not murder him. The father is the guilty party in the case of rape, not his offspring. And all such infants are equally infused with the right not to be murdered. Of course, in the first two trimesters, the baby will perish outside the womb, but the mother, in such a case, is not a murderess, since she retains sole property rights in her own person.

Next, consider this statement of our author (footnote omitted):

"Moreover, viability is not a stable point. Since Roe, the age at which prematurely born children survive in incubators has been lowered. As Justice Sandra Day O'Connor wrote, 'The Roe framework, then, is clearly on a collision course with itself.' Given current medical technology, we can talk of viability at both ends of prenatal development. Zygotes in petri dishes and embryos in cold-storage are clearly living outside the mother's womb. Indeed, if artificial wombs are eventually perfected, many children might not ever reside in a woman's body.

"Blackmun mixed technological medical problems with philosophical ones. Viability is not a test of personhood; it is a test of the level of medical technology and of the competence of medical personnel. The fact that they lack the ability to maintain a life does not give them or anyone else a right to take that life. Their inability is irrelevant to whether another's death is a homicide or not."

If and when "artificial wombs are eventually perfected" then my evictionist position, and hers of pro-life, will lead to the same results. All fetuses less than nine months old will survive until being "born;" at least none will be aborted. But it is incumbent upon us to consider the present state of medical technology, in which zygotes are "viable," that is, can survive outside of the womb, only when they have reached their seven month "birthday." What then? Gordon, the pro-lifer, wishes to compel the mother to "house" the baby until birth. It is my claim that this is a downright violation of the libertarian insistence upon the rights of private property, wombs in this case.

Her phrase "take that life" is problematic. It covers altogether too much. It includes killing, and allowing to die. It includes justified eviction and, also, murderous abortion. Let us be clear on this. The mother has only the right to separate herself from her unwanted pre-born infant; not to kill him. He will die as a result if he is in his first two trimesters, given present medical technology. That is to be regretted, since life is precious, but according to the strict interpretation of libertarianism, the mother has every right to do so. This will be an act of "letting die," not "killing." What she has no right to do is to see to it that a baby in the third trimester, in addition to being evicted, is also murdered.

I have been "having at" Gordon for a while, now. It is time for a change of pace. Here is an absolutely brilliant and incisive statement of hers:

> "Abortion choicers often insist that 'capacity' refers only to … the ability to demonstrate reason and choice right now. If this were its only meaning, then what about people generally recognized as persons, such as people who are profoundly retarded, people in coma, stroke victims, and the senile? They might not be able to reason or choose at a given moment. In fact, under such a definition, we all have grounds to worry if we sleep too soundly."

In football, the rules prohibit "piling on." But there are no such requirements here. So let us consider yet another brilliant insight of Gordon's: "A woman who miscarried does not say she lost her fetus. She says, 'I lost my child,' or 'I lost my baby'." This is very telling. There is a human being in there, not mere a blob of cells.

It is now time to renew my critique of this author. She approvingly quotes Posner (1990, p. 350) as follows:

> "Thomson is right that we don't force people to donate kidneys to strangers, or even to family members. But normally the potential donor is not responsible for the condition that he is asked to alleviate, in the way that a woman (unless she has been raped) is responsible, although only in part, for the fact that she is pregnant. The difference in evidentiary difficulty between asking who hit X and asking who failed to save X is a strong practical reason against liability for failing to be a good Samaritan. So although bystanders are not required to rescue persons in distress, someone who creates the danger, even if non-tortiously, may be required to attempt rescue, and perhaps that is the proper analogy to the pregnant woman who wants to terminate her pregnancy."

One difficulty is that the rights of all pre-born infants are identical, whether the product of rape or voluntary sexual intercourse. They are all equally innocent, and, equally residing inside of the property of someone else. When welcome, all is well; when not, they are – not to put too fine a point on the matter – trespassers. Therefore, Posner's claim about "responsibility" fails. The rape victim is certainly not "responsible" for the existence of the fetus. Therefore, she owes him no debt, according to this author. But given that all fetuses have equal rights, no mother owes any zygote any obligation to keep him "on board" for nine minutes, let alone nine months.

Secondly, Posner maintains that creating someone is to place him in danger. But compared to what? To non-existence? No. The transition from non-existence to existence is an improvement not a detriment. The "danger" consisted of not being created in the first place. So, the mother owes no obligation to her baby to keep him safe inside of her until birth, or, at least, the third semester on that ground. So this analogy of Posner's fails, along with Gordon's support of it.

In Gordon's view: "Contrary to Thomson (1990), the zygote is not an attacker." Would Gordon care to repeat that claim, were she to give cognizance to the case of rape? Would she deny that the human baby who results from an invasive attack on the mother by the father is not an innocent trespasser? So, this baby, at least, is a stowaway, an intruder, a squatter, an interloper, a gatecrasher. But if all pre-born babies have equal rights, then each and every one of them can be characterized in this manner – not a rights bearing person. Thus, it is proper to evict, but not kill, all of them, contrary to her view.

Gordon enmeshes herself in difficulty when she opines as follows:

> "…what about the mother's needs in such difficult circumstances as, for example, when her life is in danger? This issue is a 'life-boat' problem. In such situations, everyone's life is at risk, but none of them is at fault. Because nobody has a right to attack the innocent, nobody caught in a dire circumstance has a right to attack any of the others. The mother's right to self-preservation does not turn her child into a mere 'thing' that she may destroy at will. The doctor's goal should be to save both patients, mother and child, but they can only do the possible. The goal of premature deliveries is to help both. The goal of an abortion, however, is a dead fetus."

When the mother's life or health is threatened by her pre-born baby in the third semester, the solution is clear; she may evict, but not abort (evict plus murder). The same holds true in the first two semesters, although in this situation the infant will not survive. But suppose that the only way to rid herself of this menace to her physical well-being is to actually kill the zygote while still in the womb or during the process of eviction. Then, we arrive at the life-boat situation where one must die so that the other can live. Gordon appears to think that then "all bets are off" ("everyone's life is at risk,") but this is not the case. Consider the actual life-boat scenario. There are two swimmers and only one small piece of wood. If both grab it, each will drown. What is the libertarian to say about such a situation? It is simple; we resort to the second foundation of this philosophy after the non-aggression principle: private property rights! Who owns that stick of lumber? He, the owner, not the other swimmer, has a right to it. If no one owns it, then following libertarian homesteading theory, the first one to seize it is the proper owner of it. In justice, the other must perish, given our rigid assumptions. It is only when both reach the life-saving wood at the exact same moment that libertarian theory must remain silent.[1]

Contrary to Gordon, both have "a right to attack the innocent" in this case; remember, both swimmers are "innocent" but given our stringent assumptions, one of them must perish. But there is no such difficulty in the life-boat situation between the mother and child: the former is the clear owner of the property rights in question, her womb. She "got there" by a long way first. Thus, the baby must die; but this would not be abortion, defined as unjustified killing, e.g., murder. Rather, this would be a killing in self-defense. Gordon is thus incorrect when she asserts in such a case, that "The mother's right to self-preservation does not turn her child into a mere 'thing' that she may destroy at will." She most certainly does have a right to terminate her young pre-born child; self-defense gives her this right. Of course "The doctor's goal should be to save both patients," but by stipulation in the case under consideration, he cannot do this. What then? Gordon vouchsafes us no response.

Our authoress also leaves the libertarian ranch when she asserts:

> "What abortion choicers are saying is that in any pregnancy, the woman's liberty is paramount. However, liberty is not paramount. Life and liberty are equal rights; both are merely forms of the same basic right: the right to be free from aggression."

Au contraire, there is no right to life. That is a positive "right." For libertarians, there are only negative rights: the right not to be murdered, raped, stolen from, kidnapped, etc.

Finally, this scholar directs her intellectual opprobrium at the thesis presented elsewhere in this present book:

> "Interestingly, some libertarian abortion choicers insist they favor only an "eviction" abortion: the child is removed intact and alive; if she does not survive, that is too bad. Some try to deal with conflicting needs by noting the common understanding of the non-aggression principle: Although we may not aggress against one another, we have no positive obligation under rights to help one another. The eviction argument, however, overlooks at least two important distinctions: 1) killing versus letting die, and 2) who is causally responsible?
>
> "Killing versus letting die
>
> "Letting die at least does not shut off the possibility of survival, however theoretical and remote this possibility might be. For example, in hysterotomy abortions (which are similar to Caesarian deliveries), children have emerged alive.
>
> "In the real world, however, the evictionist's position gives only lip service to the moral distinction between intentional killing and letting die, and those who give such service are playing let's pretend with somebody else's life. Most abortions are intentionally destructive, not simple "letting die" procedures. Abortions do not merely place children in grave danger of death. In fact, the entire point of abortion is intentional destruction of the fetus."

---

[1] In baseball, the tie goes to the runner. Libertarianism, unfortunately, has no such tie breaking principle.

There are difficulties here. The phrase "eviction abortion" is a contradiction in terms. An abortion consists of an eviction plus murder. The former is compatible with libertarianism, the latter, of course, not. Thus, there can be no such thing as "eviction abortion." As well, Gordon misconstrues the evictionist position as countenancing, of all things, murderous abortion. If she wants to criticize the evictionist viewpoint, well and good. But she would be well advised to disparage the actual position, and not confuse it with "abortion choice," which is anathema to it. Further, libertarianism can fairly be construed as a branch of morality, the narrow sliver of it which deals with the justification of the use of physical violence. But that is its only connection with morality. Thus, libertarians are not concerned with the moral distinction between intentional killing and letting die. Rather, we are involved in analyzing what the law should say about these two concepts. And the answer is clear: intentional killing, except in self-defense, is murder, and should be severely punished. On the other hand, "letting die" is not a crime. There are hundreds of people who perish every day around the world, especially in poor nations. We in the west "let" this occur, when we do not donate all of our possessions and wealth to them, so as to put a stop to this. Are we criminals, murderers, for failing to stop this carnage? Of course not, at least not under libertarian law. Nor does the evictionist play "let's pretend" with anyone's life. There is simply no pretense here. The position, rather, is a very straightforward one: it simply states that apart from when it is necessary to save her life, or protect her health, the pregnant woman may only evict her pre-born child from her body, not murder him. Of course "abortions are intentionally destructive, not simple 'letting die' procedures." But it is difficult in the extreme to understand why this charge should be leveled at the evictionist position, since it utterly and totally rejects abortions.

Nothing loath, Gordon continues:

> "In theory, we could enact a law that limits abortion to intact removal. On the surface, such a law would seem to reflect the non-aggression principle. When the cord is cut at birth, the parents can passively abandon their child by walking away. Eviction, however, is not passive; it is an active intervention against the child. Both attack and negligence can be forms of aggression.
>
> "Nonetheless, the heart of the eviction argument must still be addressed. What if the mother could leave right after conception as easily as the father? With in vitro fertilization, everyone can walk off without anyone attacking the child. If they do walk off, they put the child, of course, in harm's way. Have parents a right to leave children unattended in hazardous situations? If their children die, is that simply regrettable, like famine victims dying because no one gave them assistance? For parents, as regards obligations, is there no difference between their own children and the children of strangers?"

Here, our author is changing the subject. She is no longer focusing on eviction. Now, she raises the issue of whether the parent may "walk off," that is fail to care for, feed, diaper, their baby. And the answer from the libertarian evictionist is that no, they most certainly may not do any such thing, and still have their inaction be compatible with just law. Why not? This is due to the fact that in doing so, they would be precluding other parents who wish to adopt the infant from doing so. They would be exercising property rights over the guardianship of the child without doing the "homesteading" required to justify such ownership. These inattentive parents should be legally obligated to bring their unwanted children to an orphanage, or a church, or a police station or a fire department or some such institution which would care for the baby until adoptive parents are found.

Gordon continues her critique of evictionism:

> "To abandon one's child in the petri dish is similar to putting her on board one's airplane and then jumping out, leaving her on the plane to crash, and doing all this without the child's consent. Perhaps a stranger with a suitable womb will happen by who is willing and able to adopt her. However, what if this does not happen?"

This writer in a creative and interesting manner inverts the usual criticism of evictionism, which is, the baby is stowed away on the airplane, and then the owner of it kicks the child out, to his death. This will sound callous, but if property rights are to be upheld, they must be upheld; there must be no exceptions. If the owner of an airplane, or a womb, does not want a trespasser to remain within his, or in the latter case, her, premises, then the libertarian, *qua* libertarian, may not gainsay this decision. Gordon does precisely that, in her attempt to pull at our heartstrings. One utilitarian refutation of her position is the query: under which system will more infants perish: one which respects private property to the ultimate degree, or one that does not? When put in this manner, it is difficult not to answer this question with support for private property rights. Practically the entire edifice of economics speaks with but one voice on this matter.

Gordon opines:

> "Interestingly, even most abortion choicers consider gross neglect and outright abandonment to be criminal behavior. When children have medical emergencies in the middle of the night, most parents do not go back to sleep saying, 'So what if my child might die? I have the right to control my own body, don't I?'
>
> "It is true that the means a woman must use to mother her child before birth are quite different from the means she uses after birth. But what difference does it make, in principle, whether her child is in the crib or in her womb? When she nurses her infant or carries her in her arms, she is using the same body she used to carry that same child to term.
>
> "As even most abortion choicers know, parent and good Samaritan are not analogous roles. Parents owe their immature children support and protection from harm. Why are they obligated? Did we have the right before birth to be in our mother's womb?"

There are numerous errors here. Let me count some of the ways. First, there are no positive obligations, at least not in libertarianism. In maintaining that there are, Gordon thus, but only to that limited extent, relinquishes her claim to be a representative of this philosophy. Second, there is a gigantic difference between "gross neglect and outright abandonment." The former is and should be a crime. Allowing a baby to starve while under parental control is to illicitly assert ownership of guardianship rights. These may only be maintained by continually caring for the baby. In sharp contrast, there is nothing at all legally wrong with the latter: transferring guardianship rights to new parents through adoption.

Gordon fires yet another shot across the bows of the position offered in the present volume:

> "To conceive and then abort one's child – even by mere eviction – is to turn conception into a deadly trap for the child. It is to set her up in a vulnerable position that is virtually certain to lead to her death. Conception followed by eviction from the womb could be compared to capturing someone, placing her on one's airplane, and then shoving her out in mid-flight without a parachute. The child in the womb is like a captive; she is in the situation involuntarily, and she cannot fend for herself. A captive is not trespassing on the captor's property, by definition. (Evicting or abandoning one's child cannot be regarded as releasing her from captivity, because this does not terminate childhood inability.)"

Nice try, but no cigar. There are serious dis-analogies between the mid-flight toss out and eviction. First, consider, again, rape. Here, there is no question that the mother set up anyone in a "vulnerable position." Yet, given that all babies have the same rights, and the ones who came into this world as a result of compulsory sexual intercourse have no such standing, then neither do any others. Gordon mistakenly asserts: "Inhabiting the mother's body is a direct byproduct of the parents' volitional act, not the child's." Yes, in ordinary circumstances, this is true. But not when rape occurs. And, since all babies, no matter what their start, have equal rights, they must be treated in the same manner.

Second, a better comparison would be A pushes B out of the way of an oncoming truck, and thus saves his life. Unfortunately, the road is near a river, into which B, a non-swimmer, falls, after being so pushed, and A either cannot swim, or does not wish to save B's life a second time. Or, perhaps, C first scoops D from drowning, places D in C's plane, and then later decides that there is no room for D in this aircraft, and pushes him out, again, without benefit of a parachute. A did not "capture" B any more than C "captured" D. Rather, A and C were the beneficiaries of B and D; they saved their lives, that is, gave them life in the first place, in much the same way as the non-raped mother first gave life to her baby. Vulnerable schmulnerable. Third, the pre-born infant was not "captured" by the mother. Rather, he was created by her, with a little help from the father. So, this analogy falls apart. Yes, "The parents are the causative agents of both the pregnancy and their child's dependence" but no one "captured" anyone else in this tableau.

According to this eloquent supporter of the pro-life position: "The fact of parental agency refutes any assertion that the child is a trespasser, a parasite, or an aggressor of any sort." False. Posit that the baby results from voluntary sexual intercourse, not rape. "Parental agency," then, consists of voluntary coitus. But why should this "refute" any such assertion? In the libertarian philosophy, there are no positive obligations. People are only "obliged" to refrain from threatening or initiating violence against others, their persons or their property. So far, the act of sexual intercourse does not obligate the parents to care for a baby; does not "refute" the claim that the unwanted baby is in effect a(n innocent) trespasser. There is only one exception to this genesis of obligations: contract. I borrow money from you; I am therefore contractually obligated to pay you back; this stems from the lending contract to which we both had agreed. But there was, cannot be, any "contract" between the parents and the fetus, certainly not at the time of intercourse, for there was no baby in existence at the time.

Gordon is not without a riposte to this sally: "Since a prenatal child is where she is because of her parents' actions, she can be said to be acting as her parents' agent – which places her alleged 'guilt' squarely on her parents' heads." But agency can only arise due to contract. Again, there can be no such thing as a contract with a very young infant, let alone with one who does not at all exist as of yet, since it takes some time after ejaculation, for the sperm to reach the egg. Then and only then may it fairly be said that a new human has been created. Surely, even Gordon would not subscribe to the notion that an egg and a sperm together constitute a human person, before physical penetration of the former by the latter?

Gordon further asserts that:

> "Under libertarian principles, parents have the same negative obligation towards their children that they have to strangers: non-aggression. The question is whether it follows that even given that parents are responsible for (caused) their child's existence, are the parents also responsible (accountable) for her support? Some abortion choicers claim that when parents let their child starve to death, they have not violated any positive right of the child and committed aggression. They are mistaken."

It is improper to resort to "Some abortion choicers..." I am here doing her the honor of quoting copiously from her publication. 'twould be far better, more considerate, more scholarly, were she to return the favor. If this unattributed criticism of hers were applied to me, I would vociferously deny it. No, there are no positive obligations in all of libertarianism, but there is such a thing as preclusion: owning something without homesteading it. What are the specifics? What crime is being committed by parents who "let their child starve to death?" They are on the one hand, the parents. This means that while they cannot of course own their children outright, they can indeed own the right to be their guardians. And how pray tell do they establish such rights: by continuing to guard, care for, their progeny. But parents who do not feed their children are claiming ownership over something, guardianship, to which they no longer have the right. If they do not anymore wish to fulfill the role of parent, in order not to commit the crime of owning something to which they have no right, they are required to take these babies to an orphanage, a hospital, a police station, etc., which will see to it that these dependents are cared for.

Next, consider this statement:

> "Parental obligation does not arise out of contract, tort, the mere fact of conception, or out of the biological relationship of parent to child. It arises because the parents voluntarily (even if they did not intend it) gave themselves a life-or-death control over their child. To withhold their support is to endanger the child. Parents owe support because they have no right to use their control to cause danger and then let the harm happen."

This is incompatible with the libertarian philosophy eloquently espoused by Gordon herself. For in that perspective, obligation can indeed arise out of contract, or tort, or criminal behavior. But it most certainly cannot be based upon holding "a life-or-death control over" someone else. The doctor holds "a life-or-death control over" a sick person. Without the ministrations of the physician, the ill man will perish. But in the absence of a contract requiring the former to treat the latter, there is simply no requirement, anywhere within even the furthest reaches of libertarianism, for him to do so. Gordon is making this up as she goes along. Yes, if the parent no longer wishes to guard the child he is compelled to notify others, the orphanage, the hospital, of this situation. But he has no libertarian obligation to continue guardianship.

Gordon avers that "if we endanger innocent people without their consent, we must protect them from the harm because of our obligation not to aggress." Yes, yes. But the female parent does not "endanger" the fetus. Rather, she improves the situation of the latter, by giving him life. Again, we resort to the case of A who saves the life of B by pushing him out of the path of the onrushing truck, whereupon B falls into the river and drowns, A refusing, or is unable, to save the swimmer. A improved the life of B, by giving him a few more seconds of life. A is not guilty of murder if he declines to further save the drowning B.

But our author denies this contention:

> "Some abortion choicers say that life is a gift to the child by the parents, a gift that does not bind the parents. A 'gift,' however, implies the option to refuse to take it, and beginning life is not an option for the child."

This, however, is erroneous. When A pushed B out of the path of the onrushing truck, A gave B a gift. This cannot be denied. However, B had no "option to refuse to take it." A's act was instantaneous, instinctive. B had no time to decide upon whether he wished to accept this gift of A's. If A had first asked B if he would like to have the gift of being pushed out of the path of the truck, B would have long ago been hit by it and killed.

Gordon is not through with her criticism of the perspective that animates this book. She avers: "Even simple eviction from the womb initiates force and violates the child's rights." Yes, of course eviction implies the use of force, but not the initiation thereof. X punches Y in the nose, gratuitously, and criminally. Y, in defense, returns the favor. Both used "force." But only X "initiated" it. Our authoress is arguing in a circle. She assumes as correct the very issue under contention: that the supposed right of the baby not to be killed supersedes the property right of the mother who does not wish to house the infant. But to reiterate, who is the proper owner of the rights seemingly in conflict. The libertarian theory of property rights maintains that the first to occupy given premises is the proper owner, not the second. But the mother was "there" first. She has been the owner-occupier of her body lo these many years. The baby is a Johny-come-lately, a long way second in these property rights sweepstakes. Once again, Gordon operates on the basis counter to the libertarianism she otherwise espouses.

It is time to end this refutation of Gordon's attempt to place the pro-life position as more in accord with libertarianism than is evictionism. She has made a valiant attempt, filled with love for the downtrodden, the helpless, the pre-born infant. But I cannot help believing she has failed in this mission of mercy.

References

Branden, Nathaniel. 1962. What Are the Respective Obligations of Parents to Children, and Children to Parents? *The Objectivist Newsletter* 1 (12, December): 55.

Gordon, Doris. 1999. Abortion and Rights: Applying Libertarian Principles Correctly. *International Journal of Sociology and Social Policy* 18 (3/4): 96–126.

Posner, Richard A. 1990. *The Problems of Jurisprudence*, 350. Cambridge: Harvard University Press.

Thomson, Judith Jarvis. 1990. *The Realm of Rights*. Cambridge: Harvard University Press.

Chapter 5
Response to Friedman on Narveson on Abortion

Friedman (2017) is a response to Narveson (2016). The former starts out with the following words:

> "Professor Jan Narveson objects to my claim that abortion on demand up to the moment of birth is not a policy prescription that follows naturally from the basic principles that undergird libertarianism. For the reasons set forth below, I continue to hold this view, even in the face of Narveson's thoughtful criticism."

I object to Friedman's characterization of Narveson's (2016) essay as "thoughtful." My own account of the latter work does not describe it in any such way; it is far more critical. Now, I appreciate Friedman's attempt to be polite. This is important not only amongst libertarians, nor even limited to scholars and academics, but should be generalized to all. However, there is that matter of truth, also, to consider. Perhaps a better word than "thoughtful" with which to have described Narveson's essay would have been "interesting," or "thought-provoking," or "attention-grabbing," "remarkable," "stimulating," or even "exciting." But "thoughtful," a positive pejorative, it was not.

Although I view Friedman's essay more positively than Narveson's, I cannot refrain from yet another criticism, this one far more important, and substantive. The former author maintains:

> "The crux of my original analysis (Friedman 2015: 157–58) is that the rights-based approach to resolving this issue must focus on the relative strengths of the mother's claim to bodily integrity and the fetus's putative right to life. Central to this inquiry is the question of when, if ever, the latter obtains full moral status (FMS) or near-FMS."

What is the difficulty here? It is that this statement assumes the correctness of the notion that rights can clash. Otherwise, who would care about the "relative strength" of incompatible claims. If and only if rights can clash, then we must, if we seek justice, weigh the two of them, one against the other. The nod, then, presumably, would go to the one with more power, or greater strength. But this is inconsistent with the clearly stated goal of Friedman to adhere to "the basic principles that undergird libertarianism." For these principles rule out any clash in rights. If there

W. E. Block, *Evictionism*, https://doi.org/10.1007/978-981-16-5014-7_5

seems to be one such, it is because either one or the other or both of these "rights" is mis-specified.

I fully agree with this author, however, that "when, if ever, the (fetus) obtains full moral status (FMS) is of crucial importance." And here, again, I depart from both Friedman and Narveson. The former maintains that "while a three-week-old embryo may be the same biological organism as the adult it becomes, it is a qualitatively different being: "it is not the same individual, in the morally relevant sense, as the person it develops into" (Friedman 2015: 239n25)."

The latter, with the approval of the former, characterizes the fetus as a "clump of cells." If the preborn child were properly categorized in this manner, then the crime of forcibly trimming someone's hair, or forcibly clipping her fingernails, would be no more serious a crime than killing her new-child-to-be-while-still-in-the-womb against her will. Yet, it is difficult in the extreme to take seriously any such contention. As to the former, Friedman, too, is "not the same individual, in the morally relevant sense, as" he was, oh, eight and a quarter months ago. Would it be justified to draw any principles of law from this difference? Hardly. Yes, the baby, will physically be very different after the passage of this time period; Friedman, himself, will likely change not at all as much. But the baby will be the same person before and after this passage of time, and so will Friedman.

I must also part company with Friedman when he emphasizes the importance of the "future value of its life" of the fetus. That is not why it is against libertarian law to murder this preborn child. First of all, if Austrian economics teaches us anything, it is that "value" is subjective. What is one man's meat is another man's poison. *De gustibus non disputandum*. Secondly, Terri Schiavo, blessed be her memory, had no future value of life, at least in the subjective tastes of most people. She was in a coma, brain dead, kept alive only by artificial means (Block 2018). Suppose someone had taken a pistol and shot her to death while she lay in her hospitable bed helpless. According to Friedman and Narveson, this gunman would not have been a murderer, since she had no future awake existence, no will, no nothing of that sort. I regard this as a *reductio ad absurdum*. No, human life starts with the fertilized egg, one millisecond after the sperm intersects with the egg, since that "cluster of cells" is now a human being. Friedman takes an altogether different view:

> "My conclusion was that libertarian theory provides no decisive reason to reject the majority opinion that "at some point in its development (perhaps at the point of consciousness), the fetus enjoys or nearly enjoys FMS, and that good cause must then exist to justify an abortion" (Friedman 2015: 159)."

It is difficult to wrap one's mind around the concept of "nearly enjoying FMS." Yes, there are continua all over the place in political, legal philosophy. But it strains the imagination to think that the same could apply to human beings and murder. Either the person is alive or not. If so then the person has FMS. There is no such thing, as Friedman acquiesces in, as "near-FMS."

I note, also, Friedman's rather cavalier attitude regarding the claim that "an infant may rightfully be starved to death by its (sic) parents." If that is not cold-blooded murder of perhaps the most despicable sort possible, then nothing is. It is puzzling that an accomplished libertarian can go so far wrong.

At this point in his essay, Friedman goes into a long, complicated exegesis concerning pain. Does the fetus feel any, is the question to which he addresses himself. I regard this as entirely irrelevant to the point at issue. There are several painless ways to murder someone, mainly by use of drugs. Take an overdose of sleeping pills and you will perish, without feeling the slightest bit of pain. If I slip them into your food, I am a murderer, and I have caused you no pain at all. Please do not misunderstand me. I totally oppose the imposition of pain on victims. There is perhaps nothing so cruel. Also, there are some, masochists, who actually enjoy pain. Marathon runners, boxers, immediately come to mind. The issue is thus not pain, but, rather, property rights: who is the proper owner of the womb. The mother of course. The unwanted fetus is a trespasser. The mother may evict him from her premises, but not murder him since he is an innocent trespasser. But evict him she may do.

Here, at last, is a passage of this author with which I at least partially agree. I note that he has the advantage over Narveson:

> "... by any reasonable measure, a third-trimester fetus is no longer a mere 'clump of cells.' At this point, it is a radically more evolved, sophisticated, 'purposeful,' and recognizably human organism.... it is highly plausible that any physiological differences between the late third trimester fetus and the newborn are morally irrelevant."

I strongly endorse the last statement. There is indeed no difference in the FMS of a fetus in the last stages of pregnancy and the newly arrived child. They are for all intents and purposes the same human being; they are only geographically separated, particularly a few minutes before and after birth. This commonsensical similarity is endorsed by Friedman, but not Narveson. However, I do not see the fetus, no matter how well developed as "purposeful," nor, even, the newborn babe. "Purpose" indicates intention, planning, thoughtfulness. Anyone who has ever held a recent arrival in their arms knows full well they are just a blob, not to say a clump of cells who (sic) is a rights-bearer. But purpose they have not.

Friedman comes truly into his own in his lambasting of Narveson. First, he does so regarding the attempt of the latter to derive an ought from an is: "the most important thing to emphasize about the contractarian approach is that it hopes to generate moral principles for societies out of non-moral values of individuals (1988: 166, emphasis in original)."

This is a philosophical howler of the worst sort and Friedman enjoys a "gotcha" moment at the expense of the guilty party. Second, the former taxes the latter as follows:

> "... it is perfectly natural for Narveson to assume his contractors would not wish to be inconvenienced by the moral demands of nonpersons: fetuses and newborns alike. The implication of this stance is that parents are seemingly incapable of criminally wronging their infants, regardless of how prolonged or horrific this abuse may be."

Why is this? It is because, in Narveson's view, even the newborn is altogether too similar to his "clump of cells" to be fully rights-bearing. If so, just as it is impossible to perpetrate a crime against the aforementioned "clump of cells," this applies, also, to the newborn infant. Presumably, there would be no such thing as child abuse in the libertarianism of Narveson.

Friedman continues his reprimanding of Narveson:

> "… it is clear that Narveson's theory cannot support government intervention to shield newborns, infants, and young children from even the most dreadful abuse by their parents. First, societal 'self-defense, broadly construed' does not apply to an entire range of cases where children are simply murdered before reaching the age that qualifies them for contractor status, or are terribly mistreated but then isolated by their parents from the rest of society during their adult lifetimes. In such circumstances it appears that the state is impotent in the face of monstrous evil."

As an anarcho-capitalist, I pass lightly over Friedman's reliance on the state, of all institutions, to do justice. But his point, otherwise, is totally sound. The logical implication of Narveson's viewpoint is surely that parents can literally get away with murder if they confine their evil to their own children. But more. Why limit this to their own progeny? There are an awful lot of "cell clusters" running around out there in their diapers. All of them would appear to be fair game, whether they are your children or not. Clusters of cells are only clusters of cells, after all.

Alas, once again Friedman slips up. He mentions "the property rights that parents hold in their offspring." But according to libertarian theory, at least the way I understand it, the father and mother have no such property rights. To have property rights in someone is to own him. If this were true, then, indeed, there logically could not be any such crime as child abuse, as Narveson would have it. But, no, parents are not the proprietors of their progeny. Rather, children occupy an intermediate position between cows and cars, on the one hand, which may indeed be owned, and, on the other hand, adults, who may not be. Mothers and fathers may not own children, but they may have property rights in guardianship over them. How do they attain them? First, by giving birth to their progeny. This establishes a homesteading right, not to them, of course, but to the right to bring them up. While there is such a thing as absentee ownership over land and buildings, but not over children; cease to guard them, and you lose your rights to be their guardian. Second, by purchasing these rights from their proper owners. There is no "what is best for the children" mandate in the libertarian philosophy. Bill Gates, we might well imagine, can give Tom Smith's children a better life than he can. However, as long as the latter continues to bring up the children, guard them, care for them, feed and clothe them, he owns the guardianship rights to them, and Mr. Gates may not take them away from him, even though, we stipulate, he can give them better lives.

But once again Friedman gets back on the right track in his reproving of Narveson. He avers: "… we should remain unsatisfied even if Narveson could somehow persuade us that his system would protect newborns. Surely, we do not object to parents' torturing their infants out of our fear of what the victims may become, but because torture is a monstrous injustice."

No truer words were ever said, and it is a shame that they even had to be said. But be said they must, if we are to explore the implications of libertarianism on this matter. Once again Narveson's utilitarianism rises to the fore, and Friedman will have none of it on deontological grounds. Parents abusing children violates the libertarian non-aggression principle, one of the key foundations of that philosophy.

I cannot resist quoting this magnificent upbraiding of Narveson by Friedman, along lines I myself have long treaded: "While it is true that infants cannot appreciate or assert their right to life, neither can persons asleep or in a reversible coma. Nevertheless, homicide laws are routinely applied in such cases as we rightly impute to such individuals the desire to live. I see no reason why a similar attribution should not be made on behalf of newborns."

What more can possibly be said about this. Narveson falls asleep upon occasion. Presumably, every night. During those times he is far from being able to "appreciate or assert (his) right to life." If he were done away with while he was semi-comatose, as we all are, he could have no objection, at least based on his version of libertarianism.

I cannot resist quoting in full Friedman's last *tour de force* against Narveson:

> "The critical point here is that Narveson's stance on infants also impugns his position on third-trimester abortion in that he has no credible way of distinguishing the two types of cases. The same three-step argument he makes with respect to the impossibility of murdering a fetus also shows that it is impossible to murder a newborn, since it also plainly lacks the 'defining properties' of personhood. And because, as argued above, Narveson cannot consistently hold that unwanted newborns, but not late stage fetuses, enjoy indirect rights, he is put to the hard choice of either permitting parental infanticide or allowing that third-trimester fetuses may also have moral status (based on the features they share with newborns).
>
> "This is the rock on which most extreme pro-choice theories run aground. It is impossible, it seems, to formulate an argument that permits third-trimester abortion on demand without also excusing infanticide… Thus, Narveson's contractarianism is either implausible for most libertarians or does not exclude pro-life arguments."

However exhilarating, I must end on a critical note vis-a-vis this author. He opines as follows:

> "It is perhaps worth stressing again that my purpose is not to take sides in the abortion controversy. Rather, it is simply to show that no particular policy prescription follows ineluctably from libertarian first principles. Essentially, in my judgment, natural-rights libertarianism—as a political theory—has nothing useful to say about the key question, fetal moral status."

This is more than passing curious. This author shows familiarity with several publications of mine on this subject by citing them in his paper and devoting an entire paragraph to my views. Undoubtedly, he is familiar with many more of them. There is not a single one of them, perhaps, in which I do not maintain that evictionism and only evictionism "follows ineluctably from libertarian first principles." I can only wonder why he did not see fit to demonstrate that I am mistaken in this conclusion of mine.

References

Block, Walter E. 2018. Judith Jarvis Thomson on Abortion; A Libertarian Critique. *DePaul Journal of Health Care Law* 19 (1): Article 3, 1–17.

Friedman, Mark D. 2015. *Libertarian Philosophy in the Real World*. London: Bloomsbury.

———. 2017. Libertarianism and Abortion: A Reply to Professor Narveson. *Libertarian Papers* 9 (1): 130–144. http://libertarianpapers.org/friedman-abortion-narveson/

Narveson. 1988. *The Libertarian Idea*. Philadelphia: Temple University Press.

———. 2016. Resolving the Debate on Libertarianism and Abortion. *Libertarian Papers* 8 (2, January): 267–272. http://libertarianpapers.org/wp-content/uploads/2016/09/post/2016/09/lp-8-2-6.pdf

Chapter 6
Comment on Narveson on Friedman on Abortion

In this chapter, I will comment on contributions by two libertarians, on the philosophically vexing problem of abortion. To wit, on Narveson (2016) and on Friedman (2017). Let us start with the former.

Narveson (1988) is one of the best books ever written on the libertarian philosophy. Therefore, I had expected better from Narveson (2016). I am sadly disappointed in the latter. It is one thing when a non-libertarian misconstrues the phrase "right to life." Their philosophies do not abhor the very thought of a positive obligation. It is quite another when a libertarian of the standing of Dr. Narveson makes this rookie error. Rights imply obligations. If I have a right not to be murdered, raped, stolen from, you have an obligation to cease and desist all such activities. No one has a right to life; if they did, others would be legally obligated to preserve the lives of other people. But under libertarianism, there are only negative rights: everyone has a right not to be murdered, not to be stolen from, not to be raped, kidnapped, etc., but not to be fed, cared for, by other people, against their will.

Narveson next "resoundingly denies Friedman's claim that no position 'flows naturally from the basic principles that undergird libertarianism.'" And here, happily, I agree with my long time fellow libertarian, Narveson, in this critique of his regarding Friedman. There is indeed a position on abortion that "flows naturally from the basic principles that undergird libertarianism." To wit, it is evictionism. Narveson, instead, adopts the pro-choice viewpoint:

> "Fetuses have none of the interactive psychological properties we ascribe to all human persons. There is no excuse for ascribing inherent liberty rights to things that have none of those features. You can only qualify for a right to general liberty if you have a 'will' that can be thwarted by others' actions."

But sleeping people have no "will." Nor do the comatose. Nor do the elderly senile. Nor do very young post-born children. Would this philosopher maintain that none of them have a right to "general liberty?" If so, this would be difficult to reconcile with libertarianism.

W. E. Block, *Evictionism*, https://doi.org/10.1007/978-981-16-5014-7_6

But this author goes further. He opines that no one: "… has reason to attribute rights to clumps of cells. Rights are for persons, not organisms or DNA encodings… You cannot murder a clump of cells."

How is that again? "Clumps of cells." If I went over to Narveson, held him down and forcibly, against his "will" clipped his fingernails,[1] I would be guilty of assault and battery, a serious crime. But I would have only relieved him of "clumps of cells." If I employed my special ray gun that kills fetuses residing in pregnant women, without in the slightest interfering with these adults in any other way, would I have been guilty of the same sort of thing I perpetrated on Narveson? That would appear to be the logical conclusion of his claims on this matter. Yet, it is difficulty to reconcile this conclusion with common sense, let alone with the high regard in which libertarianism holds human life, a position that "flows naturally from the basic principles that undergird libertarianism." Am I arguing in a circle here, assuming the very thing under dispute, the claim of humanity on the part of the pre-born infant? I think not. If I were, I would be guilty of the very same crime regarding fingernails and fetuses. There is more than a "dime's worth of difference" between the two.

Narveson continues in this vein: "Libertarianism gives every person the right to run his or her own life. But fetuses are not able to 'run' anything. They are not participants in the agreements among us that constitute morality, and not yet participants in communities."

Perhaps he has never had children, or, noted them in the few weeks and months of their lives while in their cribs. They do not "run anything" quite yet, except for their noses and also at the other ends of their bodies. And this applies to the severely mentally disabled, the comatose, people when asleep.

Continues Narveson (footnote omitted):

> "There might be reasons why a given society would want to insist on carrying fetuses to term, but those reasons have no grounding in 'fetal rights,' and it is difficult to think of any that would pass muster with libertarians, who (rightly) deny that 'society' has any business coercing individuals for any other purpose than mutual protection. And in the case of society versus individual nonparents, that's certainly what it would be. We should remember that many societies have not even extended rights to newborns. For example, they have routinely exposed to the elements newborns who were defective or even simply one too many for the limited resources available."

Talk about circular arguments. Here this author is assuming the very point under contention, namely, that fetuses do not qualify for "mutual protection." He is of course correct in contending that under libertarianism those in charge of law and order do indeed have "business coercing individuals for … mutual protection." But this hardly demonstrates that the pre-born do not thereby qualify.

Of course primitive societies allowed unwanted newborn babies to perish. That is because no one else in their environment wished to care of them or was able to do so. But suppose there were such generous people available, and the parents would still not allow others to take on these responsibilities. Then these parents would be

[1] I would do a good job. I wouldn't hurt him.

flat-out murderers. And the same applies to modern societies. Only, now, there are numerous people, organized in religious and other pro-life organizations, who stand ready to bear this burden.

Moreover, this author is way off the mark when he asserts that

> "… there is in fact a major difference between fetuses and newborns, as any parent knows. Even very young infants begin to have some of the features that identify one as a person and not just a clump of cells. But even so, there is no fundamental basis for attributing rights to nonminded, nonpersonal beings."

Consider a "very young infant" 15 minutes after being born, and compare him with what he was, a half hour ago, 15 minutes before birth. What "major difference" can Narveson possibly have in mind? Features? Not a bit of it. There is no more difference between this present baby a half hour ago and now, and he himself now and 30 minutes ago. Yes, babies change more than do adults in a given time period, but not by that much. And, if my time calculations are erroneous, we can always compare the baby five minutes before and after birth, with Narveson a week or a month or year ago before today. The pre- and post-born baby changes less, in his "features" or anything else. The only difference is that the baby necessarily changes his "address" in the interim, while this philosopher need not do so, although he certainly could.

Our author opens himself up to the counterargument of sleeping people, the comatose, the senile, the severely mentally handicapped when he avers: "… it is our choices and agreements, not the physical thing that presumably is our operating substructure, that create and ground rights."

It cannot possibly be stressed sufficiently that the aforementioned people do not make any more "choices and agreements" than does the fetus. If the latter cannot have rights, this disparages those of those mentioned above. Would Narveson really like to declare open season on such people? Does he, himself, never go to sleep? His perspective would render such an activity of his very perilous from a legal standpoint. No one could possibly murder him then, for he himself would then be, insofar as "choices and agreements" are concerned, a mere "clump of cells" ready to be eradicated with no criminal penalty on the part of the perpetrator. If he is killed, not murdered by his own lights, he will be hoisted by his own petard.

References

Friedman, Mark D. 2017. Libertarianism and Abortion: A Reply to Professor Narveson. *Libertarian Papers* 9 (1): 130–144. http://libertarianpapers.org/friedman-abortion-narveson/

Narveson. 1988. *The Libertarian Idea*. Philadelphia: Temple University Press.

———. 2016. Resolving the Debate on Libertarianism and Abortion. *Libertarian Papers* 8 (2, January): 267–272. http://libertarianpapers.org/wp-content/uploads/2016/09/post/2016/09/lp-8-2-6.pdf

Part IV
Response to Non-libertarian Critics of Evictionism

Chapter 7
Rejoinder to Boonin on Abortion

I have two problems with this book right from the start. Boonin's subject is abortion, but he never defines that term.[1] Is it the eviction, the removal, of the fetus? If this is what is meant, we must say that at the present level of medical technology, this will spell the death knell of the infant during the first two trimesters of its life, but not during the third. If so, partial birth abortions in the last trimester would be banned. Or is abortion to be defined as killing this tiny human being?[2] In that case the young person may justifiably be done away with at any stage of its development during his nine month gestation period. This author does not vouchsafe us an answer to this very important issue.

As for me, I define abortion as eviction plus unjustified killing, e.g., downright murder. I claim the former is always justified,[3] based on the fact that the mother is the legitimate title holder to the property in dispute, her womb, and therefore the unwanted baby is a trespasser.

Secondly, Boonin sees the issue as a "moral dispute" (p. 1) but offers no definition of "morality." Is it niceness? Propriety? Congruence with local mores? Our author fails to inform us.

In contrast, I approach the issue of abortion from the perspective of but a small slice of morality; the libertarian emphasis on justice, based in turn upon private property rights and the non-aggression principle (NAP). Namely, what is the proper use of force, or violence? Answer, only in defense against, or in retaliation at, a prior initial use thereof. That is, what is proper law? And the response, emanating from

---

Why spend so many words on this one book, when there are so many "out there" that deal with abortion? Simple. I regard Boonin (2003) as *the* best defense of the pro-choice perspective, head and shoulders over the next best treatments. This book brings me in mind of Bohm-Bawerk (1959) in its thoroughness (on the interest rate in that case), and I regard that as a very powerful compliment to Boonin.

---

[1] Never, ever, not once, in his entire book, which is otherwise stupendously meticulous.

[2] Both Boonin and I posit that the fertilized egg starts human life, him, arguendo, me, out of belief.

[3] The latter, never.

W. E. Block, *Evictionism*, https://doi.org/10.1007/978-981-16-5014-7_7

this philosophical quarter is, whatever is compatible with the NAP is allowed, all else is banned. So, murder, theft, kidnapping, rape, etc., are outlawed, everything else is legal.[4] With this introduction, we are now ready to evaluate Boonin (2003).

Boonin does not define morality, but does give some examples thereof (p. 4)[5]:

> "'Should abortion be legal or illegal?' In principle, these are importantly distinct questions. There are actions, such as jaywalking, which we may think to be justifiably illegal and yet not immoral, and there are actions, such as adultery, which we may think to be immoral and yet not justifiably illegal. Still, as a practical matter, it is difficult to avoid the conclusion that, at least in the case of abortion the moral question is the more fundamental. If almost everyone believed that abortion was perfectly moral, it is unlikely that there would be much public demand for laws criminalizing abortion or that such laws would be effectively enforced if they were passed. And if almost everyone believed that abortion was morally on a par with murder, it is unlikely that women wishing to have abortions would find that they were easily available, even if they were technically legal. Since the moral question of abortion is the more fundamental in this respect, an inquiry into the subject should begin with it. And since the moral question of abortion is a difficult enough question on its own, I will limit my focus in this book to it alone."

I find this unsatisfying. First there is no definition offered, merely instances of how he uses this term. But without a definition, a map as it were, we are left to our own devices as to how to apply it to cases other than the ones he mentions. Second, some of us may think jaywalking "justifiably illegal" (p. 4), while others may not. In my view, the government, the de facto owner of the road, is not a licit organization. Therefore, its rules are invalid, unless in agreement with libertarianism.[6] Prohibition of jaywalking does not necessarily conform to this criterion. It is certainly conceivable that the private owner of the street (Block 2013a, b, c, d) may allow, even encourage, this practice. Moreover, if adultery is seen as a contract violation, it would be against the law in the libertarian society.[7] The moral question is very important for Boonin, but for the libertarian the *only* issue is its *legality*.[8]

---

[4] Libertarianism defines private property rights on the basis of homesteading theory. See on this: Block 1990, 2002a, b, c, 2007, 2011b; Block and Edelstein 2012; Block and Nelson 2015; Block and Yeatts 1999-2000; Block vs Epstein 2005; Bylund 2005, 2012; Grotius 1625; Hoppe 1993b, 2011; Kinsella 2003, 2006, 2009a, b, c, d; Locke 1948; Paul 1987; Pufendorf 1673; Rothbard 1973a, b, 32; Rozeff 2005; Watner 1982.

[5] All cites to, quotes from, Boonin are to his one book (2003); his footnotes are eliminated, unless otherwise specified.

[6] That is, limited to prohibiting violations of the NAP such as murder, rape, theft, etc.

[7] It would be akin to a tort.

[8] States Rothbard: "Libertarianism is not and does not pretend to be a complete moral, or aesthetic theory; it is only a political theory, that is, the important subset of moral theory that deals with the proper role of violence in social life. Political theory deals with what is proper or improper for the government to do, and the government is distinguished from every other group in society as being the institution of organized violence. Libertarianism holds that the only proper role of violence is to defend person and property against violence, that any use of violence that goes beyond such just defense is itself aggressive, unjust, and criminal. Libertarianism, therefore, is a theory which states that everyone should be free of violent invasion, should be free to do as he sees fit except invade the person or property of another. What a person does with his or her life is vital and important, but is simply irrelevant to libertarianism." And again: "The fundamental axiom of libertarian theory is

Our author takes another hack at morality (p. 4): "Consider an imaginary billionaire named Donald[9] who has just unexpectedly won a million dollars from a one-dollar lottery ticket. He is trying to decide what to do with the money and has limited himself to the following options: (1) donating the money to several worthy charities, (2) putting it in his savings account, (3) buying a gold-plated Rolls Royce, (4) putting up billboards across the country that read 'I hate Ivana,' and (5) hiring a hitman to kill Ivana. One thing we are likely to say about this list is that there is a morally relevant sense in which the choices become progressively worse. We would be entitled to aim more moral criticism at Donald for choosing (4), for example, than for choosing (3)."

But he offers us no *reason* why when we go from one to four the acts are less and less moral. More and more selfish? Yes. But if our author is using selfishness as a synonym for morality, why does he not clearly say so? And, why refer to morality at all, since selfishness is far more clear. When Boonin tries to explicate this morass, he runs into a bit of trouble. He writes (p. 5):

> "…there is a difference in kind between (5) and the others. The difference might be put like this: Even though it is his money, and so there is some sense in which he is entitled to spend it in any way he wants, still he is not entitled to spend it in *that* way. This is the distinction I have in mind in saying that (5) is impermissible while (1)-(4) are permissible."

Yes, of course, there is a gigantic chasm between 1–4 on the one hand, and 5 on the other. But this has little or nothing to do with *morality.* Rather, it addresses, full bore, the libertarian concern with the NAP. None of the first four violate this stricture, which the fifth is a paradigm case of such a desecration. For the libertarian, one through four should be legal, but, of course, not five. If this is Boonin's main concern, and it is difficult to see why it is not, at least not at this stage of his analysis, then, contrary to his explicit statement, his book is not at all about morality; instead, it is an attempt to address the libertarian issue of what should the law be.

Seemingly, he deduces from these considerations that "a woman's having an abortion violates no rights" (p. 5). My fear is that he proceeds all too quickly in arriving at this conclusion. Boonin is quite correct that "… the claim of such critics is not that her having an abortion rather than bringing her unwanted pregnancy to term is like Donald's buying a gold-plated car rather than contributing his winnings to charity; it is that it is like his hiring a hitman to kill his ex-wife" (p. 5).

But if abortion is as I have claimed – evicting the fetus from the mother's "premises" *plus* killing the baby – it would seem difficulty for our author to defend his position. Killing an unwanted trespasser, when the owner of the property in question

that no one may threaten or commit violence ("aggress") against another man's person or property. Violence may be employed only against the man who commits such violence; that is, only defensively against the aggressive violence of another. In short, no violence may be employed against a non-aggressor. Here is the fundamental rule from which can be deduced the entire corpus of libertarian theory." Source: Vance 2016. That author applies these basic building blocks to racism. In this review essay, I attempt to apply it to abortion.

[9] Boonin's book was published in 2003, long before the advent of Donald Trump in U.S. politics; one wonders, then, at his prescience, to mention the present president of this country.

could have as easily limited herself to merely removing this tiny person, evicting him, separating herself from the child, would appear to be a blatant violation of the NAP. In terms of Boonin's five part series, it would appear most akin to number five, hiring a hit man to commit murder.

Consider this viewpoint of Boonin's (p. 7): "…the conclusion that someone (presumably the fetus) does have a valid moral claim against an abortion's being performed need not entail that abortion should be illegal. Not every valid moral claim is one we would wish to see enforced by the law. If I promise to help you move next week, or not to see anyone else while we are dating, then this provides you with a legitimate moral claim against me, but we may nonetheless think there is good reason not to treat it as one that the courts may enforce" (p. 7).

But promising to "help you move" resembles Donald's choices one through four. Aborting the fetus, as opposed to merely evicting the youngster, is in the same category as his fifth option. It would appear that this Boulder, Colorado professor is contradicting himself with regard to what he said about Donald's fifth choice. Presumably, Ivana has not only a "valid moral claim" against Donald's hit man, but one, also, "that the courts may enforce." And, no "may" about it, either. The judiciary, if it is to follow the most basic elements of the rule of law, *must* indeed enforce it.

Morality would appear to be a sometime thing; sort of like trying to nail jelly to the proverbial tree. Boonin states (p. 8, fn. 4): "It is perfectly consistent to believe that abortion (or prostitution, or pornography and so on) should be safely available because it is permissible, but rare because it is (or is often) criticizable (though one could, of course, also believe that it is not morally criticizable either, but should be rare merely because it is undesirable from a purely prudential point of view."

But if "one could, of course, also believe that it is not morally criticizable either," then this concept cannot be of much help to distinguish between what is moral and what is not; ditto, "criticizable." One man's meat is another man's poison, according to the hoary aphorism. What one man may criticize another may applaud. That jelly keeps running down the tree. "Moral intuitions" (p. 10) are all well and good, but are not of that much use in making fine distinctions between that which ought to be legal and that which ought to be prohibited.[10] Should not a scientific examination of so important an issue as abortion be predicated on something a bit more substantial?

Moving along, Boonin opines: "In framing the question to be addressed in this book, and in selecting a methodology for evaluating the various arguments that purport to answer it, I have attempted as much as possible to allow the critic of abortion to frame the debate" (p. 14).

Well and good. I, as a libertarian am a staunch and even bitter opponent of abortion, but unhappily Boonin's "framing" of this debate is not at all conducive to that

[10] Huemer 2007, would disagree.

philosophy.[11] For example, the very first argument he puts forth (p. 15) is "P1: the (typical) human fetus has a right to life." But note how "rights" work. If I have a right to X, you have an obligation, a duty, to respect it. This applies to all rights, without exception. We now divide rights into the positive and the negative. In the former case, what I have a right to is something you must give me, or support me in, otherwise you are a rights violator. If I have a right to health care, you (and others, of course) must give it to me. If I have a right to shelter, you (and/or others) need to house me. And, if I have a right to life, you (and again others) are legally obligated to keep me alive. If I die, you and these others; are murderers. These are all positive rights, rejected, entirely, by all libertarians. In the latter case, what I have a right to is that you *refrain* from acting. I have a right not to be robbed. You[12] are thus constrained not to rob me. I have a right not to be raped. The logical implication is that you have a duty not to invade me in that manner. I also have a right not to be murdered. Given this, you may not engage in homicide against me.[13] Negative rights of this sort are the bedrock of libertarianism. The point is, if Boonin wanted to "frame" the argument in terms inclusive of the libertarian critic of abortion, he would have characterized the fetus's rights negatively, not positively. He would have had as his basic premise not his P1, but, rather: "the (typical) human fetus[14] has a right not to be murdered." He never would have stated that "the (typical) human fetus has a right to life." Yes, perhaps, many scholars would agree that "the (typical) human fetus has a right to life." But no *libertarian* opponent of abortion, such as the present author, would accept any such claim. Consider the following statement (p. 16): "A defense of abortion will be more effective the more it can work from premises that critics of abortion accept, and surely most critics of abortion believe that you and I do have a right to life." Well, yes, this is probably true of "most critics of abortion." But not at all of libertarians. Are we to be frozen out of this dispute?

At last we arrive at a statement (p. 21) that Boonin and I completely share: "I will assume that the claim that a new human being comes to exist at the moment of conception is true." However, his follow up is problematic (p. 22–23):

> "Since every human fetus is a member of the human species, this would in turn imply that every human fetus acquires a right to life at the moment of its conception. Since this article appeals to the claim that appealing to our humanity provides the most parsimonious explanation of why you and I have a right to life, I will refer to it as the parsimony argument.

[11] One of the minor flaws of this book is that although there is a large literature on the libertarian analysis of abortion, Boonin completely ignores it. Some of it, of course, post-dates the publication of his book in 2003. But, there are several that pre-date it. See for instance: Akers 2012a, b; Block 1977a, 1978, 2001a, 2004a, 2008, 2010d, e, f, 2011a, c, d, e, 2012, 2014a, c, d, e; Block and Whitehead 2005; Davies 2012; Dyke and Block 2011; Feser 2004; Goodwin 2014; Mosquito 2014a, 2015; Parr 2011, 2013; Rothbard 1978a, b; Sadowsky 1978; Shaffer 2012; Vance 2008, 2012; Wisniewski 2010a, b, 2011, 2013.

[12] And others, as in the former case.

[13] Nor hire a hitman to do so, as in Donald's fifth option.

[14] And everyone else for that matter, too.

> "The parsimony argument should be rejected because species membership in itself does not provide a satisfactory explanation for the consensus that both sides of the abortion debate will reach in the case of the ten individuals you would have selected. Suppose, for example that it turned out that one of the people you brought back as an uncontroversial example of an individual with a right to life turned out not to be a human being after all. Although exactly like a human being in every other respect, he is in fact an alien from another planet whose DNA structure is slightly different from that of human beings. No matter what our views on abortion, it is extremely difficult to believe that this discovery would make us think it any more permissible to kill him. He has all of the same properties we thought he had before; he simply got them from alien parents instead of human ones. And suppose, on the other hand, that one of the people you identified as an uncontroversial example of an individual with a right to life was a human being who subsequently suffered the permanent destruction of the higher regions of his brain but who was nonetheless able to be kept alive on a life-support machine. There might prove to be some reason to think it morally criticizable to remove such a person from life support, but surely the claim that he would continue to have the same right to life as you or I would be extremely controversial at best. A defender of the claim that the typical human fetus has a right to life cannot appeal to an argument that entails that people in such conditions do as well. And so a critic of abortion cannot appeal to the parsimony argument. The fact that the only actual uncontroversial cases of individuals with a right to life are human beings provides no support for the claim that all human beings have a right to life."

The way libertarians define a human being has little or nothing to do with DNA. Rather, our species is defined as rights bearing creatures, because we have the capability, willingness, to respect the core essence of this philosophy, the NAP. If we found a *person* who looked like a giraffe, or a snake, or an octopus, but who[15] acted in accordance with this doctrine, it would be improper, *illegal* under libertarian law, to murder him. He would of course not have any more "right to life" than anyone else, but that is entirely a different matter. I thus cannot see my way clear to agreeing with Boonin that the parsimony argument is invalid. Once we admit, both of us, Boonin and me, that the fertilized egg is a rights-bearing human being, and is on a legal par with every other creature, human or not, who is capable of behaving in accordance with the NAP, then and only then do we start out with a crucial agreement. No longer will we pass each other as ships in the night. Now, perhaps, we can attain real disagreement.

Consider this statement (p. 32): "And the same seems to go for the fetus from the moment of conception. To say that one should treat the fetus with reverence is not the same as saying that killing it is morally impermissible. It is to say in one's deliberations one must not treat it as just another collection of cells."

Boonin, here, contradicts himself. He stipulated that the fetus, from conception onwards, is a human being. Now, "killing it" is morally permissible? And what is it

---

[15] For the most part; after all, not all of us with human DNA respect the NAP. This goes along with the species, not the individual. After all, babies, the senile, the unconscious, the mentally handicapped, criminals, are not able to alter their behavior to conform to the NAP. What percentage of the species would have to pass this hurdle? Suppose there was one mosquito who would not bite or otherwise molest us. Would the entire species gain the right not to be killed by us? No. How about 95% of them. Yes. Hey, our species does not do much better than that, if we can attain that level at all. We have here the insoluble continuum problem. See on this Block and Barnett 2008.

with this "it" business? This "collection of cells" is a human being! Not only, under libertarian law, would it be murder to kill these "cells," but they are deserving of more than an "it." How about a "he?"[16]

In the view of this University of Colorado professor (p. 33): "…if the zygote is taken to be worthy of awe, it is extremely difficult to avoid the conclusion that a sperm and an egg are also. After all, they have the ability to produce a zygote, which is in turn worthy of awe. This suggests that this version of the sanctity of human life argument could succeed only by also showing contraception to be morally on a par with abortion. Since critics of abortion, even those who also oppose contraception, do not believe that contraception is morally on a par with abortion, this counts as a further reason to conclude that they cannot successfully appeal to this argument."

"Awe" might be a little bit of a reach[17] but given that the zygote is a human being, as is the mere fertilized egg, this is not too far off the mark. But this does not at all apply to "a sperm and an egg." The former, left in a proper environment,[18] turns into a child and then an adult. Place the sperm and an egg anywhere you wish, apart from with each other, and this result does not obtain. There is all the world of difference, then, between the sperm that has fertilized the egg and these two cells apart from each other. Killing the former is murder, but the latter have no rights at all. Preventing them from "meeting" each other through contraception is thus not a rights violation. Dare I suggest that to even mention abortion and contraception in the same sentence, let alone to place them "on a par" as far as the law is concerned is immoral?[19]

Sayeth my debating partner (p. 33): "If the considerations marshalled thus far are correct, then the fact that a human fetus is a member of the same species as you and I cannot ground an argument conferring upon it the same right to life as you and I."

Yes, I agree. No one has any (positive) right to life. We all, including very, very, young pre-born babies, have, only, the (negative) right not to be murdered.[20] But the fact that the human fetus is a member of the same species as you and I most certainly "confers" on him the right not to be done away with.

Nor can we allow this argument to pass unscathed (p. 41): "The slippery slope argument was supposed to show that the claim that the fetus has a right to life from its conception follows from the conjunction of the fact that there is a relation of continuity between it and the adult it gradually develops into and the claim that the

[16] I confess that in my past writings I have made this error myself. And, even, in the writing of the present essay, my first draft violated this suggestion of mine. Even now, I have not ferreted out all such usage, so it is a bit harsh on my side to criticize Boonin in this manner. But at least I try. It is so ingrained in all of us. But, given that the fertilized egg is a (very young) human being, we all ought to strive mightily to use the correct language.

[17] But only by a teensy little bit; each human life if precious. If "awe" is not justified, then, at least, "respect" is.

[18] We *all* need a proper environment. Take away our air, and we survive for only a bare minute or so. Without any water, our life expectancy drops to a day or two. Ditto for temperature, a place to sit or stand, etc.

[19] I take this back. I will readily substitute "howler" or "problematic" for "immoral" since libertarians do not deal in the latter.

[20] Unjustifiably killed.

adult itself has a right to life. But the right to life of the acorn does not follow from the fact that there is a relation of continuity between it and oak tree it gradually develops into even if we assume that oak trees have such a right. The acorn objection to the slippery slope argument therefore survives the objections that have been aimed at it. Its persistence is well earned."

There are two things wrong here. First, Boonin is again going back on his word.[21] Previously, he stipulated that the fetus was a rights-bearing entity,[22] and that even on the basis of this assumption abortion would be justified. Now he repudiates this claim, seemingly, without realizing it.

Secondly, if mature oak trees really, really did have rights, why would this not apply to teen-aged members of this species, e.g., saplings? Do not teen-aged human beings have rights[23] solely because one day, presumably, they will be fully rights bearing adults? Pushing the envelope a bit, if oak saplings have (always negative, not positive) rights for this reason, what is the argument that acorns do not? Our author supplies no justification for this contention of his.

Yes (p. 41) "… if we confer a right to life on oak trees because they are members of an 'appropriate species' … then we will grant that right to acorns since they are members of the oak species as well. But notice that in either case our attributing a right to life to the acorn will do absolutely nothing to vindicate the slippery slope argument: We will be led to attribute a right to life to the acorn not because such a right follows from the conjunction of the claim that oak trees have a right to life and the claim that acorns develop gradually into oak trees, but rather because we agree that acorns themselves already possess a property (a certain kind of life force, membership in an appropriate species) that is itself sufficient to warrant such attribution."[24]

But just because one argument is correct (acorns have rights because they belong to the oak species) does not mean that the other is invalid. We are not precluded from arguing, *also*, that acorns have rights *because* they will eventually become rights bearing oak trees. This argument has indeed "persisted" in the literature, but it is by no means "well earned."

Boonin is off base, too, with regard to his potentiality argument, at least if he relies on this erroneous interpretation (p. 48): "…being a doctor and having the rights of a doctor are essentially conventional properties. Someone might know everything that a doctor knows and be every bit as good as a doctor is at diagnosing and treating illnesses, but if he did not graduate from medical school and receive the appropriate credentials, we call the person an imposter rather than a doctor and do not grant him the right to practice medicine that we grant to doctors. Thus, even if we agree that medical students have some of the rights that doctors have, this will not be an example of the sort of natural right that the potentiality argument seeks to

[21] Is this immoral? It is not illegal, at least not under libertarian law.

[22] Negative ones, not positive ones, I would insist.

[23] Especially if they clean up their rooms.

[24] This line of reasoning is strangely parallel to the money regression theorem of the Austrian school of economics. See on this Mises (1949) "The Determination of the Purchasing Power of Money."

ascribe to the fetus. It will only show that sometimes we extend conventional rights to those who potentially possess them while at other times we don't."

Our philosophy professor is certainly correct if we resort to conventional law. There, acting as a physician is a privilege, which can only be earned by graduating from an accredited medical school, passing certain exams afterward, etc. But as a matter of libertarian law, matters are quite different. These legal requirements are an infringement on the right of consenting adults to act in any manner agreeable to both parties,[25] up to and including the right to offer and receive medical advice and service without any license whatsoever from the state apparatus. Indeed, present regulations constitute a restriction on entry, a set of rules that mainly serve to boost doctor's salaries.[26] What of the potentiality argument against abortion in this context? Boonin's use of medical licensing laws undermines his rejection of this argument.

He maintains (p. 48): "The fact that I now have the right to own property, or to watch anything I want on television, does not mean that I had the right when I was a small child." Under libertarianism the rights of children are constrained; paternalism is justified for the very young, just not for everyone. But even extant law mandates that if a child receives a bequest, it is to be held for him in trust until he reaches the age of maturity. This means, if it means anything, that the child has rights because he will *potentially* become an adult, one day in the future. But the same is true, of course, for the zygote, and, also, for the fertilized egg at the very beginning of human life.

A word about the difference between conception, when the sperm connects with the egg, and implantation, when the fertilized egg connects to the lining of the uterus. In the libertarian view, at both stages of development, the young human being has acquired the (always negative, it cannot be repeated enough) right not to be murdered. Why is there no relevant difference between them, such that to kill the former is equivalent to contraception and only the latter to abortion? This is because of medical technology. At the time of this writing in 2020, the baby is not viable outside of the body of his mother. But as medical technology improves, the fetus will be viable outside of the womb earlier and earlier in his life. At present, this applies only in the last trimester. However, gradually, this will occur in the 6th, 5th and 4th months, and so on. True, these improvements will likely also effect when the fertilized egg "becomes firmly embedded in the uterine wall" (p. 92) before it impacts the sperm still floating in the fallopian tube, but our level of medical skill is surely separate from rights issues and irrelevant to them.[27]

According to Boonin (p. 91): "Critics of abortion have failed to provide a good reason to believe that a zygote has a right to life. But I am assuming, at least for the sake of the argument, that you and I do have such a right, and that we developed

---

[25] Nozick (1974, p. 163) mentions "capitalist acts between consenting adults."

[26] See on this Block 2003f; Friedman 1962 (ch. 9); Hamowy 1984; Herbener 1996; Holly 2013; Hoppe 1993a; Johnson et al. 1998; Laydon and Block 1996; Salerno 2016; Terrell 2003.

[27] The cave man had as many rights, and of the same variety, as modern man, and ditto regarding the space man of tomorrow.

gradually from such zygotes. So if we did not acquire this right at the moment of our conception, there must be some point after conception at which we did. The question that remains, then, is: When is that?"

The answer emanating from libertarian theory is that neither the zygote, nor "you and I" ever gain the right to life. But we also do indeed, all of the three of us, have the right not to be murdered, and we all gain it precisely when the sperm fertilizes the egg. This occurs not one second before this point in time, but only afterwards. Birth is merely a change of address. Whether the heart beats or not, or whether we even have a heart, whether there are brain waves, or we even have a brain yet,[28] is irrelevant.[29]

In contrast, our philosophy professor writes (p. 92): "I will attempt to provide a positive defense of one of these positions, the claim that the fetus acquires a right to life when its brain reaches a certain level of maturity." This, to be sure, has certain advantages. It comports, well, with legal definitions of the time of death. But it is not reconcilable with the future-oriented criterion I am employing. One minute before the infant in the womb's brain waves are elevated to the level that satisfies Boonin, he still has all the world of life ahead of him.

In the view of our author (p. 93): "…the claim that pregnancy begins at implantation has the implication, which is then sometimes made explicit, that methods of birth control that prevent implantation should be understood as methods that prevent pregnancy, rather than as methods that terminate pregnancy. And so it might be thought that this consideration shows that such methods are morally on a par with contraception, rather than with abortion.

> "This line of reasoning may be tempting, but it is flawed. If we agree that pregnancy begins at implantation rather than at fertilization, this is only because we are distinguishing pregnancy as a state of the woman's body from pregnancy as the condition in which a new individual member of our species has come into existence."

I am in full agreement with Boonin on this point. Why, then, in this review, dedicated to undermining his pro-choice thesis, do I even mention it?[30] I do so on the ground that it is crucial to my own analysis to distinguish contraception and abortion, and he does so brilliantly. Contraception is entirely justified from the evictionist perspective. For in that case the sperm is prevented from entering the egg and the result thus becoming a human being, my definition of the fertilized egg. In contrast, abortion is the murder of a person (in addition to evicting him from the premises owned by the mother).

Boonin asks (p. 95): "Why should whether or not an individual has the same right to life as you and I depend on what the individual looks like?" I will now edit

---

[28] In the Jewish tradition, the fetus becomes human only when he graduates from medical school.

[29] How to define death at the end of life is not entirely irrelevant to this determination. What they have in common is future prospects. If there is any chance of recovery, improvement, development, any probability at all, the person is not yet dead. He is still a person. For more on this see Block (2011a), which deals with the case of Terri Schiavo, see below.

[30] There are numerous other overlaps between the two of us from which I abstract. Why? This is because "I come not to praise but to bury" the pro-choice position.

this statement substituting "right not to be murdered" for "right to life" since the former is a licit negative right, while the latter is an illegitimate positive one. When I do so, I have him saying this: "Why should whether or not an individual has the same right *not to be murdered* as you and I depend on what the individual looks like?" Boonin is talking about a fetus, who more and more comes to resemble other members of his species as it grows older and matures. He quite properly rejects this "lookism" as determinative of rights. I would go further, and apply this important insight to other species as well. When we arrive at other planets and find creatures who look like snakes or rats or clouds or trees, what shall be our criterion for determining if they have (negative) rights or not? Surely, this would turn on whether or not these (strange looking) *people* can petition for these rights, and respect ours. States Rothbard (1982): "What of the 'Martian' problem? If we should ever discover and make contact with beings from other planets, could *they* be said to have the rights of human beings? It would depend on their nature. If our hypothetical 'Martians' were like human beings – conscious, rational, able to communicate with us and participate in the division of labor – then presumably they too would possess the rights now confined to 'earthbound' humans.

> "There is, in fact, rough justice in the common quip that 'we will recognize the rights of animals whenever they petition for them.' The fact that animals can obviously *not* petition for their 'rights' is part of their nature, and part of the reason why they are clearly not equivalent to, and do not possess the rights of, human beings. And if it be protested that babies can't petition either, the reply of course is that babies are future human adults, whereas animals obviously are not."

Next, Boonin (p. 112) considers the symmetry argument which "…begins with what seems to be an extremely plausible assumption: that there must be a kind of symmetry between when the right to life begins and when it ends. More specifically, we might say that the property whose permanent loss makes an individual no longer possess a right to life is the same as the property whose initial acquisition makes an individual possess a right to life in the first place." He (p. 112) continues: "Even if we do agree that an individual loses his right to life when brain death occurs…".

But not all of us agree to that by a long shot. First, for the libertarian, no one ever has any right to life, only a right not to be murdered.[31] Second, is it really true that people no longer have the right not to be murdered when all brain functioning ceases? Not, at least, for the libertarian! Take the case of Terri Schiavo, a woman for whom, unfortunately, this applied. The legal issue arose as to whether or not to pull the plug on her, which was in effect the equivalent of murdering her. The court ruled that the husband had the right to make this determination, and that, indeed, was his decision. Why was the husband chosen to play this very important role? Presumably, because he was his wife's guardian. But the proper function of a guardian is to *guard*. That, in turn, implies doing what is best for the ward. Murdering the latter, pulling the plug on her, hardly qualifies for this honorific. If anything, the very

[31] Am I running this into the ground, with my constant repetition of his point? Yes and no. Yes, anyone of the meanest intelligence has long ago grasped this point. No, this is justified, since Boonin continually makes this error and an awful lot of substance turns on it.

opposite is the case. That is, the decision that he made about her should have *per se* and immediately disqualified him from making it. Fortunately for Terri Schiavo (McFadden 1985), her parents and siblings were very much opposed to the doing away of their beloved relative. As long as they would have paid for her care and upkeep, the libertarian would have supported their right to do so, and for Terri Schiavo too, and thus keep her out of the clutches of her would-be murderers, her husband and the court that ruled in this manner.[32]

But suppose, just suppose, that instead of taking her off the machines that were keeping her breathing and her heart pumping blood, a hit man had entered Schiavo's room and simply shot her in the head. If I understand Boonin's position, while he might well consider this an immoral act,[33] he would not count this as the cold-blooded murder it most certainly would be. Brain functioning be damned, say I. Murder is murder is murder. Period.

Next (p. 131): "Consider, for example, an adult human being with a particular form of brain injury that has caused him to lapse into an irreversible coma. Most people would agree that he does not have the same right to life as you and I. But it is of course possible that technological advances might someday make it possible to bring people with precisely the same form of brain injury out of their comas. Were that to happen, we would surely say that the individual did have the same right to life as you or I, since this is what we say of people who are only temporarily unconscious. This would be to make his moral standing relative to the existing state of technology, and in a way that seems perfectly appropriate."

But this is to render legal (not moral) standing relative to the degree of technological sophistication. "Most people" may indeed agree with this contention, but it is anathema to the libertarian philosophy. In this latter view, rights are timeless. No matter what epoch in history we occupy, we all have identical, indistinguishable rights: that is, the negative right not to be murdered, trespassed upon, stolen from, raped, etc. Rights are not like hemlines, altered with every change in tastes. And this applies, too, to technology.

What are we to make of this argument of Boonin's (p. 127): "I have argued that, on the account that does best by the critic of abortion's own standards, the fetus acquires the right to life that you and I have when it begins to have conscious desires, that this occurs when it begins to have a certain kind of electrical activity in its cerebral cortex, and that this occurs at some point from 25 to 32 weeks after fertilization. If all of this is correct, then the vast majority of abortions take place well before the point at which the fetus acquires a right to life. This does not in itself demonstrate that such abortions are morally permissible, but it does show that the rights-based argument against abortion fails to show that they are impermissible."

Not so fast. One flaw here is that it makes no never mind what *proportion* of abortions occur at any given time. For the evictionist, they *all* count as murder. The

[32] Donald Trump, were he a libertarian, would have characterized the latter as these "so-called judges" (Wang 2017).

[33] It is difficult to tell since no definition of immorality is ever forthcoming from him.

argument is whether *any single* abortion, at *any* stage of fetal development, constitutes unjustified killing. And, of course, it does. Nor has this anything to do with when consciousness ticks in. Rather, as our author himself concedes if only for the sake of argument, it is due to the fact that the fetus, from the fertilized egg stage and onward, is a rights-bearing human being. Again, there was no "kind of electrical activity in its cerebral cortex" of Terri Schiavo and it would have been murder to shoot her to death.

With this discussion of viability, Boonin comes closer to, but still does not touch, evictionism. He opines (p. 129): "Viability refers to the point at which it becomes possible for a fetus to survive outside of the womb. The exact moment at which this occurs cannot be determined precisely, but it is generally acknowledged to occur at some point toward the end of the second trimester, between 20 and 23 weeks after fertilization. Since the vast majority of abortions occur well before even the most conservative estimates for viability, greater specificity is unnecessary for our purposes. If the fetus acquires a right to life when it becomes viable, then on any plausible account of when viability occurs it will turn out that the vast majority of abortions do not involve the death of an individual with a right to life."

Again with the "vast majority." The lover of liberty never counts noses. Rights are rights are rights. Their violation to even one person, at whatever age,[34] is a rights violation; something to be opposed. In any case, this statement is wrong: "the vast majority of abortions occur well before even the most conservative estimates for viability." What he should have said is that "the vast majority of *evictions* occur well before even the most conservative estimates for viability." Why so? This is due to the fact that an abortion is an eviction plus a(n unjustified) killing. In the first two trimesters, an eviction will result in a *justified* killing, since the fetus is not yet viable outside of the womb, and the mother has every right to evict the (baby) trespasser.

In the view of our author (p. 137): "Once it becomes clear that the right to life does not include or entail the right to life support, that is, it becomes clear that it is not enough for the critic of abortion to establish that the fetus has a right to life: 'We need to be shown also that killing the foetus violates its right to life, i.e., that abortion is unjust killing. And is it?'"

Do we not have a "right" to precision of language from accomplished philosophers? What else should a "right to life" mean other than, precisely, the right to "life support?" If I have a right to a pencil, it is my property, I necessarily have the "support" of the law to ensure that I can keep it if I wish, that if anyone steals it from me, the forces of law and order will ideally return it to me, or if it is lost or broken at the very least punish those who took it from me. If I have a right to this pencil, and I do, you have an obligation not to steal it from me. If I have a right not to be molested, and I do, then you have an obligation not to molest me. If I have a right to life, which I most certainly do not, you have an obligation to support me, feed me, clothe me, etc., which you do not.

[34] This includes "pre-birth" ages.

Next in the batter's box is this statement (p. 139): "So let me assume for a moment that you agree that there is no morally relevant difference between the violinist case and the case of a typical unwanted pregnancy, and that you also agree that it would be morally permissible for you to *unplug* yourself from the violinist. If you accept both of these claims, then it might seem obvious that I would be entitled to conclude that you will also, even if grudgingly, accept the conclusion that *abortion* in the case of a typical unwanted pregnancy is morally permissible. But this would be premature. For you might simply reject the authority of such arguments from analogy to begin with."

I have italicized two words here, "unplug" and "abortion." My contention is that, contrary to this author, they are not analogous. Synonyms for the first word include "separate from," "disassociate from," "part company with" "eject." This fits in very well with "evict" and the evictionist viewpoint. "Abortion," I never tire of saying, is something *very* different. It is not a one but a two-stage affair. The first stage is to evict; the second is to kill, or, rather, murder. Boonin's failure to see this point mars an otherwise sterling analysis of this phenomenon. Nor is he always unaware of the distinction between evicting and killing. He mentions (p. 149) "the right to expel the fetus." Surely, this phrase bespeaks cognizance of the difference between these two very diverse acts. Yet, when push comes to shove, he jettisons this distinction and conflates the two.

We now move on to consider (p. 159): "... the case of a woman who freely chooses to have an embryo implanted in her. This does seem to be a case in which she voluntarily brings about the state of affairs in which there is a fetus making demands on her body, rather than one in which she merely foresees that her action may lead to such a state of affairs. It thus seems plausible to think of it as a genuine case in which, if one believes in tacit consent, one will have good grounds for thinking that consent has been given. The other is what might be called the case of intentional conception, one in which the woman deliberately refrained from using contraception because she wanted to become pregnant. She does seem to do more than merely foresee that the subsequent state of affairs may arise, and so it can again seem plausible to suppose that in this case she has consented to it."

I have one difficulty with this analysis. I am not all that much interested, for this purpose, in whether or not the woman has "consented" to being the hostess of the infant now in her body. In cases of rape, obviously, she has not, and in virtually every other situation she has. No, my focus is on whether or not she has *obligated* herself to carry the child inside her person for nine months. And she can only have such a *legal* obligation if she has *contracted* to do so. She logically *cannot* have made any contract with the baby at the time of sexual intercourse since the latter was not even in existence at that time.[35] But is there any such example at all? Yes, in the case of a paid host mother for an infertile couple. They in effect hire this woman to "baby-sit" their child for them for nine months. Then and only then is the latter

[35] It takes a while for the sperm to travel up the fallopian tubes and enter the egg. And, here, we posit the possibility of making a contract with a very young person, a fertilized egg, a truly heroic assumption.

obligated to keep the baby for the full term. Not only may she not abort, kill, the infant, she may not even legally evict him. Why not? This is because she had *contractually obligated* herself to do no such thing.[36]

We now launch ourselves against yet another problematic aspect of this author's analysis (pp. 165–166): "Suppose that because of your unique compatibility, the violinist will die unless you undergo a series of nine painful bone marrow extractions over the next nine months, and with a clear understanding of the nature of the procedure and its potential risks, you freely volunteer to undergo the first extraction. After the second round of extraction, however, you find that the burden is considerably more than you are willing to bear on his behalf. Do you really believe that it would now be morally impermissible for you to discontinue providing aid to the violinist merely because you began providing aid voluntarily? To say that doing so would be impermissible would be to say that the violinist's right to life does not entitle him to seven more extractions of bone marrow from you if the first two were done involuntarily, but that it does entitle him to seven more extractions from you if the first two were done voluntarily. It is extremely difficult to believe that critics of abortion will be willing to endorse such a view."

I have no opinion, whatsoever, as to whether or not starting in this manner, and then stopping, is "morally impermissible." Libertarians do not truck in such matters. However, a case can certainly be made, at least under certain circumstances, that stopping in midstream, so to speak, would actually constitute criminal behavior, punishable by law. For example, suppose there were any number of donors willing to engage in nine monthly painful bone marrow extractions, but that for some reason they all had to be made by the same contributor. No other benefactor could be substituted for the one who begins this process. Then, if the first one reneged after two or three transfers, the violinist dies. Posit that a contract was signed by the original giver and that payment from the recipient violinist was already made. Then, in the case of non-fulfillment, the contract violator is not guilty, merely, of "letting die," but of actual downright murder.[37] Boonin has two possible defenses for this position of his.

---

[36] What of the objection that specific performance contracts are invalid? For a refutation, see Andersson 2007; Block 1979, 1999, 2001b, 2002b, 2003e, 2004b, 2005, 2006a, 2007, 2009a, b, 2016c; Frederick 2014; Kershnar 2003; Lester 2000; Mosquito 2014b, 2015; Nozick 1974, pp. 58, 283, 331; Steiner 1994, pp. 232; Thomson 1990, pp. 283–84.

[37] Forget about the contract. There is a drowning child out there in the water. There are several good swimmers on shore. One of them, without saying a word, starts strongly swimming in the direction of this person in trouble. The others rely upon him for his lifeguard abilities. But when the latter arrives near the youngster, he stays a few feet away from him, and lets the child drown. When asked about this afterward, he states that he just likes a close up view of people dying. Had he not swam out toward the child, one of the other swimmers certainly would have done so, and, we stipulate, saved the life of the child. Was the first swimmer a murderer? A strong case can indeed be made in this direction, since by his human action, coupled with implicit societal understandings, he signaled he was swimming out there on a mission of mercy. But he violated this common interpretation. (Here is a similar case of implicit agreement: you order a cup of coffee, drink it down, and then are presented with a bill for $1 billion. Need you pay it? Certainly not. If the vendor wishes to charge such an unusual amount of money for this beverage, it is up to him to ascertain

First, if donors, under these circumstances, know full well that once they start this nine-part process, they must continue until the entire job is done, there will be far fewer of them coming forward to aid their fellow creatures. But this is mere utilitarianism, frowned upon, severely, by all right-thinking deontological libertarians. Yes, perhaps, likely, even, fewer donors will start down this arduous path if they know they will be compelled by law to "dance the whole dance." However at least the recipient of this benefit will not find his source of succor fatally interrupted. And if there is only one possible donor and he is unwilling to obligate himself for the entire nine month process, a contract can possibly be signed that allows him to discontinue. From the point of view of the violinist (fetus) this will be his best (only) option.

Second, Boonin avers (pp. 166–167): "I have been assuming to this point that the right to control one's body is an alienable one, a right that is at least in principle possible to give away by consent. My claim has simply been that the fact that her engaging in intercourse was voluntary provides no good reason to suppose that she has in fact done this. But the assumption that the right to control one's body is alienable is itself open to doubt. Suppose, after all, that a woman made the following explicit agreement: Give me some money today, and tomorrow you can use my body in any way that you want even if by that time I have changed my mind and no longer want you to. Most of us would think this sort of contract to be simply invalid. As at least one writer sympathetic to the good Samaritan argument has urged, "one cannot legitimately enslave oneself by waiving in advance one's right to control one's own body" (Long 1993: 189). And if this is so, then even if we thought that by her actions the woman could legitimately be understood as *attempting* to consent to waive this right, we would still have to conclude that she had not in fact done so."

There can be little doubt that our author's assessment of the masses of people is correct. "Most of us would (indeed) think this sort of contract to be simply invalid." But are they correct? Hardly. Long inaccurately calls this enslavement, but, surely, if it is voluntarily undertaken, it differs from the "curious institution" in relevant ways.

I am a tightrope walker. I perform 100 feet in the air. I hire you to hold a net under me. We sign a contract to that effect. Consideration has already passed hands. Half way through my act you withdraw your services. Did you merely "let me die" after I fall to my death, with no net any longer beneath me? No, you are an out and out murderer, guilty of a most foul deed.[38]

agreement of the customer). On the other hand was this swimmer with strange tastes the only one on the shore, he could have acted exactly as he did, with no criminal implications. For, then, there would have been no one else around, by stipulation, to save the drowning baby. Suppose it was not a baby, but an adult. And, the swimmer, with no one else in sight, offered to save that man, with the understanding that the latter would be his lifetime slave. Would this be a valid contract? Yes, of course, at least from the libertarian viewpoint. This of course should be sharply distinguished from actual coercive, not contractual, slavery, which all men of good will, not only libertarians, must bitterly oppose.

[38] See supra for a refutation of Long's perspective.

Another difficulty with Boonin's presentation is that he contradicts himself with regard to the issue of whether or not it is a benefit to the fetus to be conceived and then aborted, vis-a-vis never coming into existence in the first place. On p. 178 our author cites Davis (1983, p. 277) in support of the non-benefit viewpoint: "[T]o be killed is bad, so bad that merely being brought into existence for a time is not necessarily enough to make up for it. We would not, I take it, allow a scientist to kill a ten-year-old child just because the scientist had ten years ago 'constructed' the child out of a dollar's worth of chemicals, had reared it for ten years in such a way as to make it impossible for the child's care to be given to anyone else for another eight years, and now found the care of the child a far greater burden than he had expected."

Whereupon Boonin proceeds, quite properly, to utterly annihilate this perspective in his next few pages. Our author's tour de force is a quote of his (p. 179) from Nagel (1970, p. 1): "… as Nagel has pointed out 'If death is an evil at all, it cannot be because of its positive features, but only because of what it deprives us of.'"

But then, a few short pages later, Boonin takes it all back (pp. 184–185): "In particular, there is the following difference between a woman who voluntarily conceives and then aborts a fetus, and you when you voluntarily cure and then later refuse to save an ailing violinist: In curing the violinist, you greatly benefit him, providing him with several more years of valuable experiences that he would otherwise not have had. When the woman conceives the short-lived fetus, she does not benefit it at all, since it will not go on to have any valuable experiences that it would otherwise not have had."

I am a strong supporter of Boonin-Nagel, but not Boonin-Davis. In my view, life is precious, even a second of it.[39] It cannot be denied that (p. 185) "the short-lived fetus, she does not benefit it at all, since it will not go on to have any valuable experiences that it would otherwise not have had." But to say this is profoundly anti-life, the preservation of which against murder is one of the basic pillars of the libertarian philosophy. In any case, once conceived, even if intended to be aborted, the fetus has a *chance* to be formed into a person and lead a fulfilling life. Who knows, maybe the woman who intends to have an abortion will change her mind, or, perhaps, be precluded from doing so based on her changed medical condition. Without conception, there is no probability at all of this occurring. So, there are benefits even in such a contrived example.

We now take up the issue of positive obligations.[40] According to our philosophical writer, nothing he has said (pp. 183–184):

> "… implies or presupposes that a woman who declines to bring her newborn home has no duty to care for it at all. Suppose that she gives birth to a child in an abandoned field. One might hold the view that there are no positive duties to assist others, in which case one will hold that if she does not wish to raise the child herself she is morally free to walk away and leave the infant to die. But a proponent of the good Samaritan argument need not hold this view. One could believe that there are positive duties to assist others, at least in cases where

[39] I make an exception for a person who is in excruciating, endless pain, for which the morphine or other such drug no longer works.

[40] This is in sharp contradistinction to positive rights.

the burden is relatively small and the benefit relatively great, and so hold that the woman would at least be obligated to incur the cost of carrying the child to town and providing for it until it could be taken to a hospital or shelter. But one who holds this view will also hold that she would have this obligation equally even if she were to come across a newborn that someone else had abandoned in the field, so this will again fail to support the claim that the good Samaritan argument is undermined by the difference between the voluntariness of intercourse in nonrape cases and the involuntariness of the kidnapping in the violinist case. And, in addition, it would hardly follow that a woman would therefore be obligated to sustain her pregnancy since the burdens of a typical pregnancy are far more intimate and extensive than the burden of dropping a baby off at a hospital or police station. Of course, one might endorse the existence of a positive duty to assist another who will otherwise die even where the burden to you in doing so is quite substantial, provided that (a) the benefit to the other still significantly outweighs the burden to you and (b) you are the only one who can save the individual. This would justify a duty to continue the pregnancy even granting that the burden is substantially greater than what we are typically required to undergo for the benefit of others. But then it will equally follow that you are obligated to remain plugged into Thomson's violinist for nine months, since the benefit to him significantly outweighs the burden to you and you are the only one who can save him. So even this view of positive rights would fail to undermine Thomson's analogy."

All of this is in sharp contrast to the libertarian view. It is not at all a matter of the differential costs[41] between carrying a child for nine months in one's body and taking him to the nearest hospital.[42] To the libertarian, there are only negative rights: the right not to be murdered, raped, enslaved, stolen from. How then, in this view can we preclude the mother from bringing her newborn home, and then failing to feed him? It is due to the fact that were she to engage in this neglect, she would be guilty of the crime of forestalling, or precluding. In similar manner, no one would be allowed to homestead land in a donut formation, leaving empty territory in the middle of his new holdings. Both would be guilty of controlling a valuable asset (a baby, territory), without homesteading him, it.[43] However, this would not apply to a passerby, nor any stranger, regarding a newborn "in an abandoned field." Libertarianism does not subscribe to the Good Samaritan requirement. To rescue such a baby would be supererogatory: over and above the call of legally required duty.

When our author discusses hysterotomy (p. 183) he comes close to the libertarian theory on these matters, evictionism. But he cannot be awarded a cigar since there is still an important difference between the two principles. Boonin defines terms (p. 193) thusly: "Hysterotomy involves removing the living fetus through an abdominal incision of the uterus and allowing it to die." Evictionism, in sharp

[41] A core principle of Austrian economics is that costs are subjective. See on this Barnett 1989; Block 1988; Buchanan and Thirlby 1981; Buchanan 1969, 1979; Butos and Koppl 1997; Cordato 1989; DiLorenzo 1990; Garrison 1985; Gunning 1990; Kirzner 1986; Mises 1998; Rizzo 1979, 1980; Rothbard 1979, 1997b; Stringham 2008.

[42] Boonin's emphasis on differential costs channels Coase (1960). For a critique of that article, see Barnett and Block 2007, 2009a, b; Block 1977b, 1995, 1996, 2000, 2003d, 2006b, 2010a, b, c; Block et al. 2005; Cordato 1989, 1992a, b, 1997, 1998, 2000; DiLorenzo 2014; Fox 2007; Hoppe 2004; Krause 1999; Krecke 1996; Lewin 1982; North 1990, 1992, 2002; Rothbard 1982, 1997a; Stringham 2001; Stringham and White 2004; Terrell 1999.

[43] For more on this see Block 2016a.

contrast, also involves removing the live fetus from the pregnant woman, but is entirely silent on whether or not he[44] subsequently perishes. Under medical technology of the year of this writing, 2020, the baby will indeed expire if evicted in the first two trimesters but not at all necessarily in the third.[45] This difference is stark. Under evictionism, the lives of all third trimester babies can automatically be saved. It would be against the law to have an abortion at this stage of development. This does not hold for hysterotomy.

Boonin's phrase (p. 193) "abortion by hysterotomy" is not in and of itself a logical contradiction. This is so because at the end of the hysterotomy process the infant necessarily dies. That is what "abortion" means: eviction plus downright murder. However, if we redefine hysterotomy so as to leave it as an open question as to whether or not this small human being perishes,[46] we then arrive at evictionism, the libertarian solution to the problem.

We cannot allow to pass without comment this author's analysis of the trolley challenge (p. 191–211). The streetcar example is an outright attack on the very essence of libertarianism. Boonin's solution misses the point. The scenario, at its most basic, involves the actor murdering an innocent person in order to save large numbers of other equally innocent people. Since libertarianism opposes murder, period, this places us in a very non-enviable position. "Justice though the heavens fall" sounds attractive, but as a practical clarion call it leaves something to be desired. How can we have our cake and eat it too? How can we cling to the NAP, and not counsel death for the entire human species[47]? It is simple. Some hero murders the innocent man, and is dealt with as are all other murderers. He is put to death,[48] unless the heirs of the victim wish to forgive him, given these extenuating circumstances. Yet, another libertarian solution to this critique of libertarianism is to resort to private property rights. We ask who owns this means of transport. We allow him to decide, positing that all customers have agreed beforehand to be bound by his decision. It is the same with all lifeboat challenges to libertarianism. He who owns the vessel makes the decision as to who will live and who will die. A third option is that the only person who can switch the trolley's path from killing many to killing one, simply does nothing. Then, he will not be in violation of any law that a libertarian must respect.

What are we to make of this clearly fallacious statement (pp. 215–216):

> "A defender of the good Samaritan argument could, I suppose, maintain that in typical cases of abortion, the woman merely wants to be relieved of the unwanted burden of carrying the

[44] Not "it."

[45] As medical technology improves, this cross-over point will occur earlier and earlier.

[46] Is allowed to "let die" in Boonin's vernacular.

[47] In the extreme, that is potentially the number of people whose lives lie in the balance in the trolley challenge.

[48] For support of the death penalty for murder on philosophical grounds, see Block 2003a, b, c, 2006c; Rothbard 2011; Whitehead and Block 2003; on practical or pragmatic grounds, e.g., it reduces the murder rate: Ehrlich 1972, 1973, 1974, 1975, b, 1976a, b, 1977a, b, c, 1978, 1979, 1981, 1982; Ehrlich and Gibbons 1977; Ehrlich and Posner 1974.

developing fetus and would have no objection to the removed fetus then being safely transferred to an artificial incubator or another woman's womb, if that were possible. Since such transfers are not currently possible this response would argue, she foresees that the fetus will die as a result of its removal, but this is no part of her intention. On this account, her intention would run parallel to that of you when you unplug yourself from the violinist, and so the violinist analogy would not be determined by the moral relevance of the distinction between intending death and foreseeing it. Whatever the merits of this empirical claim might prove to be, however, it is difficult to believe that a typical critic of abortion will be willing to accept it. If part of what divides critics and defenders of abortion is their sense of what motivates women to have abortions in typical cases, then a response to the intending versus foreseeing objection that rests on such a claim will be viewed by critics of abortion as begging the question, and with at least some justification. I believe, therefore, that a defense of abortion that attempts to engage critics of abortion on their own terms should concede, at least for the sake of the argument, that in typical cases of abortion, the pregnant woman wants more than merely to be relieved of the burden of the pregnancy itself. She wants to be relieved not only of the burden of pregnancy, but also of the burden of knowing that she has produced an offspring being raised by someone else somewhere in the world. For her, the death of the fetus developing inside her is a part of her intention in seeking an abortion."

One, the facts are clearly erroneous. Even babies targeted by abortions sometimes live nonetheless; sometimes, they exit the womb alive, despite the efforts of the doctor to the contrary. Further, medical technology at present enables life in the third trimester for evictees.

Let us now consider this writer's view of intentions. He states (p. 220):

"After all, imagine that you are the doctor in Violinist III. The person plugged into the violinist has called you over to his bed demanding that you unplug him from the violinist. You are about to unplug him, since you agree that the violinist has no right to use this person's kidneys to stay alive, but then at the last moment you discover that not only does the person intend to liberate himself from the hospital by being unplugged from the violinist, but he also intends to improve his chances of becoming first chair in the local symphony by bringing about the death of his main rival. Could you really maintain that you must now leave the person plugged into the violinist because one of his intentions is unacceptable? This seems an extremely implausible position to take."

For the most part, I agree with his analysis. I would only substitute the word "nonsensical" for "implausible." Why? This is due to the role of intentions in libertarian law. They do play some part but not the vast one as Boonin would have it. If I run you over purposefully with my car while you are crossing the street, I am a murderer. If I do this by accident, I am merely a tort-feasor; I owe your heirs financial compensation. If you as a pedestrian jumped out in front of my moving vehicle from between two parked cars, and I had no time to avoid hitting you, I am entirely innocent.[49]

"Hate crimes" would play no role in our deliberations whatsoever. As long as A kills B purposefully, not by accident, he is a murderer. A can do so for sport, to answer a dare, on a bet, for money, for hate, it should make no never-mind. A is

[49] I abstract from the possibility that the private owner of the road (Block 2009e) might have set up other rules and regulations.

equally guilty of criminality in all such cases, and the same goes for (p. 220): "… a woman whose reason for seeking an abortion is not merely that it will relieve her of the burdens of an unwanted pregnancy but that it will cause the death of the fetus. I suppose we can imagine cases in which a woman's intention is *only* to cause the death of the fetus and has nothing at all to do with the effects of the pregnancy on her body. We might, for example, picture a woman who has always wanted to experience the physical transformations involved in pregnancy and who would enjoy carrying a pregnancy all the way to birth, but who is deterred from doing so only by the fact that she does not want to raise children and does not want to have offspring of hers being raised by others."

This woman has a right to *evict* her fetus at any time during her pregnancy, for *any* reason, up to, or, rather, down to, "hate," at any time, but no right to abort, ever, at any stage. Her reasons for her choice, her motivations, are entirely irrelevant to her status or non-status as a criminal.

Now consider this statement (pp. 220–221): "How, they ask, would a woman who seeks an abortion respond if after the procedure was over she were told that the fetus had successfully been removed, but that it had been kept alive and would be brought to term and raised by someone else? Presumably, many women would feel that they had not gotten all they had asked for. And this counts as good reason to conclude that, in such cases, the woman's intention in seeking an abortion does include the death of the fetus and not merely its removal."

Boonin and I again diverge on this matter. He defends abortion against its many critics. Presumably, he would grant this woman in question not only the right to evict the fetus and acquiesce in the notion that the child could be brought up by someone, but, also, in addition, the right to prevent that, by seeing to it that this tiny human being perishes. The libertarian, in sharp contrast, would of course go along with this first option, but would cavil, mightily, at the second.

Our author avers the following (p. 225): "That this is so can again perhaps best be seen by considering a further variation on Thomson's story. Suppose you agree that you are permitted to unplug yourself from the violinist in a way that foreseeably leads him to die. But you then discover that you can save yourself a fair amount of harm and reduce your risk of death by intentionally killing him first and then unplugging yourself."

Let us break down this scenario into two parts. First, take the case of a woman in the first two trimesters, when the baby is not viable outside of the womb. Then, I will concede to Boonin that yes, the mother has a right to kill the baby while still in her womb. She has every right to evict the baby, at that stage or at any other, and if she does, the infant will surely die. And, as Boonin says, he is unconscious and could not care less if he perishes now or a few minutes later.

I wrote the foregoing, but then realized it, too, goes against the libertarian prohibition of violating the NAP. To repeat: every second of life is precious, conscious or not.[50] It belongs to its owner, to no one else. The initiation of violence against

[50] It would be a rights violation to murder an incurably unconscious person.

innocent people, at whatever stage of development they find themselves in, is contrary to the NAP. Who knows? In the 10 minutes between the murder of the fetus in the womb, and his later eviction, technology might have improved so much that this very young person might now be viable on the outside, on his own. So, yes, eviction, but no partial birth abortion. The case is even clearer in the third trimester. Suppose I can save my life by killing you. Do I have a right to do so? To ask this is to answer it: of course not. No more does the woman have the right to engage in a hysterotomy. Murder is murder is murder, and must not be treated in any way other than murder.

That is, this is all true under ordinary circumstances. However suppose A is trespassing in B's house. B asks A to leave. A says that if he leaves B's house, he will die. We stipulate this is true. Does B still have the right to evict A from his house even though A will thereby perish? Yes. A is a criminal trespasser. B is obligated to remove A from B's premises only in the gentlest manner possible (Parr 2011), lest he violate A's rights. However, in this case, the *only* way to secure his own private property right in his house is for B to remove A in a manner that will cause the death of the latter. Does B have a right to do so? The only answer compatible with the libertarian emphasis on private property rights is in the affirmative.

A is the baby, B is the mother. The aforementioned thus translates into the question: Does the mother B, still have the right to evict the baby, A, from her "house" even though the baby will thereby perish? We must again answer in the positive.

Now let us try this example the other way around.

Suppose A is trespassing in B's house. B again wants A to leave. But for some reason the only way to evict A is to first kill him, A. If B does not kill A, A cannot leave, and remains a trespasser. May B kill A? Again, we must answer Yes. Therefore, partial birth abortion is justified in cases where it is the only way to save the mother's life.

Let us try again.

Suppose A is trespassing in B's house. B wants A to leave. A is willing to do so. However, for some reason, if A leaves while he, A, is still alive, B will die. The only way B can stay alive is by first killing A, and then evicting A. Does B have a right to kill A? Yes. Had it not been for the evil A trespassing on the innocent B's property, B would have been alright. So, B may kill A and then kick him out of his, B's house, and it should not be considered murder. Therefore, partial birth abortion to save the mother's life is licit.

Of course, if the mother (B) may first kill the trespassing baby (A) before evicting him to save her life, the question arises as to whether or not she may do so for a lesser gain; for example, to improve her health, or, even, to save money. In the latter case, it is easy to see a way to save the baby: the adoptive parents may pay whatever additional funds the mother would have been charged for engaging in the more expensive eviction.

However, the mother most certainly may not engage in a partial birth abortion for any other reason. For example, she may not do so because she does not want "that man's" progeny to see the light of day. Should motive play so important a role in distinguishing licit from illicit acts? Yes, of course. It is only motivation that distinguishes the purposeful murderer from the accidental killer; it is only motivation that distinguishes the motorist who purposefully crashes into your car from the one who does so accidentally. *Mens rea* may not be all there is to law, but it certainly plays an important, no, crucial, role.

Boonin writes (p. 225): "Again, it is not his death that you are using as a means to your end in this case, but rather your causing his death by one means rather than your causing his death by another means."

This is at least roughly the case in the first two trimesters. The baby will die, either inside the womb, or, a few minutes later, outside of it. However, this is not at all the case in the third trimester. Then, it is a matter of life or death, not between death at one point of time, and another, slightly later.

We move on, now, to a consideration of this distinction (p. 226): "…killing the fetus rather than foreseeably causing its death."

Yes, there indeed are these two options. But Boonin never once mentions a third alternative, evicting the fetus and keeping him alive. True, this can only occur[51] in the third trimester, but so what? This is the core of the libertarian position, and our author gives it short shrift. No, unfortunately, he gives it no shrift at all.

Consider (p. 233) "A woman who leaves a newborn child in a garbage dumpster when she could instead leave it at a hospital or police station does something reprehensible, but this is true even if the newborn is not hers, but one that is left on her doorstep."

Reprehensible? Yes, of course. But, the libertarian is not interested in such issues. Rather, we focus on the proper use of violence, e.g., law, so we ask instead, Regarding the woman who leaves her baby in a dumpster there to die, is she a murderer? And, the clear answer is Yes of course she is, since the fetus will (soon) decease due to her action. Another interesting question in this vein is, suppose A, a stranger, sees a baby in a dumpster, soon to expire, should he have any legal obligation to bring him to a hospital or some such institution, thereby saving his life? Here, the answer must be in the negative. There are no positive obligations to pluck newborns out of dumpsters or anywhere else. But, suppose the baby is your own. The infant is born. You take him from the hospital, where it is presumably safe, and place him in a dumpster. This is a pretty clear case of murder. If you take someone else's baby and do so, you could add kidnapping to the criminal charges. Now consider a woman who takes her baby home from the hospital and then places him in his crib, but does not feed him. Here, there is no outright murder. Instead, she is guilty of the crime of forestalling, or precluding. In carrying home the baby, she has taken on the role of guardian, but does not live up to its requirements. It is as if she homesteaded land in a donut format, leaving empty, but under her control,[52] the land in the middle.[53]

---

[51] Given present medical technology circa 2017.

[52] We assume there are no helicopters, nor any ability of others to bridge over, or tunnel under, her property so as to be able to access the virgin land in the middle of the donut.

[53] For further elaboration of this point see Block 2016a.

Even the pregnant woman who was raped may only evict her baby, not murder him. She, too, is required to bring her baby to the hospital, orphanage or church if she had a home delivery and does not want to (continue to) be the guardian. Otherwise, she would be in illicit control of "property" the baby in this case who is desired by others.[54] She would not deserve to continue to be the newborn's guardian, unless she engages in "homesteading" acts sufficient to deserve that status, such as feeding, clothing and otherwise caring for the baby.

Boonin is almost as almost as thorough in his coverage of abortion as is Bohm-Bawerk (1959) on interest theories.[55] But not quite. There are no lacunae in Bohm-Bawerk. However, this cannot be said of our present author. He discusses abortion, thoroughly. But, not ever, eviction. This is more than passing curious in that (p. 243) he does mention whether or not the woman may "unplug" herself both from Thomson's violinist and also whether or not she may "unplug herself from the fetus." But "unplugging" is pretty much synonymous with "evicting."

We next turn to yet another fascinating contribution by Boonin (p. 244):

> "Adam and Eve, through some unspecified process, each acquire the use of adjoining plots of land in a very hot climate. Adam's plot contains a tall, leafy tree, which produces shade over much of Eve's plot of land. As a result, the plot of land acquired by Eve is cool and its remaining cool requires the use of the tree on Adam's plot of land. But this does not mean that Eve has acquired the use of the tree. Only Adam has acquired that. As a result, what Eve has acquired through the process in question does not justify a claim against Adam if Adam decides to chop down the tree. Suppose that keeping the tree alive is a substantial burden to Adam; it would make life much easier for him to kill it or to remove it and let it die. But Eve will die from exposure to the sunlight unless Adam waits nine months, after which Eve will have developed sufficient resistance to the sun. The fact that Eve has acquired the right to her plot of land, the fact that the land she has acquired the right to is currently cool, and the fact that her land's remaining cool requires the use of Adam's tree does not justify the claim that she has acquired the right to the use of Adam's tree. Similarly, it does not follow from the facts that through some process George has naturally acquired a supply of blood (which is at present healthy) and that the use of the liver in your body is necessary for the blood to remain healthy, that George has acquired the right to the use of the liver in your body. The facts are equally consistent with saying that what he has acquired is healthy blood coursing through his veins, blood that will continue to be healthy just in case the band between you and George remains intact. And on this account, you are within your rights to withdraw George's use of your liver. This does not demonstrate that George has not acquired the right to the use of the liver. But it does show that the facts as described do not provide any particular support for the claim that he has."

In our author's view, Eve acquires no rights at all to the life-giving shade. For the libertarian, in contrast, matters are not at all that clear. It all depends upon who was there *first*; who was the *initial* homesteader. Boonin abstracts entirely from this crucial issue. If for example, Adam initially mixed his labor with this plot of land, Eve is plain out of luck. But, if she were the initial settler, and Adam only came afterward, then her claim to the shade of the tree, not the tree itself, is vastly strengthened. Adam can only lay claim to his plot of territory if he leaves that tree strictly

---

[54] Just as would be the virgin land in the middle of the donut formation property.

[55] See for example fn. 68 of Boonin's ch. 4. I mean this as an enthusiastic compliment.

alone.[56] This is especially true if Eve cared for the tree, watered it, protected it from insects, etc., before the arrival of Adam. Matters are quite different between mother and baby, however. Which is the "tree" in this case? Why it is the mother's womb. And who, pray tell, was there first? To ask this is to answer it: the mother, of course.[57] Thus, here, B's position is strengthened by the libertarian reliance on the first come first served homesteading theory. Boonin, too, veers in the direction of saying that the baby has no claim on the mother's property, just as Eve has none on Adam's tree. This is because the latter, in both cases, was the initial homesteader.

Nor is Boonin unsympathetic to this libertarian argument. He states (p. 245): "The organs inside her body were provided to her by nature well before the fetus began to make use of them, just as the organs inside your body in Thomson's story were provided to you by nature well before the violinist began to make use of them." Boonin just does not realize that this applies to Adam and Eve too.

Our author sees a gigantic chasm between a violation of the person and theft of his property (p. 251): "If the state determined that it would be in the public interest to build a new highway, for example, it would hardly follow from the claim that it would be morally permissible for the state to take some of the money that workers earn to help pay for the highway that it would also be morally permissible for the state to force such workers to help to build the highway."

Libertarians can only go along with him on this part way. Yes, ceteris paribus, an attack on the person is more serious than that on mere physical property. There is a lower rung in hell built for murderers and rapists than for pick-pockets, fraudsters and muggers. And yet. If the state sets tax rates at 99%, many people will die. In the old west, horse thieves were properly visited with the death penalty, since loss of this "mere" property could well mean the difference between living and dying.

Boonin (pp. 251–252) continues in this vein: "The state's taking control over a person's body is fundamentally different from the state's taking control over some of the money that a person earns while freely controlling that body. This is a claim that critics and defenders of abortion both accept."

Yes, different, but only somewhat. *Both* are violations of the NAP of libertarianism. Nor is it necessarily the case that a violation of the former is always worse than an infringement of the latter. To borrow a leaf from this author, "most people" would presumably rather rake leaves for the state one day per year than continue to have roughly half of their earnings taken away from them through taxes, as at present.

Thus, Boonin's rejection of the child support argument is overdone. He accepts (pp. 252–253)[58] that the state may compel monetary child support but not the

---

[56] On a libertarian theory of ownership of shade, see Block 2014e.

[57] For an analysis of why she, and not her parents, the baby's grandparents, is the proper owner of this, and all other parts of her, see Block 2016b; Kinsella 2006; Steiner 1994, pp. 242–248.

[58] "...the existence and presumed legitimacy of child support laws, even if they are construed as evidence of an underlying moral obligation to provide such support, does nothing to undermine the good Samaritan argument. There is no inconsistency in holding both that reluctant fathers (and mothers) should have a legal obligation to provide financial support for their offspring and that pregnant women should have no legal obligation to carry their pregnancies to term And there is

physical variety (nine months of pregnancy). But if there is a continuum (Block and Barnett 2008) between physical invasions and financial ones, not a hard and fast unbridgeable gap between them, this argument falls to the ground. No. If Boonin wishes to make his point, he must object at the outset, as would all libertarians, to *any* assault of the person or his property, financial *or* physical. He must reject the requirement that parents financially support their children in the first place. Our author instead doubles down on his view. He maintains not only that an attack on the body does not only not constitute a difference in degree, but a difference in kind from a financial depredation, but that this applies to some types of bodily infringements vis-a-vis others. He states (p. 254): "But while most people would agree that in, say, committing first-degree murder, the woman had forfeited her right to live freely in society, surely no one would insist that she had thereby forfeited her right not to be impregnated against her will."

Again with the "most people would agree" argument. But there is a difficulty here. Suppose the following. Woman A murders pregnant woman B, the wife of Mr. B. According to libertarian principles, a great deal of the proper punishment for A lies with the heir of Mrs. B, in this case Mr. B. It is to a significant degree up to Mr. B how Miss A may be punished. Yes, the former may impose the death penalty on the latter.[59] Or, B may compel A to serve as his slave for the rest of her life. In this regard, B may also, or, separately, require A to bear his child, to replace the one he lost when A murdered Mrs. B. It is difficult to see why Mr. B may not do precisely that, the views of "most people" to the contrary notwithstanding. After all, Mr. B now *owns* Miss A. He may, presumably, do with her exactly as he wishes with no exceptions.[60], [61] Surely, a forced impregnation, via rape, is a far lesser punishment than the death penalty. If Mr. B may exact the latter on Miss A, surely he should be legally permitted to impose on her the former.

I lied. I previously wrote that while Boonin was very thorough in his analysis of abortion, he all but ignored the libertarian solution to the controversy, namely evictionism. It took him until page 255 to do so, but do so he eventually did. Unhappily, he misconstrues this viewpoint, so it is not fully clear that he actually does deal with it, even at this point in his book. He quotes numerous advocates of all sorts of other theories on this topic verbatim, and, presumably, accurately. He neither quotes nor cites any libertarian adherent of evictionism, however he does aver (p. 255):

> "…abortion as a medical procedure is typically defined in terms of the expulsion and not the death of the fetus, and so in this sense the distinction between abortion and extraction is

---

therefore no inconsistency in holding both that reluctant fathers (and mothers) have a moral obligation to provide financial support for their offspring and that pregnant women have no moral obligation to carry their pregnancies to term."

[59] For a libertarian justification of the death penalty, see this material: Block 2003a, b, c, 2006a, b, c, 2009c, d; Rothbard 2011; Whitehead and Block 2003.

[60] Well, maybe, one. If Miss A dispatched Mrs. B in a clean kill, no prolonged torture, then Mr. B may not subject Miss A to that sort of punishment.

[61] Whether "most people" would agree with this or not can only be determined by a survey, which, to my knowledge, has never been done.

empty. But the force of the objection is nonetheless clear: To the extent that women who currently seek abortions want the fetus that they are carrying to die and not merely to be extracted and then raised by others, it would follow that the good Samaritan argument does not establish the moral permissibility of what they wish to do. This objection, if it is to be accepted as such, makes three distinct claims: that it is possible for such technology to become available; that if it becomes available, its availability will prevent the argument from justifying the permissibility of a woman's ensuring the death of her fetus and not merely its removal; and that this result counts as a reason to be dissatisfied with the argument. I will respond to these points in reverse order."

This is not quite accurate. The advocate of evictionism has no views, qua libertarian, none at all, as to what is "morally worse" than something else. Rather, his concern, his entire concern, is with the *legality* of any given action.[62] However, it would appear, finally, that Boonin "gets it," despite the fact that he uses the phrase "right to life" and the word "abortion" in a different way than I do. Unfortunately, this is not the case. He and I are still passing each other like ships in the night. He never quite cottons on to the fact that the pregnant woman has the right to evict the fetus at any stage of its development, never to murder him, and that at the present state of medical technology only babies in the third trimester will be legally guaranteed not to perish, under libertarian law. Not so for human beings in the first two trimesters.

What, then, are Boonin's arguments against evictionism, e.g., in defense of what he calls "the good Samaritan argument?" He starts off in this manner (p. 254–255): "They believe that aborting a viable fetus is morally worse than aborting a nonviable one, but find it difficult to accept the claim that the fetus acquires a right to life at that point. Whether or not a fetus is viable seems to be more a fact about its environment and the existing state of technology than about its own nature, and so it is difficult to see how being viable could make the difference between its having a right to life and its not having a right to life."

But this is neither here nor there. The fetus never had "a right to life at that point," or at any other time. The issue is, instead, Should it be illegal for the mother and her doctors to kill this very young person? The level of technology is irrelevant. It merely determines whether, if evicted at any given stage of development, the fetus can survive outside of the womb.

This philosopher avers, in his attempt to come to grips with what he misconstrues as evictionism (p. 255): "…the right the pregnant woman has is not the right to kill the fetus but the right to unburden herself of it, even if this must involve its death. If the fetus is viable, and thus can be safely removed, then the woman has the right only to have it removed, not to have it killed. That aborting a viable fetus is impermissible while aborting an unviable fetus is permissible, therefore, is consistent with the assumption that the fetus acquires a right to life at some point before viability, including the moment of its conception."

---

[62] It cannot be maintained that Boonin is unaware of this distinction between what is moral and what should be legal. Although he spends 99.9% of his book on the former, he does mention this distinction.

No, no, no. The fetus, it can never be repeated too often, never has any right to life. This is a positive right, abhorred by libertarianism. No one has any such right. But all persons, certainly including the pre-born, have a *negative* right not to be murdered. It is equally a homicide to kill a viable and an unviable fetus. It is licit to remove, evict, separate from, unburden oneself of, an immature baby at *any* stage of his development. The only difference is that in the one case the infant will perish, and in the other, not.

Next consider (p. 255) this contribution of Boonin's: "Since it is at least imaginable that technology might one day produce either an artificial womb capable of sustaining fetal life from conception onward or a procedure by which a fetus could safely be removed from one woman and reimplanted in another, it would follow from what has been said that under such circumstances women would never have a right to kill their fetuses but only to have them removed alive. As one such critic has put it, "Thomson's argument is not really a defense of *abortion*, it is a defense of *extraction* (Levin 1985: 125)."

No, this is not quite right, whether on the part of Boonin, or Levin. To the contrary, Thomson does allow a case of what I have been calling abortion, which included eviction, alright, but, plus the downright killing of an innocent fetus, that is, murder. This is the case of the fetus who comes into being as the result of the rape of his mother.

Let us now pursue Boonin's response to what he regards as the three steps of the argument; we follow him in the reverse order he addresses them (as per usual, I delete his footnotes). He rejects the third outright (p. 255–256): "So far as I can see, the third claim should simply be rejected. As one writer has put it, 'There is no reason to think of the death of the fetus as something the [defender of the permissibility of abortion] passionately wants so much as something, given what he does want, he is prepared to accept' (Ross 1982: 233). This is clearly Thomson's view: Your right to unplug yourself from the violinist, she emphasizes, does not entail that if by some miracle he survives the procedure you may then go ahead and slit his throat. And similarly, 'The desire for the child's death is not one which anybody may gratify, should it turn out to be possible to detach the child alive' (1971a, b, c: 126). Indeed, even if we do not assume that the fetus has the same right to life as you or I, it may still seem reasonable to believe that it would be wrong to kill a viable fetus when it could instead be removed and cared for by someone who is willing to care for it."

This sounds good to the libertarian ear, at the outset. But, remember, Thomson, who Boonin relies on, does not accept this argument. Nevertheless, I must admit for the first time, this is an accurate rendition of the evictionist position. However, Boonin rejects it.[63] He opines (p. 256):

> "How might a proponent of the abortion versus extraction objection respond? In order for the objection to retain its force, we must believe that when a woman is in a position to have her fetus removed either dead or alive, and when someone else will care for the child if it is removed, she has the right to have the fetus removed dead. I can imagine only one kind of consideration that might seem to support this contention. One could appeal to the claim that

[63] Sad, as President Trump might say.

> the woman has a right to kill the viable fetus she is carrying because if she does not do so, she will then suffer the mental distress of having an offspring of hers out in the world that she is not caring for."

Mental distress? Is this for real? I was mentally distressed by the possibility of Hillary Clinton beating Donald Trump for the presidency of the United States. Therefore, I have the right to decide upon which one takes that office? This is not only nonsense, it is dangerous nonsense. But the same applies to the distraught pregnant woman. Let her go seek help from a psychologist, or other such mental health professional. To think that her unhappiness justifies murder is surely at least very highly problematic.

But then our author appears to reverse course, like an excellent broken field runner in a football game. He asserts (p. 257):

> "…the claim that the woman has such a right would entail that if the baby survived an attempted abortion, or was born prematurely, before the woman had an opportunity to have the abortion performed, then she would still have the right to have it killed. And this is plainly unacceptable. It may well be true that many women who seek abortions do so because they want the fetus that they are carrying to be killed. And such women will to that extent be dissatisfied with a position on which it is morally permissible for them to have their viable fetuses extracted but not killed. But in the absence of an independent reason to think that they are entitled to have the fetus die when it is already viable, this seems to count more as a criticism of their desires than as an objection to the good Samaritan argument."

Yes, of course, this desire of hers counts as a criticism of it. It is difficult to think of a more justified case for criticism. But it *also* "counts" as a critique of Boonin's defense of abortion. What is the evidence for this contention of mine? It is the fact that my debating partner supports *abortion*, not evictionism.

Here is how Boonin deals with the second claim (p. 259):

> "Suppose that the imagined artificial life-support system has been invented and that keeping a fetus on such artificial life-support for nine months is quite expensive. Now consider a woman who has her unwanted fetus merely extracted (but not killed) under such circumstances. What will happen to the fetus? The fetus will still die unless someone is willing to take on the great burden of supporting it for nine months. The mere availability of the technology itself, after all, does not entail that the fetus will survive the extraction process."

Here is my response. First, who would that be who will care for the evicted, not the aborted, fetus? Why, it would be the first person to homestead, not of course ownership over the saved baby, but the guardianship rights thereof. It is only if there is not a single solitary person on the planet who wishes to save this newborn that he will die.[64]

Certainly, no libertarian would agree that society as a whole has any such obligation. For one thing, as we never tire of saying, there are no positive obligations incumbent upon anyone, and caring for babies is precisely an example of that. For another, this option smacks of government and taxes, phenomena anathema to the purist version of this philosophy. Moreover, this worry about who will care for the saved baby is beside the point. The only relevant issue is, Does the pregnant woman

---

[64] Given the number of pro-life movement people, this is exceedingly unlikely.

have the right to only evict the baby from her premises, and, or/also, to kill him. When put in this manner it is difficult to see how any man of good will can agree to both. Murder is murder is murder. In any case, this issue is prior to the one of who will take care of the infant once he is saved. First, let us save him; only then should we worry about who will care for the baby.

How does Boonin deal with the first point? He does so as follows (p. 260):

> "… there are two fundamentally different ways in which our ability to keep premature babies alive can improve: We can increase the percentage who survive from a given stage in pregnancy and we can decrease the level of gestation at which it is possible for at least some to survive. Impressive, even breathtaking improvements of the first sort provide no real evidence of the feasibility of the second. And, indeed, almost all of the recent improvements in the survivability of premature infants has been of the first sort. In particular, the sharp rise in survivability at 25 weeks of gestation has not been accompanied by a significant decrease in the level of gestational development at which survivability outside the womb is possible. None of this, of course, shows such technology to be literally impossible. But it should at least give pause to those who imagine that a technological resolution to the abortion controversy will be available at any point in the near future. For the foreseeable future, at least, it seems reasonable to suppose that the permissibility of extracting the fetus will continue to mean the permissibility of performing an act that results in the fetus's death. Thus, even if one thinks that a woman should be entitled to secure the death of a viable fetus and not merely its removal (again, an assumption that is extremely questionable at best), the good Samaritan argument seems to provide a justification for that for the foreseeable future as well."

This is evasive. To say this is to attempt to ignore the power of the evictionist argument. First of all, sufficient medical technology already exists at least for babies in their third trimester. Adopting evictionism would save all babies at this stage of development from the despicable horrors of partial birth abortions.[65] But, assume this expertise did not already exist. Posit that it would never come into being. Still, we can *imagine* such a breakthrough. Boonin misses the point. This technology would then be a theoretical construct, such as a perfect gas or a frictionless system in physics, or equilibrium in economics. Even if not real, all of these theoretical constructs shed light on philosophical problems. They allow us to peer below the surface of a controversy. In this case, such an assumption helps us to perceive the difference between evil abortion, and licit eviction.

To summarize. Boonin rejects eviction and supports abortion. But his reasons for doing so are problematic. Yes, some women will be psychologically debilitated at the prospect of their progeny surviving. They do not want "that man's" child to live. But our author does not accept this argument. It is difficult to see precisely why, then, he supports the pro-choice position when every other desiderata of his, apart from this single one, can be attained by eviction.

---

[65] However, see, supra, our discussion of whether or not this is justified in order to save the mother's life or preserve her health. It does not seem likely, although, I confess, I have no direct knowledge of the medical implications of this procedure. But, from a common sense point of view, expelling the dead baby logically implies one additional procedure, killing him. Certainly, this extra step takes time, which itself can endanger the mother. Also, any extra steps, such as this one, can be done improperly, which would expose the mother to additional risk.

We cannot leave without commenting on Boonin's mistaken analysis of the lifeboat controversy, which will support only one of two seekers of the safety it affords. In his view (p. 262): "…it does seem reasonable to suppose that in a life boat dilemma each person is entitled to give preference to his own interests." Not at all. Each competitor for the lifeboat is "entitled" to no such thing. As libertarian theory makes clear, the decision as to who may make use of this life boat which can support only one person is properly made, only, by its *owner*. What if there is no such person on the scene, or he cannot be found? Then, the property right goes to the *first* homesteader. It is only if the two of them reach the boat at the same exact time that any philosophical dilemma arises.

Let us conclude by considering one last failure of Boonin to come to grips with the case for evictionism, after coming so infuriatingly close to doing so. He opines (p. 276–277):

> "…there seems to many people to be a morally relevant difference between abortion prior to the point at which the fetus becomes viable and abortion after that point. Many defenders of abortion in general are at least more hesitant to support abortion after viability and some are inclined to oppose it. And critics who oppose abortion prior to viability often believe that there is something especially objectionable about abortion after viability. Indeed, if there is anything at all resembling a common or middle ground in the abortion debate, it consists in the claim that there is a morally relevant difference of some sort between early abortions and late-term abortions on viable fetuses. Yet on the other hand, there seems to be no morally relevant difference in the moral status of the fetus itself between the last moment when it is not viable and the first moment when it is viable. Critics of abortion, of course, deny that there is such a difference, since they maintain that the fetus has the same right to life as you and I well before this point. But defenders of abortion, too, find it difficult to affirm that there is such a difference, since it is difficult to discern any relevant change in the nature of the fetus itself at this stage in its development."

But "the nature of the fetus itself" is entirely irrelevant to the case in point.[66] It is not a matter of his nature. It is an issue of *property rights*. The mother owns her womb. The unwanted preborn person is a(n innocent) trespasser. The owner of the property in question has a right to be secure in her rights. So, she may evict the intruder, but only in the gentlest manner possible. But she may not unjustly kill (murder) this infant. There is no valid reason to bring into the analysis the continuum (Block and Barnett 2008) problem of "the moral status of the fetus itself between the last moment when it is not viable and the first moment when it is viable." The only proper consideration is whether or not the evictee will survive after he is expelled. But that is a positive, not a normative, matter. It depends upon the level of medical sophistication. Do we want a *normative* point of departure? Here it is: it is the difference between the situation where there is a sperm alone, and an egg, alone, unconnected to each other, where neither will ever become a person, on the one hand, and on the other, the fertilized egg, which will, if it, he, rather, is placed in the proper environment.

Boonin continues in this vein (p. 277–278):

[66] Stipulating, as does Boonin, even if only arguendo, that the human being exists, from the fertilized egg and afterward.

> "There is a morally relevant difference between causing the death of the fetus before and after viability not because there is a morally relevant difference between the *fetus* before and after viability, but rather because there is a morally relevant difference between the fetus-woman relation before and after viability. In the violinist story, for example, it is clear why there is a morally relevant difference between the fetus-woman relation before and after viability. In the violinist story, for example, it is clear why there is a morally relevant difference between the relation between you and the violinist before and after the point at which the violinist becomes 'viable.' Prior to the point at which he recovers from his kidney ailment, he cannot survive without being plugged into you. After that point, he can. The claim that you have a right to unplug yourself from him at any point in time, therefore, entails that you have the right to do an act that will result in his death only prior to the point at which he can survive without the use of your body. Once he is cured, you can of course still choose to unplug yourself from him. But you cannot choose to kill him before or in the process of doing so. And so if we accept the good Samaritan argument's analysis of abortion, it becomes clear why the common view that there is something distinctively problematic about abortions on viable fetuses is well grounded. The claim that a pregnant woman has the right to withdraw the needed life support that she is providing for the fetus, after all, will entail that she has the right to do an act that will result in the death of the fetus only prior to the point at which the fetus can survive without the use of her body."

No, no, no. Death schmeath. Death is beside the point. Living or dying depends, only, on the level of medical ability, something irrelevant to the *normative* issue. It is crucial to focus, instead, on private property rights. Does the woman own her body, or not? If so, and libertarians, at least, maintain she most certainly does, then she has the right to eject, at *any* time of her choosing, whether or not "death" of her baby will result. We must keep our eye on the ball, given these treacherous philosophical waters. And the "ball" is the normative one of rights, not the positive one of medical technology and life or death, upon which Boonin is here fixated.

In the view of Boonin (p. 278–279):

> "A further puzzle arises from a relatively uncontroversial legal practice. If an attacker assaults a pregnant woman and kills the fetus she is carrying, he can be charged with a serious offense because of the death he has caused. Critics of abortion often point to this as evidence of inconsistency or hypocrisy on the part of the defenders of abortion. As one pro-life activist has put it, 'If a pregnant woman is murdered, we [society] want to bring the perpetrator up on double-homicide charges. However, if that same woman was to abort she would be invoking her freedom of choice. It's almost as if it's not really a baby unless you want it to be. And that, of course, is ridiculous' (Dinah Monahan, quoted in Allen 1995: 12). The implication that whether or not the fetus is a baby depends on whether the woman wants it to be a baby is, clearly, unacceptable, as is the implication that this is true of the question of whether or not it has the same right to life as you or I. We cannot justify the practice of punishing the attacker but not the woman by saying that whether or not the fetus has a right to life depends upon whether or not the woman wants it to have a right to life. If the permissibility of abortion is defended by insisting that the fetus is just a blob of tissue, however, then it may indeed prove difficult to justify the practice of charging the attacker with a second serious offense. Destroying a blob of tissue, after all, is not generally a serious crime.

> "But on the analysis provided by the good Samaritan argument, the coherence of this practice, too, is clearly illuminated without raising problems for the claim that abortion is morally permissible. If you do choose to allow the violinist to use your kidneys in Thomson's example, after all, the fact that you could also have chosen not to do so does not give someone else the right to unplug the violinist from you against your will. If I murder you in

your bed, causing the violinist to be deprived of the use of the kidneys that you have agreed to let him use, then I am guilty of unjustly killing you and of unjustly killing the violinist by depriving him of life support that he had acquired the right to use. In this respect, it is no different from a case in which I kill a violinist by destroying a life support machine to which he was attached and which he had acquired the right to use. If you choose to unplug yourself from the violinist, on the other hand, causing the violinist to be deprived of the use of your kidneys, you are not guilty of such an unjust killing, since in that case you do not deprive the violinist of something to which he was entitled."

I cannot see my way clear to acknowledging that this answer is responsive. Either the fetus is a mere blob, similar to a tumor, or it is a human being. If the former, when someone kills a pregnant woman, he murdered two people, not one person and one blob. If the latter, then partial birth abortion is justified in any and all circumstances. The connection between this consideration and destroying a life support machine is rather distant.

Nor is Boonin's response to the challenge to his theory altogether convincing. He states (p. 278):

"A second and related problem arises from the fact that the moment at which the unborn fetus becomes a newborn infant, like the moment at which the nonviable fetus becomes a viable fetus, marks no significant change in the nature of the individual involved. Virtually every defender of abortion is, at the very least, reluctant to have the permissibility of abortion stand or fall with the permissibility of killing a newborn human infant, but it can again seem very difficult to see how this linkage can be avoided. If it is permissible to abort a late-term fetus, and a late-term fetus is not significantly different from a newborn (especially a prematurely born) infant, then how could it be impermissible to kill a newborn infant? Here, again, the good Samaritan analysis provides a simple answer. The fact that it is permissible for you to unplug yourself from the violinist, after all, does not imply that if you agree to remain plugged into him for nine months, you may then kill him after he has been successfully unplugged. And so on the good Samaritan account, it is easy to see why the permissibility of abortion does not imply the permissibility of killing newborn babies."

But if the "nature" of the fetus itself has the importance Boonin places upon it, and if there is no real difference between the fetus in the womb in the eighth month and the premature newborn of that number of months of development, and it is alright to engage in partial birth abortion of the former, then it seems problematic to contend it would be improper, also, to slaughter the latter. This is a very important point. For, pro-choicers properly find abhorrent the murder of a baby outside of the womb. But, and this must be stuffed down their (intellectual) throats until they cry "uncle," there is (virtually) no difference at all between that baby, and one of equal development with a different address: still inside the womb.

To summarize. This is an important book. It is a tour de force of an important issue in philosophy. It is about as thorough as it is possible to be. His analysis reaches into issues only loosely covered in the discussion of abortion such as murder, punishment, and much, much more. Its only failure is that it gives short shrift to evictionism, the one true solution to the abortion conundrum.

References

Akers, Becky. 2012a. *Not My Definition – Or Webster's Either – Of 'Trespassing'*, September 6. http://archive.lewrockwell.com/blog/lewrw/archives/120226.html

———. 2012b. *What If the 'Fetu' Could Shoot Back?*, September 12. http://archive.lewrockwell.com/blog/lewrw/archives/120728.html

Andersson, Anna-Karin. 2007. An Alleged Contradiction in Nozick's Entitlement Theory. *Journal of Libertarian Studies* 21 (3, Fall): 43–63. http://mises.org/journals/jls/21_3/21_3_3.pdf

Barnett, William II. 1989. Subjective Cost Revisited. *The Review of Austrian Economics* 3: 137–138.

Barnett, William II, and Walter E. Block. 2007. Coase and Van Zandt on Lighthouses. *Public Finance Review* 35 (6, November): 710–733. http://pfr.sagepub.com/content/35/6/710

———. 2009a. Coase and Bertrand on Lighthouses. *Public Choice* 140 (1–2): 1–13. https://doi.org/10.1007/s11127-008-9375-x.

———. 2009b. Financial Intermediaries, the Intertemporal-Carry Trade, and Austrian Business Cycles; Or; Crash and Carry: Can Fraudulent Time deposits lead to an Austrian Business Cycle? Yes. *Journal Etica e Politica/Ethics & Politics* XI (1): 455–469. http://www2.units.it/~etica/2009_1/BARNETT_BLOCK.pdf

Block, Walter E. 1977a. Toward a Libertarian Theory of Abortion. *The Libertarian Forum* 10 (9, September): 6–8.

———. 1977b. Coase and Demsetz on Private Property Rights. *The Journal of Libertarian Studies: An Interdisciplinary Review* I (2, Spring): 111–115. http://www.mises.org/journals/jls/1_2/1_2_4.pdf

———. 1978. Abortion, Woman and Fetus: Rights in Conflict? *Reason* 9 (12, April): 18–25.

———. 1979. Review of Nancy C. Baker, Baby Selling: The Scandal of Black Market Adoptions. *Libertarian Review* 7 (12, January): 44–45.

———. 1988. Comment on Leland Yeager on Subjectivism. *The Review of Austrian Economics* II: 199–208.

———. 1990. Earning Happiness Through Homesteading Unowned Land: A Comment on 'Buying Misery with Federal Land' by Richard Stroup. *Journal of Social Political and Economic Studies* 15 (2, Summer): 237–253.

———. 1995. Ethics, Efficiency, Coasean Property Rights and Psychic Income: A Reply to Demsetz. *The Review of Austrian Economics* 8 (2): 61–125.

———. 1996. O.J.'s Defense: A Reductio Ad Absurdum of the Economics of Ronald Coase and Richard Posner. *European Journal of Law and Economics* 3: 265–286.

———. 1999. Market Inalienability Once Again: Reply to Radin. *Thomas Jefferson Law Journal* 22 (1, Fall): 37–88.

———. 2000. Private Property Rights, Erroneous Interpretations, Morality and Economics: Reply to Demsetz. *Quarterly Journal of Austrian Economics* 3 (1, Spring): 63–78.

———. 2001a. *Stem Cell Research: The Libertarian Compromise*, September 3. http://archive.lewrockwell.com/block/block5.html

———. 2001b. Alienability, Inalienability, Paternalism and the Law: Reply to Kronman. *American Journal of Criminal Law* 28 (3, Summer): 351–371.

———. 2002a. *A Libertarian Theory of Secession and Slavery*, June 10. http://www.lewrockwell.com/block/block15.html

———. 2002b. Homesteading City Streets; An Exercise in Managerial Theory. *The Planning and Market* 5 (1, September): 18–23.

———. 2002c. On Reparations to Blacks for Slavery. *Human Rights Review* 3 (4, July–September): 53–73.

———. 2003a. *The Death Penalty*, November 11. http://www.lewrockwell.com/block/block34.html

———. 2003b. *Death Penalty Essential for Social Justice*. Loyola University New Orleans Loyola University New Orleans The Maroon, October 10.

———. 2003c. Libertarianism vs. Objectivism; A Response to Peter Schwartz. *Reason Papers* 26 (Summer): 39–62.

———. 2003d. Private Property Rights, Economic Freedom, and Professor Coase: A Critique of Friedman, McCloskey, Medema and Zorn. *Harvard Journal of Law and Public Policy* 26 (3, Summer): 923–951.

———. 2003e. Toward a Libertarian Theory of Inalienability: A Critique of Rothbard, Barnett, Gordon, Smith, Kinsella and Epstein. *Journal of Libertarian Studies* 17 (2, Spring): 39–85.

———. 2003f. Socialized Medicine Is the Problem. *Surgical Neurology* 60 (5, November): 467–446.

———. 2004a. Are Alienability and the Apriori of Argument Logically Incompatible? *Dialogue* 1 (1). https://papers.ssrn.com/sol3/papers.cfm?abstract_id=1889440

———. 2004b. Austrian Law and Economics: The Contributions of Adolf Reinach and Murray Rothbard. *Quarterly Journal of Austrian Economics* 7 (4, Winter): 69–85.

———. 2005. Ayn Rand and Austrian Economics: Two Peas in a Pod. *The Journal of Ayn Rand Studies* 6 (2, Spring): 259–269.

———. 2006a. Epstein on Alienation: A Rejoinder. *International Journal of Social Economics* 33 (3-4): 241–260.

———. 2006b. Coase and Kelo: Ominous Parallels and Reply to Lott on Rothbard on Coase. *Whittier Law Review* 27 (4): 997–1022.

———. 2006c. Radical Libertarianism: Applying Libertarian Principles to Dealing with the Unjust Government, Part II. *Reason Papers* 28 (Spring): 85–109.

———. 2007. Alienability: Reply to Kuflik. *Humanomics* 23 (3): 117–136.

———. 2008. Homesteading, Ad Coelum, Owning Views and Forestalling. *The Social Sciences.* 3 (2): 96–103.

———. 2009a. Yes, Sell Rivers! And Make Legal Some Slave Contracts. *The Tyee*, July 25. http://thetyee.ca/Opinion/2009/07/24/SellRivers/

———. 2009b. *Privatizing Rivers and Voluntary Slave Contracts*, July 27. http://www.lewrockwell.com/block/block134.html

———. 2009c. Toward a Libertarian Theory of Guilt and Punishment for the Crime of Statism. In *Property, Freedom and Society: Essays in Honor of Hans-Hermann Hoppe*, ed. Jorg Guido Hulsmann and Stephan Kinsella, 137–148. Auburn: Ludwig von Mises Institute.

———. 2009d. Libertarian Punishment Theory: Working For, and Donating To, The State. *Libertarian Papers* 1: 1–31.

———. 2009e. *The Privatization of Roads and Highways: Human and Economic Factors*. Auburn: The Mises Institute.

———. 2010a. Response to Jakobsson on Human Body Shields. *Libertarian Papers* 2 (25): 1–9.

———. 2010b. A Response to Brooks' Support of Demsetz on the Coase Theorem. *Dialogue* 2. http://www.uni-svishtov.bg/dialog/2010/2.10.WB.pdf. https://www.scribd.com/document/165099141/REJOINDER-TO-BROOKS-ON-COASE-AND-DEMSETZ

———. 2010c. Rejoinder to Brooks on Coase and Demsetz. *Quarterly Journal of Austrian Economics* 13 (4, Winter): 56–73.

———. 2010d. Rejoinder to Boettke on Coasean Economics and Communism. *Romanian Economic and Business Review* 5 (3, Fall): 9–90.

———. 2010e. Objections to the Libertarian Stem Cell Compromise. *Libertarian Papers* 2: 34.

———. 2010f. Rejoinder to Wisniewski on Abortion. *Libertarian Papers* 32 (2): 1–9.

———. 2011a. Terri Schiavo: A Libertarian Analysis. *Journal of Libertarian Studies* 22: 527–536.

———. 2011b. Rejoinder to Bertrand on Lighthouses. *Romanian Economic and Business Review* 6 (3, Fall): 49–67.

———. 2011c. Response to Wisniewski on Abortion, Round Two. *Libertarian Papers* 3: Article No. 4.

———. 2011d. Response to Wisniewski on Abortion, Round Three. *Libertarian Papers* 3 (6).

———. 2011e. Evictionism Is Libertarian; Departurism Is Not: Critical Comment on Parr. *Libertarian Papers* 3: Article 36.

———. 2012. *A Not So Funny Thing Happened to Me in Tampa*, August 30. http://archive.lewrockwell.com/block/block208.html
———. 2013a. *Legalize Blackmail*. New Orleans: Straylight Publishing.
———. 2013b. *More Than Passing Curious: George Jonas and Libertarianism*, January 20. http://www.lewrockwell.com/blog/lewrw/archives/130927.html
———. 2013c. *If You're Going to Attack Libertarianism, Try Having a Clue. The Curious Case of the Non-libertarian, George Jonas*, February 8. http://lewrockwell.com/block/block216.html
———. 2013d. Rejoinder to Parr on Evictionism and Departurism. *Journal of Peace Prosperity & Freedom* 2: 125–138.
———. 2014a. Response to Wisniewski on Abortion, Round Four. *Management Education Science Technology Journal (MEST)* 2 (2): 1–14.
———. 2014b. Should Abortion Be Criminalized? Rejoinder to Akers, Davies and Shaffer on Abortion. *Management Education Science Technology (MEST) Journal* 2 (1, January): 33–44.
———. 2014c. Evictionism and Libertarianism. *Journal of Medicine and Philosophy* 35 (2): 290–294.
———. 2014d. Toward a Libertarian Theory of Evictionism. *Journal of Family and Economic Issues* 35 (2, June): 290–294.
———. 2014e. A Collection of Essays on Libertarian Jurisprudence: Sunshine and Property Rights. *Saint Louis University Law Journal* 58 (2, Winter): 541–547.
———. 2016a. Forestalling, Positive Obligations and the Lockean and Blockian Provisos: Rejoinder to Stephan Kinsella. *Ekonomia Wroclaw Economic Review*. https://repozytorium.uni.wroc.pl/Content/94352/03_Block_W_E_Butt_J_A_Forestalling_Positive_Obligations_and_the_Lockean_and_Blockian_Provisos_Rejoinder_to_Stephan_Kinsella.pdf
———. 2016b. How We Come to Own Ourselves. *Polish Academich Journal – Societas et Ius Version* 5: 7–14.
———. 2016c. Response to Feser on Libertarianism. *Journal Etica e Politica/Ethics & Politics* XVIII (3): 547–572.
Block, Walter E., and William Barnett II. 2008. Continuums. *Journal Etica e Politica/Ethics & Politics* 1: 151–166.
Block, Walter E., and Michael R. Edelstein. 2012. Popsicle Sticks and Homesteading Land for Nature Preserves. *Romanian Economic and Business Review* 7 (1, Spring): 7–13.
Block, Walter E., and Richard Epstein. 2005. Debate on Eminent Domain. *NYU Journal of Law & Liberty* 1 (3): 1144–1169.
Block, Walter E., and Peter Lothian Nelson. 2015. *Water Capitalism: The Case for Privatizing Oceans, Rivers, Lakes, and Aquifers*. New York City: Lexington Books/Rowman and Littlefield.
Block, Walter E., and Roy Whitehead. 2005. Compromising the Uncompromisable: A Private Property Rights Approach to Resolving the Abortion Controversy. *Appalachian Law Review* 4 (2): 1–45.
Block, Walter E. and Guillermo Yeatts. 1999–2000. The Economics and Ethics of Land Reform: A Critique of the Pontifical Council for Justice and Peace's 'Toward a Better Distribution of Land: The Challenge of Agrarian Reform'. *Journal of Natural Resources and Environmental Law* 15 (1): 37–69.
Block, Walter E., William Barnett II, and Gene Callahan. 2005. The Paradox of Coase as a Defender of Free Markets. *NYU Journal of Law & Liberty* 1 (3): 1075–1095. http://tinyurl.com/2hbzd4
Bohm-Bawerk, Eugen. 1959 [1884]. *Capital and Interest*. South Holland: Libertarian Press. Trans. George D. Hunke and Hans F. Sennholz. See Particularly Part I, Ch. XII. Exploitation Theory of Socialism-Communism. http://www.mises.org/store/product1.asp?SID=2&Product_ID=19
Boonin-Vail, David. 2003. *A Defense of Abortion*, Cambridge Studies in Philosophy and Public Policy. Cambridge, MA: Cambridge University Press.
Buchanan, James M. 1969. *Cost and Choice: An Inquiry into Economic Theory*. Chicago: Markham.
———. 1979. The General Implications of Subjectivism in Economics. In *What Should Economists Do?* Indianapolis: Liberty Press.

Buchanan, James M., and G.F. Thirlby. 1981. *L.S.E. Essays on Cost*. New York: New York University Press.

Butos, William, and Roger Koppl. 1997. The Varieties of Subjectivism: Keynes, Hayek on Expectations. *History of Political Economy* 29 (2): 327–359.

Bylund, Per L. 2005. *Man and Matter: A Philosophical Inquiry into the Justification of Ownership in Land from the Basis of Self-Ownership*. Master thesis, Lund University, Spring Semester, June. http://www.uppsatser.se/uppsats/a7eb17de8f/; http://perbylund.com/academics_polsci_msc.pdf;http://www.essays.se/essay/a7eb17de8f/;http://www.lunduniversity.lu.se/o.o.i.s?id=24965&postid=1330482

———. 2012. Man and Matter: How the Former Gains Ownership of the Latter. *Libertarian Papers* 4 (1). http://libertarianpapers.org/articles/2012/lp-4-1-5.pdf

Coase, Ronald H. 1960. The Problem of Social Cost. *Journal of Law and Economics* 3: 1–44. http://www.sfu.ca/~allen/CoaseJLE1960.pdf

Cordato, Roy E. 1989. Subjective Value, Time Passage, and the Economics of Harmful Effects. *Hamline Law Review* 12 (2, Spring): 229–244.

———. 1992a. Knowledge Problems and the Problem of Social Cost. *Journal of the History of Economic Thought* 14 (Fall): 209–224.

———. 1992b. *Welfare Economics and Externalities in an Open-Ended Universe: A Modern Austrian Perspective*. Boston: Kluwer.

———. 1997. Market-Based Environmentalism and the Free Market: They're Not the Same. *The Independent Review* 1 (3, Winter): 371–386.

———. 1998. Time Passage and the Economics of Coming to the Nuisance: Reassessing the Coasean Perspective. *Campbell Law Review* 20 (2, Spring): 273–292.

———. 2000. Chasing Phantoms in a Hollow Defense of Coase. *The Review of Austrian Economics* 13 (2, September): 193–208.

Davies, Jim. 2012. *Abortion*, September 24. http://strike-the-root.com/abortion

DiLorenzo, Thomas J. 1990. The Subjectivist Roots of James Buchanan's Economics. *The Review of Austrian Economics* 4: 180–195.

———. 2014. *When Did Ronald Coase Become the Ayatollah of Economic Theory?*, January 2. http://www.lewrockwell.com/2014/01/thomas-dilorenzo/the-beltarian-cult/

Dyke, Jeremiah, and Walter E. Block. 2011. Explorations in Property Rights: Conjoined Twins. *Libertarian Papers* 3: Art. 38. http://libertarianpapers.org/2011/38-dyke-block-conjoined-twins/

Ehrlich, Isaac. 1972. The Deterrent Effect of Criminal Law Enforcement. *The Journal of Legal Studies* L (2, June): 259–276.

———. 1973. Participation in Illegitimate Activities – A Theoretical and Empirical Investigation. *Journal of Political Economy* 81 (3, May/June): 521–565.

———. 1974. Participation in Illegitimate Activities – An Economic Analysis. In *The Economics of Crime and Punishment*, ed. Becker and Landes, 68–134. New York: Columbia University Press.

———. 1975. On the Relation Between Education and Crime. In *Education, Income, and Human Behavior*, ed. F.T. Juster, 313–338. New York: Mcgraw-Hill Co.

———. 1976a. Deterrence: Evidence and Inference. *The Yale Law Journal* 85 (2, December): 209–227.

———. 1976b. Rejoinder. *The Yale Law Journal* 85 (3, January).

———. 1977a. Fear of Deterrence – A Critical Evaluation of the Report of the Panel on Research on Deterrent and Incapacitative Effects. *The Journal of Legal Studies* 6 (2, June): 293–316.

———. 1977b. Capital Punishment and Deterrence: Some Further Thoughts and Additional Evidence. *Journal of Political Economy* 85 (4, August): 741–788.

———. 1977c. The Deterrent Effect of Capital Punishment: Reply. *American Economic Review* 67 (3, June): 452–458.

———. 1978. Deterrence and Economics: A Perspective on Theory and Evidence. In *Major Social Issues: A Multidisciplinary View*, ed. Milton Yinger and Stephen Cutler. New York: The Free Press.

———. 1979. The Economic Approach to Crime – A Preliminary Assessment. In *Criminology, Review Yearbook Vol. l*, ed. Messinger and Bittner. Beverly Hills: Sage.
———. 1981. On the Usefulness of Controlling Individuals: An Economic Analysis of Rehabilitation, Incapacitation, and Deterrence. *American Economic Review* 71 (3, June): 307–322.
———. 1982. The Market for Offenses and the Public Enforcement of Laws: An Equilibrium Analysis. *British Journal of Social Psychology* 21: 107–120.
Ehrlich, Isaac, and J.C. Gibbons. 1977. On the Measurement of the Deterrent Effect of Capital Punishment and the Theory of Deterrence. *The Journal of Legal Studies* 6 (l, January): 35–50.
Ehrlich, Isaac, and Richard A. Posner. 1974. An Economic Analysis of Legal Rulemaking. *The Journal of Legal Studies* 3 (l, January): 257–280.
Feser, Edward. 2004. Self-Ownership, Abortion, and the Rights of Children: Toward a More Conservative Libertarianism. *Journal of Libertarian Studies* 18 (3, Summer): 91–114. http://www.indytruth.org/library/journals/libertarianstudies/18/18_3_5.pdf
Fox, Glenn. 2007. The Real Coase Theorems. *The Cato Journal: An Interdisciplinary Journal of Public Policy Analysis* 27 (3, Fall): 373–396. http://www.cato.org/pubs/journal/cj27n3/cj27n3-5.pdf
Frederick, Danny. 2014. Voluntary Slavery. *Las Torres de Lucca* 4: 115–37. http://www.lastorresdelucca.org/index.php?option=com_k2&view=item&id=145:laesclavitud-voluntaria&Itemid=24&lang=en
Friedman, Milton. 1962. *Capitalism and Freedom*. Chicago: University of Chicago Press.
Garrison, Roger. 1985. A Subjectivist Theory of a Capital Using Economy. In *The Economics of Time and Ignorance*, ed. Gerald P. O'Driscoll and Mario Rizzo. Oxford: Basil Blackwell.
Goodwin, Jonathan. 2014. *Libertarians and Abortion*, December 23. http://bionicmosquito.blogspot.com/2014/12/libertarians-and-abortion.html
Grotius, Hugo. 1625. *Law of War and Peace* (De Jure Belli ac Pacis), 3 vols. Trans. A.C. London: Campbell, 1814.
Gunning, J. Patrick. 1990. *The New Subjectivist Revolution: An Elucidation and Extension of Ludwig von Mises's Contribution to Economic Theory*. Savage: Rowan and Littlefield.
Hamowy, Ronald. 1984. *Canadian Medicine: A Study in Restricted Entry*. Vancouver: The Fraser Institute.
Herbener, Jeffrey. 1996. Socialized Medicine, Take Two. *The Free Market* 14 (7, July). http://www.mises.org/freemarket_detail.asp?control=172&sortorder=articledate
Holly, Mike. 2013. *How Government Regulations Made Healthcare So Expensive*, December 17. http://bastiat.mises.org/2013/12/how-government-regulations-made-healthcare-so-expensive/
Hoppe, Hans-Hermann. 1993a. A Four-Step Health-Care Solution. *The Free Market* 11 (4, April). http://www.mises.org/freemarket_detail.asp?control=279
———. 1993b. *The Economics and Ethics of Private Property: Studies in Political Economy and Philosophy*. Boston: Kluwer.
———. 2004. *The Ethics and Economics of Private Property*, October 11. http://www.lewrockwell.com/hoppe/hoppe11.html
———. 2011. Of Private, Common, and Public Property and the Rationale for Total Privatization. *Libertarian Papers* 3 (1): 1–13. http://libertarianpapers.org/2011/1-hoppe-private-common-and-public-property/
Huemer, Michael. 2007. *Ethical Intuitionism*. Palgrave Macmillan.
Johnson, Clint, Walter E. Block, and Thomas Oxner. 1998. Notes on Health Care Financing and Free Markets. *Journal of Accounting, Ethics and Public Policy* 1 (3, Summer): 488–502.
Kershnar, Stephen. 2003. A Liberal Argument for Slavery. *Journal of Social Philosophy* 34 (4): 510–536.
Kinsella, N. Stephan. 2003. A Libertarian Theory of Contract: Title Transfer, Binding Promises, and Inalienability. *Journal of Libertarian Studies* 17 (2, Spring): 11–37. http://www.mises.org/journals/jls/17_2/17_2_2.pdf
———. 2006. *How We Come to Own Ourselves*, September 7. http://www.mises.org/story/2291

———. 2009a. *A Critique of Mutualist Occupancy*, August 2. http://www.stephankinsella.com/2009/08/a-critique-of-mutualist-occupancy/

———. 2009b. *Left-Libertarians on Rothbardian Abandonment*, August 22. http://www.stephankinsella.com/2009/08/left-libertarians-on-rothbardianabandonment/

———. 2009c. What Libertarianism Is. In: *Property, Freedom, and Society: Essays in Honor of Hans- Hermann Hoppe*, ed. Jörg Guido Hülsmann, and Stephan Kinsella. Auburn: Mises Institute. https://mises.org/library/what-libertarianism

———. 2009d. *Homesteading, Abandonment, and Unowned Land in the Civil Law*, May 22. http://blog.mises.org/10004/homesteading-abandonment-and-unowned-land-in-the-civil-law/

Kirzner, Israel M., ed. 1986. *Subjectivism, Intelligibility and Economic Understanding*. New York: New York University Press.

Krauss, Michael. 1999. Tort Law, Moral Accountability, and Efficiency: Reflections on the Current Crisis. *Markets and Morality* 2 (1, Spring). http://www.acton.org/publicat/m_and_m/1999_spr/krauss.html

Krecke, Elisabeth. 1996. Law and the Market Order: An Austrian Critique of the Economic Analysis of Law. *Journal des Economistes et des Etudes Humaines* 7 (1, March): 19–37. Commentaries on Law & Economics, 1997 Yearbook, ed. Robert W. McGee, 86–109.

Layden, William R., and Walter E. Block. 1996. Health Security. *Nomos*, July, No. 47/48, 38–45.

Lester, Jan Clifford. 2000. *Escape from Leviathan*. St. Martin's Press. http://www.amazon.com/exec/obidos/ASIN/0312234163/qid%3D989845939/107-8070279-6411737

Lewin, Peter. 1982. Pollution Externalities: Social Cost and Strict Liability. *Cato Journal* 2 (1, Spring): 205–229.

Locke, John. 1948. An Essay Concerning the True Origin, Extent and End of Civil Government. In *Social Contract*, ed. E. Barker, 17–18. New York: Oxford University Press.

McFadden, Robert D. 1985. *Terri Schiavo, 31, Dies; Focus of '76 Right to Die Case*, June 12. http://www.nytimes.com/1985/06/12/nyregion/karen-ann-Schiavo-31-dies-focus-of-76-right-to-die-case.html?pagewanted=all

Mises, Ludwig von. [1949] 1998. *Human Action, Scholars' Edition*. Auburn: Mises Institute. www.mises.org/humanaction/pdf/HumanActionScholars.pdf

Mosquito, Bionic. 2014a. *Libertarians and Abortion*, December 23. http://bionicmosquito.blogspot.com/2014/12/libertarians-and-abortion.html

———. 2014b. *The Sanctity of Contract*, April 19. http://bionicmosquito.blogspot.com/2014/04/the-sanctity-of-contract.html

———. 2015. *Walter E. Block, Specific Performance Contracts, and Abortion*, July 12. http://bionicmosquito.blogspot.com/2015/07/walter-block-specific-performance.html

North, Gary. 1990. *Tools of Dominion: The Case Laws of Exodus*. Tyler: Institute for Christian Economics.

———. 1992. *The Coase Theorem*. Tyler: The Institute for Christian Economics.

———. 2002. Undermining Property Rights: Coase and Becker. *The Journal of Libertarian Studies: An Interdisciplinary Review* 16 (4, Fall): 75–100. http://www.mises.org/journals/jls/16_4/16_4_5.pdf

Nozick, Robert. 1974. *Anarchy, State and Utopia*. New York: Basic Books. http://www.amazon.com/Anarchy-State-Utopia-Robert-Nozick/dp/0465097200

Parr, Sean. 2011. Departurism and the Libertarian Axiom of Gentleness. *Libertarian Papers* 3 (34). http://libertarianpapers.org/articles/2011/lp-3-34.doc

———. 2013. Departurism Redeemed – A Response to Walter E. Block's 'Evictionism Is Libertarian; Departurism Is Not: Critical Comment on Parr.' *Journal of Peace, Prosperity and Freedom* 2 (36).

Paul, Ellen Frankel. 1987. *Property Rights and Eminent Domain*. Livingston: Transaction Publishers.

Pufendorf, Samuel. 1673. Natural Law and the Law of Nations (De officio hominis et civis prout ipsi praescribuntur lege naturali) De officio hominis et civis juxta legem naturalem libri duo, 2 vols, Volume 1: Text, Buffalo, NJ, Hein; Reprint of New York: Oxford University Press, 1927a.

Rizzo, Mario J. 1979. Uncertainty, Subjectivity, and the Economic Analysis of Law. In *Time, Uncertainty, and Disequilibrium*, ed. Mario J. Rizzo, 71–90. Lexington: Lexington Books.
———. 1980. The Mirage of Efficiency. *Hofstra Law Review* 8: 641–658.
Rothbard, Murray N. 1973a. Free Market, Police, Courts, and Law. *Reason*, March, 5–19.
———. 1973b. *For a New Liberty*. New York: Macmillan. http://mises.org/rothbard/newliberty-whole.asp
———. 1978a. The Editor Replies. *Libertarian Forum*, July–August, 3. http://mises.org/journals/lf/1978/1978_07-08.pdf
———. 1978b. Society Without a State. In *Anarchism: Nomos XIX*, ed. J.R. Pennock and J.W. Chapman, 191–207. New York: New York University Press.
———. 1979. Comment: The Myth of Efficiency. In *Time, Uncertainty, and Disequilibrium*, ed. Mario J. Rizzo, 91–96. Lexington: Lexington Books.
———. 1982. Law, Property Rights, and Air Pollution. *Cato Journal* 2 (1, Spring); Reprinted in Economics and the Environment: A Reconciliation, ed. Walter E. Block, 233–279. Vancouver: The Fraser Institute, 1990. http://www.mises.org/rothbard/lawproperty.pdf; http://mises.org/story/2120
———. 1997a. Value Implications of Economic Theory. In *Logic of Action I*, 255–265. Cheltenham: Edward Elgar.
———. 1997b. Toward a Reconstruction of Utility and Welfare Economics. In *The Logic of Action: Method, Money and the Austrian School*, vol. I, 211–254. Cheltenham: Edward Elgar.
———. 2011. *For a New Liberty: The Libertarian Manifesto*. Auburn: Mises Institute. http://www.mises.org/rothbard/newliberty.asp
Rozeff, Michael S. 2005. *Original Appropriation and Its Critics*, September 1. http://www.lewrockwell.com/rozeff/rozeff18.html
Sadowsky, S.J., James. 1978. *Abortion and Rights of the Child*. Libertarian Forum, July–August, 2–3. http://mises.org/journals/lf/1978/1978_07-08.pdf
Salerno, Joseph P. 2016. *Laura Hillier, RIP*, February 11. https://mises.org/blog/laura-hillier-rip
Shaffer, Butler. 2012. *Of Children and Fetuses*, September 17. http://archive.lewrockwell.com/shaffer/shaffer259.html
Steiner, Hillel. 1994. *An Essay on Rights*. Oxford: Blackwell Publishers. https://drive.google.com/file/d/0B2mi4-xFgT7NNWhEQWNhbXB6enc/view
Stringham, Edward. 2001. Kaldor-Hicks Efficiency and the Problem of Central Planning. *Quarterly Journal of Austrian Economics* 4 (2, Summer): 41–50. http://www.mises.org/journals/qjae/pdf/qjae4_2_3.pdf.
———. 2008. Economic Value and Cost Are Subjective. In *The Handbook of Austrian Economics*, ed. Peter Boettke. Cheltenham: Edward Elgar Publishing. http://mises.org/journals/scholar/stringham4.pdf.
Stringham, Edward Peter, and Mark White. 2004. Economic Analysis of Tort Law: Austrian and Kantian Perspectives. In *Law and Economics: Alternative Economic Approaches to Legal and Regulatory Issues*, ed. Margaret Oppenheimer and Nicholas Mercuro, 374–392. New York: M.E. Sharpe. http://www.sjsu.edu/stringham/docs/Stringham.and.White2005.pdf.
Terrell, Timothy D. 1999. Property Rights and Externality: The Ethics of the Austrian School. *Journal of Markets and Morality* 2 (2, Fall). www.acton.org/publications/mandm/mandm_article_114.php
———. 2003. Socialized Medicine in America. *The Free Market* 23 (11, November). http://www.mises.org/freemarket_detail.asp?control=458&sortorder=articledate
Thomson, Judith Jarvis. 1971a. A Defense of Abortion. *Philosophy and Public Affairs* I: 47–66.
———. .1971b. *A Defense of Abortion*. University of Colorado at Boulder, Fall, 2007, March 4. http://spot.colorado.edu/~heathwoo/Phil160,Fall02/thomson.htm
———. 1971c. A Defense of Abortion. *Philosophy & Public Affairs* 1 (1, Fall); Reprinted in Intervention and Reflection: Basic Issues in Medical Ethics, 5th ed., ed. Ronald Munson (Belmont; Wadsworth 1996), 69–80.
———. 1990. *The Realm of Rights*. Cambridge: Harvard University Press.

Vance, Laurence M. 2008. *Is Ron Paul Wrong on Abortion?*, January 29. http://archive.lewrockwell.com/vance/vance133.html

———. 2012. *Libertarianism and Abortion*, July 17. http://archive.lewrockwell.com/vance/vance297.html

———. 2016. *Libertarianism and Racism*, August 16. https://www.lewrockwell.com/2016/08/laurence-m-vance/libertarianism-racism/

Wang, Amy B. 2017. *Trump Lashes Out at 'So-Called Judge' Who Temporarily Blocked Travel Ban*, February 4. https://www.washingtonpost.com/news/the-fix/wp/2017/02/04/trump-lashes-out-at-federal-judge-who-temporarily-blocked-travel-ban/?utm_term=.edd464773843

Watner, Carl. 1982. The Proprietary Theory of Justice in the Libertarian Tradition. *Journal of Libertarian Studies* 6 (3–4, Summer/Fall): 289–316. http://mises.org/journals/jls/6_3/6_3_6.pdf

Whitehead, Roy, and Walter E. Block. 2003. Taking the Assets of the Criminal to Compensate Victims of Violence: A Legal and Philosophical Approach. *Wayne State University Law School Journal of Law in Society* 5 (1, Fall): 229–254.

Wisniewski, Jakub Bozydar. 2010a. A Critique of Block on Abortion and Child Abandonment. *Libertarian Papers* 2 (16). http://libertarianpapers.org/2010/16-wisniewski-block-onabortion/

———. 2010b. Rejoinder to Block's Defense of Evictionism. *Libertarian Papers* 2: Art No. 27. http://libertarianpapers.org/articles/2010/lp-2-37.pdf

———. 2011. Response to Block on Abortion, Round Three. *Libertarian Papers*. http://libertarianpapers.org/2011/6-winiewski-response-to-block-on-abortion-round-three/; http://libertarianpapers.org/articles/2011/lp-3-6.pdf

———. 2013. Abortion, Libertarianism and Evictionism: A Last Word. *Libertarian Papers* 5 (1): 153–162. http://libertarianpapers.org/2013/6-wisniewski-abortionlibertarianism-and-evictionism/

Chapter 8
A Response to Beckwith's (1993) Book Review of Boonin (2003)

Beckwith (1993) starts off this very important essay of his with a paean to Boonin (2003):

> "It is difficult to believe that another book on the abortion controversy could contribute anything new to what appears to be an intractable dispute whose resolution is not imminent. David Boonin proves this notion wrong in his book A Defense of Abortion. Although I am an abortion opponent, and thus I come to much different conclusions than does Professor Boonin, I found myself admiring his careful and rigorous method and his philosophical creativity, and learning much in the process."

Beckwith ends on this note:

> "A Defense of Abortion is a significant contribution to the philosophical literature on the subject. It is arguably the most important monograph on abortion to be published in the past twenty years. Although one may find oneself disagreeing with Boonin, as I do, one cannot help but be challenged by, and impressed with, the author's mastery of argument and his honest grappling with the various cases for the position he opposes."

I find myself in full and enthusiastic agreement with Beckwith's assessment of Boonin (2003). I, too, appreciate the latter, but cannot bring myself to fully agree with that splendid essay. I offer my own assessment of Boonin (2003) in Chap. 7 of this book. The present chapter is devoted to an evaluation of this article of Beckwith's.

The first topic with which I take issue with Beckwith is the "brainless human being." This author explains:

> "Another, though similar, problem with the desire account is its inability to account for the wrongness of purposely creating brainless human beings for an apparent public good. David W. Brock, for example, cites Carol Kahn's proposal for a possible use of human cloning, in which she suggests that "[a]fter cell differentiation, some of the brain cells of the embryo or fetus [clone] would be removed so that it could then be grown as a brain-dead body for spare parts for its earlier twin." According to Brock, "this body clone would be like an anencephalic newborn or presentient fetus, neither of whom arguably can be harmed, because of their lack of capacity for consciousness." Yet, Brock maintains, "most people would likely find" the practice of purposely creating non-sentient human beings "appalling and immoral, in part because here the cloned later twin's capacity for conscious life is

W. E. Block, *Evictionism*, https://doi.org/10.1007/978-981-16-5014-7_8

destroyed solely as a means to benefit another." It is not precisely clear, given the desire account of rights, what would be wrong with cloning brainless human beings for the purpose of harvesting their organs. That is, if there is no injustice done to another and someone receives a benefit, it is difficult to know where exactly the wrong is to be located in the act. I suspect that some would locate it in the moral intuition that the pre-brain embryo is deprived of something to which he is entitled. But if that is the case, then desire (whether current, dispositional, actual or ideal) is a condition that is not necessary in order for a human being to possess both rights and a present capacity to be harmed. Yet, what follows is that the intentional creation of brainless children (or embryos) for the purpose of harvesting their organs is a serious wrong. But if we were to extract from this insight the principle that seems to ground this wrong–it is prima facie wrong to destroy the physical structure necessary for the realization of a human being's present capacity for the exercisability of a function that is a perfection of its nature–then the pre-brain embryo is a subject of rights even if it has no desires."

The difficulty, here, is that it is indeed possible to create the brainless human being (BHB) to serve as a source of spare parts, for his clone-donor, without violating the rights of anyone, any person, any entity, any human being. At least this is one way of looking at the matter. How can this be attained? Certainly not by removing "some of the brain cells of the embryo or fetus [clone]." To do so would clearly be to violate the rights of the zygote from whom these brain cells were "removed." However, an egg is not a human being, nor is a sperm. I take it that the beginning of the human person occurs when the latter of these two human body parts intrudes into, or interacts with, the former one. Before that act takes place, we have only the sperm and the egg to contemplate. I have no idea whether present medical technology is sufficiently advanced to accomplish this task, but, one, day, presumably, it will be. Even if this never occurs, we can still contemplate the possibility. The possibility of what? The possibility of deleting those parts, and only those parts, of both the sperm and the egg, which will in due course turn into brain cells. When the BHB which results from this procedure is born, it, not he, will be a mere shell of a human being. It will consist, only, of arms, legs, kidneys, lungs, a heart, etc., and nothing more. It will not have even the potential to attain consciousness. Thus, it will be able to be used as a source of spare body parts without any rights violation.

That is one possible analysis. Here is another one. Who knows? Maybe, one day, science will advance to the point that very BHB will be able to function, will be able to be a person, even suffering from this lacuna. Who, then, is the owner of the BHB at present? Well, no one can initially own another human being.[1] However, parents may indeed own the guardianship rights of small children. How do they first attain them? By giving birth of course. May they become "absentee owners" of these guardianship rights, in a manner similar to absentee owners of real estate? No. Proprietors of housing own these properties outright, not merely guardianship rights over them. With children, the guardianship rights must be earned every day, and when these obligations are not consummated, those rights are lost.

Terri Schiavo (Block 2001a, b) was for all intents and purposes a BHB. Her brain was of course present, but it was completely non-functioning. She was kept alive

[1] For the case in favor of voluntary slavery, see fn. 64.

only through artificial medical means. Her husband wanted the plug pulled, and her put to death as a result. The court supported this decision of his. But this case was judged improperly, at least from a libertarian point of view. Because he wished her to die, he demonstrated that he was no longer her proper guardian. The function of a guardian is to guard, and with his decision, the husband renounced his guardianship rights in one fell swoop, over his wife. Her parents wanted to keep her alive, and a proper judicial finding would have supported them. If they had declined, then her siblings, then friends, then, whoever.

Suppose that though super cloning a human baby is born without a brain; all of its other body parts are functioning, with or without artificial help, it matters not. Stipulate that he has no potential, none at all, to think, to desire, to engage in any human emotion whatsoever. Someone, Smith, goes to this baby's crib and shoots this young person to death, or slits his throat to the same end. Has Smith committed a crime? It would certainly appear that he has done so. Its parents are furious with Smith. Has he committed murder? It is difficult to avoid this conclusion.

I am not sure which is the correct way to look at this matter. I lean in the latter direction: it is murder to kill this BHB; therefore, he, not it, has rights. Why publish mere musings about it then? Well, we all have to start somewhere. I do so in the hope that someone will read this, add to it, and move us that proverbial one millionth of an inch closer to the Truth, someone who, without reading these preliminary remarks, might not have been able to do so.

Next consider this view of our author (245–246):

> "...the pregnant woman has a special obligation to care for her unborn child. This obligation does not arise from explicit choice or intention to produce a child, but rather, it arises from the fact she engaged in an act, sexual intercourse, which is naturally ordered to result in the foreseeable consequence of the procreation of a dependent human being that requires her care. Because we hold the father responsible for child support for postnatal children even if he did not intend for his sexual encounters to result in offspring, therefore, it follows that the pregnant woman has the same obligation prenatally.
>
> "Consider the following story. Suppose a couple has a consensual sexual encounter that is fully protected by several forms of birth-control short of abortion (condom, the Pill, IUD, etc.), but nevertheless results in pregnancy. Instead of undergoing an abortion, the mother of the conceptus chooses to bring the pregnancy to term although the father is unaware of this decision. After the birth of the child the mother pleads with the father for child support. Because he refuses, she seeks legal action and takes him to court. Although he took every precaution to avoid fatherhood, showing that he did not wish to accept such a status, according to nearly all child support laws in the United States he would still be obligated to pay support precisely because of his relationship to this child. As Michael Levin points out, 'All child-support laws make the parental body an indirect resource for the child. If the father is a construction worker, the state will intervene unless some of his calories he extends lifting equipment go to providing food for his children.' These laws are grounded in deep moral intuitions, that seem prima facie correct, that ground our notion that parents have a natural, pre-political, obligation to care for their child even if the child's existence was not the result of a conscious plan to bring the child into being. Our intuitions about parental obligation to children, and society's obligation to its vulnerable immature members, seem to be more well-grounded intuitions than the autonomy to which abortion rights advocates appeal."

Perhaps the moral of this story is that there are intuitions, and then, other intuitions. If I may speak of a "libertarian intuition" it is in direct conflict with the one espoused by Beckwith and Levin. Namely, in the liberty philosophy, there are no positive obligations. None whatsoever. The only obligations we have are negative: we must keep our mitts off of the persons and property of other people, unless we have their permission. We may not threaten them with rights violations. And that begins and entirely ends what we owe to other people. Once we embrace the noxious doctrine of positive obligations, we are at sea without a rudder. Positive obligations are never-ending. The father, and the mother too, violated no one's rights by engaging in voluntary sexual intercourse. All of a sudden, well nine months later, there is another human being in great need of care. Neither parent, we posit, along with Beckwith, desired any such outcome. Indeed, they took steps to prevent it. There is nothing in all of libertarian law that would make criminals of these two people if they refused to raise this baby. Levin is entirely correct that "All child-support laws make the parental body an indirect resource for the child." But what of it? Are we embracing legal positivism, according to which all extant laws are just? That it is a logical contradiction to stipulate that the law says X, and yet to question its legitimacy? At least not in the libertarian tradition.

Beckwith (246–247) continues in this vein:

> "But this obligatory relationship is not based strictly on biology, for this would make sperm-donors morally responsible for children conceived by their seed. Rather, the father's responsibility for his offspring stems from the fact that he engaged in an act, sexual intercourse, which he fully realized could result in the creation of another human being because reproductive organs are ordered to result in reproduction if they are functioning properly, although the father took every precaution to avoid such a result short of abstaining from sex. This is not an unusual way to frame moral obligations, for we do so even in cases where a particular result is merely foreseeable and not naturally ordered. For example, we hold drunken people whose driving results in manslaughter responsible for their actions, even if they did not intend to kill someone prior to becoming intoxicated. Such special obligations, although not directly undertaken voluntarily, are necessary in any civilized culture in order to preserve the rights of the vulnerable, the weak, and the young, who can offer very little in exchange for the rights bestowed upon them by the strong and the powerful."

But this is out and out socialism. It is certainly not within the scope of libertarianism to compel "the strong and powerful" to, against their will, "help the vulnerable, the weak, and the young" unless of course the former violated the rights of the latter in the first place, and this lien on their wealth is a form of compensation. But which rights of the baby did the parents violate by conceiving their child? None whatsoever. If anything, they gave their progeny a boon: life itself. Why should they be asked to do more? They have already done far more than their "fair share." They have already done far more than anyone else for this baby. Now, it is time for others to step up to the plate and care for this infant if it is anyone's positive obligation to do so, which it decidedly is not.

Beckwith (246–247) continues:

> "An anonymous referee asks: 'Why should sperm donors be so different from a man having sexual intercourse? The act of the donor more surely leads to conception than the contracepted sex of the man having intercourse.' I'm not sure sperm donors are so different. After

all, such donors typically sign contracts that relieve them from responsibility for, and surrender parental rights over, the children that result from their donated seed. These children are often brought up by two parents, one of whom is the adoptive father. It is to this individual that the sperm donor transfers his paternal responsibilities and obligations. Consequently, if these sperm donors had no responsibilities or obligations to the children they sire, as the referee suggests, no contracts that transfer their responsibilities and obligations would be necessary. Moreover, if the donated sperm is being used by unmarried women to bring children into single-parent homes, I think one can question the ethics of men who provide genetic material that bring fatherless children into the world."

I am with the anonymous referee in his criticism of Beckwith. As he says, the donor intends the birth of the baby, the father does not. So, if intent, *mens rea*, is a deciding factor, the former, not the latter, should be responsible. And what is this business of the donor "contracting" away his supposed responsibilities. A contract is an agreement between two consenting parties in which each gives up something for something else he regards more highly. If the donor, by virtue of that fact, had a responsibility, to whom did he give it up, and what amount of money did he have to pay to rid himself of this responsibility? This analysis has matters backwards, for the donor is paid for his aid in the reproduction process, he pays nothing to be relieved of his so-called obligation. But, suppose the contrary to fact conditional to be true. The donor is now relieved of his duty. On whom does this devolve? Of course, to the mother, not the father. The donor donates his sperm to her, not to him. Yes, the husband may pay for the donor's services, but, the biological interaction takes place between the male donor and the female recipient; the (possible) husband of the donor plays no role whatsoever in this matter, biologically speaking.

Beckwith questions the "ethics of men who provide genetic material that bring fatherless children into the world." And here I agree with him. But not *qua* libertarian, which philosophy is concerned, solely, with what the law should be, not with general ethical matters. The issue, the only issue here, is, is the parent a criminal if he or she refuses to pay for the support of the baby. Beckwith and Levin never confront this crucially important question, although, reading in between the lines, it is easy to discern where their views lie: in a non-libertarian direction.

The next issue concerns whether an act is an improvement or not. States our author (249–250):

"The physician, by giving the violinist the drug to extend his life for at least another five years, decreases his patient's net neediness, since, after all, the violinist was given the drug at the edge of death. An already existing state of affairs was improved. On the other hand, in the case of pregnancy, net human neediness is increased, for a child-with-neediness, a joint condition, is actualized by an act which is ordered in such a way that its proper function (though not its only function) is to produce a child-with-neediness. In the case of the violinist, the physician helps a violinist to be less needy than he otherwise would have been. In the case of pregnancy, a needy being is brought into existence that otherwise would not exist if not for its progenitors engaging in an act ordered toward producing needy beings.

"Consider this scenario. Imagine a scientist has discovered a procedure by which he can clone human beings for infertile couples, but there is a glitch: all of the children conceived by this procedure will develop a genetically caused, yet correctable, heart condition. The procedure is elective, the scientist and the parents do not desire that the cloned children have this condition, but the children cannot be brought into existence without this defect. The scientist's procedure results in simultaneous existence and neediness, just as in an ordinary pregnancy, but with more neediness than what is typical. It seems to me that the scientist and/or the clone's parents have a responsibility to make sure that the children receive the proper care, that the children's neediness is remedied. In that case, the degree of neediness is not relevant in requiring that those who caused the neediness provide a remedy. So, if one agrees that the scientist and the children's parents are responsible for the cloned children's neediness, then one must agree that parents of ordinary non-cloned children are just as responsible for their neediness."

In my view, in contrast, it all depends upon the starting point. Yes, indeed, there is a net improvement in the violinist's situation; that is not debatable. But there is a difficulty with his stance regarding pregnancy. First, let us compare the situation of the baby inside the womb, with what will befall him outside. In which geographical place is he more "needy?" It seems difficult to deny that when he is born, he, like the violinist, is less needy. The infant still in his former "address" is very disadvantaged. He depends, entirely, on the health of the mother. Once he moves into his new residence, outside of the womb, he is far less so. He now has many other potential care-givers upon whom he can rely. Second, compare his situation before and after – not birth, but conception. In the first instance, he does not exist. His future parent's genetic material has not yet met. Now, happily for him, he exists, as a fertilized egg. Under which condition he is more deprived? In the first instance he is in need of his very existence. That is a very serious lacuna. In the second case, he now exists. Surely his position has been improved, not worsened.

The same analysis applies to the newborn with the correctable heart condition. Yes, this youngster is in a far more perilous position than he would have been without this malady, but, his welfare has increased compared to the situation where, one, he did not exist at all, or, two, was still in the womb, with no alternatives but to depend upon his mother.

As to the responsibility of parents "to make sure the children receive the proper care" that is an instance of positive rights, of which there are none, at least not in the libertarian philosophy, from which we are viewing all contributions to the issue of abortion in this book.

Our author asserts (p. 250): "in the case of the fetus, his neediness is the direct result of his parents engaging in an act, because the act is ordered to bring needy persons into existence." Here is an economics joke: The economist was asked how was wife? Came the answer: "compared to what?" Yes, of course, a nursling is "needy." But, compared to what? To when he was in the womb? To before the time he even existed? No. The parents have reduced neediness. The non-existent person was really in dire straits. He needed his very existence. This is something often very difficult to attain. There are literally zillions of "people" out there, who have not yet been conceived. In contrast, the newborn merely needs some medical and non-medical care.

We next encounter a disanalogy. In the view of Beckwith (252):

"Imagine you are a physician whose patient is a violinist. … your patient is healthy and also happens to be your lover. After arriving at your office for his yearly physical, you suggest to him a vitamin regimen in order to maintain his health. You offer him what you think is a sample of the vitamin, but it is really a narcotic to which the violinist is highly allergic. You hand him the samples, he swallows one right there in your office, and then moments later he has a severe allergic reaction. He is rushed to the hospital and soon after his arrival the chief of neurology gives you the tragic news: 'Your patient, the violinist, will survive, and live quite a long time. However, he has suffered serious brain damage that has resulted in his losing all his memories, abilities, and skills. He will remain in a coma for nine months, but upon awakening he will be able to relearn all his abilities and skills and acquire new memories. It should take about a decade to accomplish this. This means that he is effectively in precisely the same position as a standard fetus.' According to Boonin, you are clearly responsible for your patient's neediness and your patient is entitled to your assistance."

Where is the disanalogy? The narcotic reduced the violinist's welfare; it violated his rights. He was in effect poisoned. Whereas, in very sharp contrast indeed, getting pregnant, giving birth, does none of this. It is an improvement in the subject's situation. It does not at all violate his rights.

Moreover, the word "responsible" in this context is somewhat problematic. It could refer to a causal agent. Or it could mean that the person is legally required, either by tort or the criminal code, to compensate the victim. There is indeed a victim in the narcotic case, but none at all in the birth situation. Either rights were violated, or they were not. Neither the baby's nor the non-existent person's rights were disturbed. The same cannot be said for the poisoning case. Responsibility in the cause and effect situation does not necessarily impinge on anyone's liberty nor create any legal obligation.

Jones jumps two feet into the air. He is responsible for pushing the earth away from him by a miniscule amount, out of the axis it would otherwise have occupied. He is responsible alright, but is neither a criminal nor a tort-feasor. He owes no one anything. Then, a second later, he lands back on the planet. Again he very slightly shakes up the earth. He is again a causal agent, but ditto in terms of responsibility. Smith purchases a loaf of bread. He causes the price of this foodstuff to be a bit higher than otherwise would have been the case. The poor, and everyone else, must pay slightly more for this product. Smith is "responsible" for this dire outcome. But he owes no one anything for this nefarious act of his. Green buys several tons of bread. He is trying to corner the market for this staple. The analysis is the same. No rights violation, no foul.

Our author now criticizes Boonin on the following ground. This part of Beckwith's paper (253) starts off as follows:

"First, Boonin understates the force of the intuition that guides our understanding of parental obligation, namely, that explicit consent to parenthood is not a necessary condition for parental obligation. It seems to me that most people would think it bizarre to discard that intuition on the grounds that Boonin is suggesting, that parental obligation is grounded exclusively on explicit consent. In fact, most people would think that Boonin's understanding of parental obligation itself should be discarded precisely because what it affirms about parental obligation is inconsistent with our intuitions on this matter."

This passage is very far indeed removed from sound social science. Here, we are relying on "intuition," "the views of most people," what "most people would think" and then again on "intuition." This is no way to proceed. Intuition, backed up by nothing more than intuition, is highly problematic. And, relying on democratic votes to solve serious philosophical questions is also extremely dubious.

In the libertarian tradition, contrary to this author's "intuition" and citations regarding public opinion, we are obligated in two ways: not threaten or engage in violence or fraud against innocent people, and, live up to our freely agreed upon contracts. In the latter case, we give up something, in order to attain something else. If we receive, but do not yield up what the contract specifies, to that extent we have stolen from our commercial partner. So, yes, "parental obligation is grounded exclusively on explicit consent," or contract. And, since there was no fetus with whom to make a pact with at the time of sexual intercourse, there can be no question, at least in this philosophy, of any obligation on the part of either parent to care for the baby.

References

Beckwith, F.J. 1993. *Politically Correct Death: Answering Arguments for Abortion Rights*. Grand Rapids: Baker Books.

Block, Walter E. 2001a. *Stem Cell Research: The Libertarian Compromise*, September 3. http://archive.lewrockwell.com/block/block5.html

———. 2001b. Alienability, Inalienability, Paternalism and the Law: Reply to Kronman. *American Journal of Criminal Law* 28 (3, Summer): 351–371.

Boonin-Vail, David. 2003. *A Defense of Abortion*, Cambridge Studies in Philosophy and Public Policy. Cambridge, MA: Cambridge University Press.

Chapter 9
Deadlocked; a Reaction to McDonagh and Ford on Abortion

With but one major exception, I am a strong supporter of McDonagh (1996), not so much Ford (2005). As the latter is a comment on the former, let me start with McDonagh.

Part I. McDonagh

Her thesis, to put the matter bluntly, is that the fetus is an invader, a trespasser, akin to a rapist, even a slave-master. To be sure it is entirely innocent. It[1] lacks any and all elements of mens rea. Still, it occupies that precise role, even if totally inadvertently, blamelessly. Moreover, while sexual intercourse is indeed the ultimate cause of the assault, it is not the proximate cause; this is the role played only by the preborn child, not his father. She states (p. 6):

> "(F)ounding abortion rights on the conditions under which sexual intercourse occurs prior to pregnancy misses the point. The fetus is the direct cause of pregnancy, and if it makes a woman pregnant without her consent, it severely violates her bodily integrity and liberty."

I regard this insight as an important breakthrough on that author's part. After all, it is the zygote, not any other entity, which is now occupying space in territory owned, entirely, by the mother. If this is not to the latter's satisfaction, then in effect a crime is being committed against her. It may sound cruel and heartless, but, the truth is the truth, and, if we are to figure our way out of this morass, it ill-behooves us to reject a claim solely because it is shocking and unpleasant, albeit undeniable.

However, early on, McDonagh (p. 7) and I part company. She avers:

> "Even in a medically normal pregnancy, the fetus massively intrudes on a woman's body and expropriates her liberty. If a woman does not consent to this transformation and use of

[1] He. I often inadvertently, make this error, so I cannot be too harsh with this author.

W. E. Block, *Evictionism*, https://doi.org/10.1007/978-981-16-5014-7_9

> her body, the fetus's imposition constitutes injuries sufficient to justify the use of deadly force to stop it."

What is it with this "deadly force" business so early in the game? According to the libertarian philosophy, private property rights are indeed sacrosanct. And, this certainly includes the mother's womb. However, when someone trespasses on your lawn, if you immediately blow him away with a bazooka, you have over-reacted; you are the criminal, along with the intruder (to a much lesser extent). Rather, you are supposed to protect your property in the gentlest manner possible, given the side order condition that you ensure your safety. So, if it is a three-year-old child who is trespassing, you are required to be even more gentle than with an adult. As for the latter, the property owner is mandated to say something along the following lines: "Sir, do you realize you are treading on my lawn? Please vacate the premises." If he replies some along the lines of: "Oh, sorry, I didn't realize; I'll immediately step away" that is the end of the matter. No "deadly force" needed here. What could the mother do, other than engage in "deadly force" if she wishes that the fetus no longer darken her doorstep? Why, evict, eject, expel, oust, banish the baby from her premises. True, if she is in the first two trimesters of her pregnancy, the baby will die, no matter how carefully he is removed from her body. However, in the third trimester, matters are now quite different. "Deadly force" constitutes a vast over-reaction. Certainly, it is not the only option. And yet this author never mentions such an alternative, which in my view somewhat mars her otherwise splendid and important essay.

There is one other issue on which McDonagh and I differ at least partially: should the government pay for abortions? She maintains in effect that since one of the prime responsibilities is protect its citizenry against crimes, and that in effect the zygote is a criminal trespasser, then, its clear duty is to stop this sort of "home invasion" as well. In her view (p. 9):

> "Since no born people have a right to intrude massively on the body of another, … to the degree that the state stops people from harming others by intruding on their bodies and liberty, including the mentally incompetent or those in dire need of the body parts of others, similarly the state must stop fetuses that intrude on women's bodies without their consent."

I think this an excellent point on her part against libertarians who support the government. However, for anarcho-capitalists such as myself, the state should not exist in the first place. Thus, there would be no justification for it to finance evictions, certainly not abortions, even construed as self-defense against an interloper. The difficulty is that the only way the government can finance the abortions or evictions of some is by compelling others to pay for them, against their will, via taxation. Does this mean that in the anarcho-capitalist society there would be "anarchy" in the sense of chaos? Wherein criminals would be given free rein to engage in murder, rapine, theft? Of course not. Such criminals would be stopped, more efficiently, via private police forces. Thus, if a woman's contract with one of these agencies provided they would protect her from the invasion that is the result of an unwanted pregnancy, then and only then would someone else pay for, not an abortion, but, rather, an eviction. As to whether or not in the free society such contractual provisions would be made, that is an empirical question, difficult to answer.

The problem of forcing other people who bitterly oppose abortions to nonetheless pay for this operation simply would not arise in this milieu. Pro-lifers would not be compelled to finance a medical procedure they detest. This would all be done by contract, in which case there is unanimous agreement on the part of both parties, not via democratic vote, in which case the minority is obligated to adhere to the wishes of the majority.

McDonagh is not without a powerful defense for compelling others to pay for abortions against their will (p. 105):

> "If a man is raping a woman or a mugger is inflicting a severe beating on someone or one private party is killing another, of course the victims have a right of self-defense to try to stop that injury themselves, but they also have a right to state assistance to stop the private parties on their behalf … When a fetus seriously injures a woman by imposing a wrongful pregnancy, therefore, of course she has a right to stop it from injuring her, but she also has a right to state assistance in stopping it on her behalf."

Her point is that what the unwanted fetus is doing to the now pregnant woman is not only akin to what the rapist did to her, but, in some sense, even more intrusive. For the former took but a few minutes; the latter, nine months. True, there was *mens rea* in the one case but not in the other. The zygote is legally and morally innocent, but of course not the rapist. However, if we put on our moral blinders and confine ourselves to looking, dispassionately at the actual physical harm which ensues, her conclusion is not an unreasonable one. Even if matters were the other way around, the merest uninvited purposeful touching constituted a battery, if the government has a responsibility to devote resources to the stoppage of the one, it has an obligation to do so for the other. I think her argument is a seamless one, when directed at the statist libertarian. Happily for my own perspective, it leaves untouched the anarcho-capitalist version of this philosophy.

Let us now delve a bit more deeply into McDonagh's viewpoint. She makes excellent use of the distinction between ultimate and proximate causation (p. 40):

> "Whereas a man can cause a woman to engage in a sexual relationship with him, a man cannot cause a woman's body to change from a nonpregnant to a pregnant condition; the only entity that can do that is a fertilized ovum when it implants itself in a woman's uterus."

It is often the case that a sperm enters a woman's body, and pregnancy does not ensue. Therefore, while this can be the ultimate cause of a woman being with child, it is certainly not the proximate cause. The entity which is directly causing the woman's body to change, to be subject to morning sickness, etc., is thus not the sperm. Rather, it is the growing baby within her premises.

This author goes rather far out on the proverbial limb to characterize the unwanted pre-born infant as akin to a rapist (p. 44):

> "Men and women who contribute to a situation in which it is foreseeable that a fertilized ovum might be conceived and make a woman pregnant against her will contribute no more to the woman's harm than does a woman who walks down a street late at night contribute to her own rape … Men and women who engage in sexual intercourse, therefore, cannot be

held as contributing to the harm imposed on a woman by a fertilized ovum making her pregnant without consent."

In a similar manner, Hitler's parents were the ultimate cause of much human misery. Without the act of theirs that brought this evil Nazi into existence, the course of history might well have run in a different and better direction. Yet, they are not legally responsible for this deed of theirs. They are only the ultimate cause. It is, in contrast, the actions of Hitler himself that are properly blameworthy.

One would not go too far wrong in summarizing McDonagh's contribution in terms of consent (p. 66) as follows:

> "Sexual intercourse merely causes the risk that pregnancy will occur, and consent to engage in sexual intercourse with a man, for any and all fertile women, implies consent to expose oneself to that risk.
>
> "Consent to expose oneself to the risk that one will be injured by a private party, however, is not a legal proxy for consent to the actual injuries ... Consent to jog alone in Central Park does not stand as a proxy for consent to be mugged and raped, should others so attack you."

Here, she is very much aligned with libertarianism. For consent, agreement, accord, coupled with private property rights, are virtually the entire be-all and end-all of that philosophy. As to the proper owner of the property in question, the womb, there can be no doubt, at least not vis-à-vis the pregnant mother and her pre-born baby. It was she, the adult, who was "there" first. Her womb came into existence long before the fetus arrived. Clearly, she is the owner of that (human) capital equipment. Thus, it is her consent, and her consent alone, that is definitive. If she agrees to being pregnant, all is well and good. If not, she has the right to defend herself from the imposition of this small invader.

McDonagh (pp. 74–75) further elaborates upon this point. She maintains that the fetus:

> "... wholly controls her body, her freedom of movement, and her reproductive services. When a woman is pregnant, as the Court noted [in Roe], her privacy is no longer sole. She can go nowhere without the fetus; every action she takes necessarily includes the fetus. The circulation of her blood, her endocrine system, and her menstrual cycles are now controlled by the fetus. As long as it maintains a pregnant condition in her body, for up to nine months she is decidedly not let alone, and she is anything but free."

This is eloquently and truthfully said. However, this brings up one minor point of disagreement I have with this author. It centers around the concept of "privacy." She writes as if privacy is a right, part and parcel of overall property rights; and that the fetus is compromising this right of hers. Not so, not so. Rather, privacy is an aspect of wealth. If you want some, usually you have to pay for it. Typically, this takes the form of a hermit-like existence, living in a large holding of acreage. Or, occupying terrain in a high-rise apartment house, or a gated community. If privacy really were a right, then detectives would be an outlawed profession, similar to rapists or murderers.

Our Northeastern University professor of political science distinguishes between two different types of privacy. The first is "decisional autonomy" which is, in the view of Ford (p. 631) equivalent to freedom from state interference (p. 92):

> "As established in Roe, a woman's right of personal privacy as defined by her decisional autonomy is governed and limited by what the fetus is, not by what it does. As long as the fetus is previable, justification for a woman's right to an abortion rests simply on whether she chooses to have one or not ... Once the fetus is viable, however, a woman no longer has the right to exercise personal privacy by choosing an abortion, and a state may prohibit her right to choose one."

From the anarcho-capitalist point of view, privacy is indeed a right, the foregoing notwithstanding, but against only the government. This follows, logically, from the major premise that the state is an illicit organization in the first place. It is thus no small step to the conclusion that the public sector may not invade anyone's privacy, since it may not properly do anything at all!

McDonagh's second definition of privacy is as follows (p. 93):

> "The law also recognizes the right of people to use deadly force when threatened with qualitative injuries that intrude on their basic liberty or bodily integrity even while threatening no objective physical injuries per se, much less threatening their lives. Thirty-six states explicitly affirm a person's right to use deadly force when threatened with forcible rape, even when that rape is not aggravated by physical injuries. Thirty-five states legislatively recognize the right to use deadly force against kidnapping."

A problem arises here, with regard to both of these definitions: they each reek of legal positivism, the view that whatever the legislature, or the courts, decide upon is correct. From this vantage point, it is impossible to maintain that the law of the land is X, but ask if X is justified? Who cares what 35 or 36 states recognize? They could all be wrong. And, here, I define error as incompatibility with the libertarian notion of private property rights and the non-aggression principle (NAP). Of course just law would "recognize ... the right of people to use deadly force" in self-defense. This does not mean it is justified to shoot first and ask questions later; we have seen that bodily integrity should be upheld, at least initially, in the gentlest manner possible compatible with full protection.

Our author, here, seems to recognize this when she writes (p. 100):

> "(i)t is constitutional for the state to prohibit one's choice to engage in homosexual activity, to contract for prostitution services, and to sell one's organs. In addition, it is constitutional for the state to require people to obtain vaccinations in order to prevent the spread of disease and to be conscripted for military service."

Certainly, the libertarian NAP would legalize homosexuality, prostitution, organ sales" which is incompatible with laws to the contrary. Compulsory vaccinations are controversial within the libertarian community (Block 2013a, b). On the one hand, they are illicit in that they invade the bodies of non-consenting innocent people. On the other hand, a contagious person constitutes a threat of bodily injury, and the NAP not only proscribes actual crimes but also the threat thereof.

In concluding my discussion of McDonagh, I cannot ignore one other area of disagreement; albeit one peripheral to what I take as her main contribution. Ford summarizes this accurately (p. 635):

> "McDonagh acknowledges that her model is at odds with current social assumptions about abortion; for most people, to contemplate fetal personhood (even just for the sake of argument) is to throw grave doubt on the moral and legal validity of the practice of abortion. McDonagh does not, however, take this discrepancy to be indicative of any problem with her argument; rather, she is confident that it arises because our current social norms, particularly those relating to women and reproduction, derive from our cultural heritage of patriarchy, and in particular, from a combination of puritanical and bourgeois morality that reserves norms of self-defence for men while imposing norms of self-sacrifice on women."

McDonagh goes deeply off the rails at this point. From whence springs this balderdash? Presumably from the fever swamps of multi-culturalism and feminist "studies." She offers not one whit of evidence that men are allowed to defend themselves while women are not. Yes, to be sure, on average men are taller, heavier and stronger than women, and thus, presumably more able to defend themselves than members of the distaff side, but this is hardly what this author has in mind. Given specialization and division of labor, it might well inure to the benefit of women to allow men to take on the role of defender, but, again, we cannot deduce from this physical fact any normative claim against self-help on the part of females.

Part II. Ford

My comment on this author will be almost totally negative. But let me start out on a positive note: in her treatment of her foil, McDonagh, Ford was thorough, polite, sympathetic and even generous in her interpretations. She started out with an entirely accurate summary of the latter, devoting almost a full third of her paper to systematically summarizing this exemplary effort of McDonagh's. Hopefully, I can repay Ford by treating her in a similar manner: criticizing her for what she actually said, not creating any straw men, leaning over backwards in an attempt to place a positive spin on her important contribution, and most important, citing her fully and widely, etc.

Ford first launches her critique of McDonagh under the heading of self-defense. She states as follows (pp. 636–637):

> "McDonagh would also reject the argument that pregnancy is an 'invited attack'; as we have seen, she regards the action of a woman having consensual sexual intercourse merely as 'putting oneself at risk' of pregnancy, and insists that the acceptance of a risk does not necessarily entail any acceptance of the actual injuries, should they occur. Just as a jogger who chooses to run alone through Central Park accepts a degree of risk but does not consent, by any stretch of the imagination (or the law) to be mugged or raped, a woman who engages in consensual sexual intercourse accepts the risk of pregnancy, but does not consent to the actual attack of a fetus or the injury it perpetrates by invading her body and later, by effecting ever more drastic changes upon it throughout the gestational process. Although whether or not someone uses contraception may hint at their intentions regarding pregnancy,

or indicate that they are willing to accept a greater or lesser degree of risk, McDonagh would argue that, whatever degree of risk they accept, they are not consenting to the actual injury of pregnancy itself.

"McDonagh's claim that a woman's consent to sexual intercourse, and acceptance of the attendant risks, does not entail consent to pregnancy is problematic because the concept of 'risk' covers a wide spectrum of possibility. At one end there is the situation where it is possible, although highly unlikely, that certain consequences will occur if a certain action or course of action is undertaken; at the opposite end of the spectrum of risk, there is the scenario wherein, if a person behaves in a particular way, certain consequences will almost inevitably follow. For example, if a man walks along a pavement, it is possible, although highly unlikely, that a car will mount the pavement and kill or injure him. If he crosses a busy road using a designated crossing-place and paying reasonable attention to the traffic, it is more likely, but still unlikely, that he will come to harm. There are of course varying degrees of risk associated with walking on or near roads. If the same man were to jump out on a major motorway in front of a car approaching at seventy miles per hour, we can say with some confidence that he is likely to be hurt or killed. It is still not a certainty, since any number of outlandish events could intervene to rid the danger; he is still only 'at risk' of harm. But on McDonagh's analysis, we must nonetheless say that he has not consented to the actual harm he will almost inevitably sustain. This is a philosophical point; of course, the law would take a quite different view on who was responsible for the harm in such a case. What about a man who steps in front of an express train with the intention of committing suicide? His death is not guaranteed; again, unlikely events could intervene to thwart his plan. According to McDonagh, he would still be 'putting himself at risk' of injury and death, and would not have consented to any injury he sustains as a result of his actions. Moreover, if he clearly intended to bring about his own death, yet survived, horribly injured, he could claim quite plausibly, on McDonagh's logic, that he certainly did not consent to be so injured."

This is a nice try on Ford's part, but, no prize for her, at least not quite yet. For, there is a disanalogy between the two scenarios. The woman who strolls innocently into a dangerous public park commits no crime. She is entirely innocent. If she is attacked, it is the perpetrator who is the guilty party. In sharp contrast, the person who throws himself into the path of an onrushing vehicle is himself a property rights violator. The driver of the automobile is entirely innocent. He had no chance, by stipulation, to avoid the collision between man and machine. Thus, "McDonagh's logic," in this case is impervious to Ford's critique.

Nothing daunted, Ford (p. 637) continues her criticism of McDonagh in this vein:

"…one weakness of McDonagh's theory is her view of how an assumption of risk relates to responsibility for subsequent injury. In the above hypothetical examples, McDonagh would be compelled to absolve both the man on the motorway and the man who steps in front of a speeding train of any responsibility for their subsequent injury or death. She is unable, on the basis of what she proposes in Breaking the Abortion Deadlock, to distinguish between different degrees of risk, and is thus unable to ascribe responsibility to those who assume the level of risk found at the higher end of the spectrum while admitting that some levels of risk are very low and ought to entail no legal responsibility for consequences."

But no. "Risk" is not in play here. Rather, it is the initiation of violence, the violation of the NAP that takes center stage. The Central Park perambulator is an innocent victim. In the other hypothetical, it is precisely the opposite; it is the automobile or train driver whose rights are violated, not the person who is hurt by his unavoidable actions. Now, to be sure, in this uneven battle between man and machine is the former who comes off second best. There might not even be a scratch of damage on the property on the latter. Nevertheless, it was the attempted (or successful) suicide who is responsible for the impact, not the other way around.

The next arrow in Ford's quiver is as follows (p. 638):

> "Moreover, as West notes, 'an attack by a born person … threatens the peace – and hence threatens the state – in a way that the invasion of a woman by an unwanted fetus does not.' This being so, another reason for criminalizing certain kinds of behaviour – namely the state's duty to maintain public order and deter offenders – has no application in the context of wrongful pregnancy, since the fetus does not threaten public order (although it threatens the pregnant woman's internal physical and psychological order as well as the order of her social functioning) and cannot be deterred from causing pregnancy by the threat of sanctions."

But this really will not do. Why complicate matters by bringing in the state? Either an act is a violation of rights, or it is not. There is in this case a dispute as to who owns the terrain in question: the fetus "wants" to occupy it, but the mother does not wish her body to be so "occupied." If we concede that it is the adult woman, not the pre-born baby, who is the rightful owner of the property in question, then, the conclusion is simple and straightforward. The baby is a(n innocent) trespasser. If justice is to prevail, proper law would allow him to be evicted. If the state wishes to uphold proper law, well and good, it should rule in favor of the mother in this case of conflict. To be sure, the infant does not "threaten the peace" in the manner that does the murderer or the rapist. But, neither does the bad check writer, the fraud, the pickpocket. When they do their jobs "properly" no one even knows that they are robbing people. But, surely, these types of "micro-aggressions" are equally criminal, along with the "macro-aggressions" of the arsonist or kidnapper.

Next, let us consider an attack on McDonagh launched not by Ford, but by Cox (2000, note 84 at 582) who she cites (pp. 640–641). States this worthy:

> "[W]hatever the impact of pregnancy, the foetus is doing nothing apart from involuntarily staying alive in the ordinary way and hence the 'attack' for self defence purposes comes in the form of simple foetal existence. But self defence law does not entitle me to kill another if my health or life or bodily integrity is threatened by his or her simple existence."

Nothing? If the fetus was not doing anything at all, in any manner, shape or form, the mother would scarcely object to his presence. Indeed, scientists would scarcely be able to detect his existence. Let us make the heroic assumption that the fetus is not "doing anything." Still, it is acting inertly somewhere; it is occupying some geographical space. One of the mottos of real estate is "location, location, location." Yes, the fetus is merely "staying alive," by assumption not doing much of anything else, but he is doing this on the property of another person, his mother. He is not welcome there. Thus, he is a trespasser. Simple existence, yes. But where? On, or, rather, in, someone else's body.

Nothing daunted, Ford (p. 641) continues in this vein:

> "the law on self-defence to a threat posed by another's mere existence is somewhat precarious, since the situation rarely, if ever, arises wherein one person's health, life, or bodily integrity is threatened by the mere existence of another."

Au contraire, this occurs each and every time a woman becomes pregnant. She is, in all such cases, without exception, threatened by the mere existence of another person, who is now inhabiting her body. In most cases, happily, this "threat" is a welcome one.

Next, Ford (p. 642) asks if the fetus is entitled to legal due process. She mentions (Scully 1997) in this context, who avers:

> "if a fetus is a human being, it might be entitled to a legal hearing and legal counsel prior to being aborted."

Continues Ford:

> "If the fetus can be regarded as an agent or a legal person, as McDonagh is prepared to assume for the purposes of her model, then it could indeed be claimed that such an entity ought to be entitled to due process of law – a least where the pregnancy is medically normal (i.e., where it poses no immediate threat to a woman's life or health). Failing to recognize such an entitlement, it may be argued, is to treat the fetus as a 'legal person' only in the negative sense."

But this is problematic. The break and entry man invades my house. He is standing there with a gun. However, I also have a firearm, I am a crack shot, and I've got the drop on him. Am I obligated to confer on him "a legal hearing and legal counsel"? Am I obliged to grant him "due process of law?" This seems like quite a stretch for my legal responsibilities. To be sure, there is a difference between the fetus and the criminal intruder. One lacks mens rea, the other does not. But it by no means follows that either should be legally entitled to the niceties of the law. If anything, the pre-born baby is in a worse legal position. At least the adult burglar can offer some sort of excuse: he thought he was in his own home; he was attending a costume party and his gun is but a toy. None of these options are open to the zygote who is a product of rape; matters are pellucidly clear as to how he happened to come to occupy territory in the mother's body. There is no justification for the niceties of civilized law.

As to the mugger in your home, a strong distinction must be made between the time the homeowner confronts him in her home, and when he is later carted off to court. It is on the latter occasion, and only the latter occasion, that the issue of legal hearing, legal counsel, due process of law can even arise. Upon the first meeting between the two, the miscreant must rely on the benevolence of the abode's occupant, assuming she has the ability to stop him in his tracks.

We arrive now at the question of whether pregnancy is a unique case. McDonagh relies heavily on analogies. But this mode of argumentation is only coherent if being with child has similarities to other situations. Ford maintains that pregnancy is a unique condition. Ford (p. 643) wheels in Davis (1984) to underscore this point:

> "Such an objection is raised by Nancy Davis, who argues that the uniqueness of pregnancy as a condition is such that it is impossible even to characterize the issue as one where competing rights are being balanced. Davis writes, "If the relationship between the woman and the fetus is thought to be in itself a special one, then this undercuts the force of arguments by analogy."

In my view, in contrast, pregnancy is not unique in the sense that there are no strong analogs. For example, an intruder in a house, boat, airplane, owned by someone who does not welcome him. Thomson's (1971a, b, c) violinist constitutes yet another analogy, and a strong one to boot.

As it happens, Ford (p. 644) agrees with this assessment: In her view the critics are

> "making the claim that the whole set of circumstances associated with pregnancy is unique, particularly with regard to the operation and exercise of individual rights. … I ultimately agree with McDonagh that the objection from uniqueness must fail…"

At this point Ford delves more deeply into the conjoined twins (supposed) analogy. She states (pp. 645–646):

> "The case of the conjoined twins corresponds to McDonagh's model of nonconsensual pregnancy in a number of important respects. Jodie (the stronger twin) was involved in a nonconsensual physical relationship with the weaker twin, Mary; Jodie was suffering physical harm and facing certain death as a result of Mary's physical dependence on her body, and Jodie's only possible defence against the harm would be the removal of Mary, which would end the nonconsensual relationship and inevitably cause Mary's death. The relationship was beneficial only to Mary, and harmful only to Jodie, making it more similar to McDonagh's pregnancy model than to other more "symbiotic" twin conjoinments. Another similarity to McDonagh's model is that both of the twins in Re A were deemed to be "persons" in law. It is therefore instructive to examine the case for evidence of how the UK courts might approach a right to abortion based on the right to self-defence.
>
> "The court in Re A allowed the surgical separation to proceed. The rationale for this decision was complex, but can be summarized by saying that the judges, faced with a choice between saving the life of one twin or losing both, preferred the option that saved the greater number of lives – a "quantity of life" calculus, in effect. By this logic, if both twins would have survived in their conjoined state, it would seem that the court would not have sanctioned the deliberate killing of Mary. While such killing was considered permissible in order to save one life instead of none, it would not appear, on the logic of Re A, to be justified if the choice is between one life of high quality or two lives of inferior quality. The implication of this for the model proposed by McDonagh is that, unless the life of the pregnant woman was actually threatened by the pregnancy, the killing of the fetus (viewed as a legal person) would be impermissible.
>
> "While the facts of Re A do not represent a perfect analogy with pregnancy, this is not in itself a reason to dismiss it as irrelevant; it seems to be at least as strong as any of the interchangeable analogies offered by McDonagh herself. Moreover, … analogies (even if imperfect) are necessary, since to treat pregnancy as completely legally unique is to embrace a kind of particularism that is incompatible with coherent legal regulation and with the philosophical justifications underpinning the liberal legal system itself, such as non-discrimination and legitimate expectation."

I am afraid I cannot see my way clear to agreeing with Ford on this matter. First of all, minor point, all analogies are imperfect. That is why they are characterized in this manner in the first place. If they were "perfect," they would not be called "analogies." Rather, they would be identities. Second, more important, there is a gigantic disanalogy between the conjoined twin and pregnancy case. Neither twin was in any manner shape or form trespassing on the property owned by the other. Yes, what might be construed as their vital interest was incompatible with one another, but, they were both occupying space properly possessed by a third party: their mother.

Then there is the issue of "non-discrimination and legitimate expectation." The former is certainly part and parcel of "the liberal legal system" as per the twenty-first century. But, classical liberalism, e.g., libertarianism, has no truck with this concept. Rather, the right to discriminate is an integral part of this philosophy.

It is difficult to understand why Ford would find it necessary to bring in such matters which are rather irrelevant to the main issue under discussion herein: abortion. But, while we are on the topic, a few critical words. Both heterosexual and homosexual leftist are hypocritical on this matter. Each discriminates against fully half of the human race in terms of love, marriage, personal partners. Only bisexuals are innocent of this charge. Yet, where is the call from this part of the fever swamp, for compulsory bisexuality?

As for "legitimate expectation" I do not totally reject this concept. If you order a cup of coffee, drink it down, and then are presented with a bill for $1 million for this hot beverage, you do indeed have a "legitimate expectation" that you are not legally required to pay the full amount. There is, yes, an implicit contract between vendor and customer that a "normal price" will be charged; that such an unusual price must be clearly mentioned at the outset. However, there is no such implication for the issue now under analysis. The fetus, no matter how created, has no "legitimate expectation" that he shall be allowed to abide for nine months inside the property owned by someone else.

Ford's next attempt to undermine McDonagh arises in the context of father's rights. But, before she involves herself in that criticism, she introduces it as follows (p. 649):

> "Many feminist commentators have complained, rightly in my view, that theorizing about pregnancy, and in particular, the rhetoric of the fetal-rights debate, has traditionally marginalized women to the point of invisibility. Such has been the focus on the emerging "person" of the fetus and its welfare that the pregnant woman and her interests can be forgotten, or at least 'suspended' until after she has given birth."

Now, this is more than a passing curiosity. Why is it per se unjust to "marginalize" women in this or any other philosophical discussion? Perhaps, the distaff side has no particular role to play in some of them. For example, in metaphysics, epistemology, ethics, free will, the issue of "other minds," to say nothing of callings such as mathematics, physics, chemistry, it would appear that the biology of females is just about entirely irrelevant to the conversion. And, of course, the same applies to males. All of these cases concern human beings and their sex need not even be mentioned. My claim is that the very same thing applies in the present situation. As far as justice is concerned, it is only an accident that females, not males, can get pregnant. The matter may best be addressed, solely, completely and only, as a question of who owns the property rights under dispute. Gender simply has nothing to do with the matter. Neither sex is any more privileged in this discussion than the other. To assert the opposite, as both Ford and McDonagh unfortunately, do, is to commit the ad hominem fallacy.

Why, then, does Ford reject McDonagh's analysis in this context?
She states as follows (p. 650):

> "McDonagh … eliminate(es) men from the landscape of pregnancy and childbirth. McDonagh would, of course, argue that men ought not to be regarded as being involved in the pregnancy relationship anyway, since it is, by definition, a relationship between the pregnant woman and the fetus. Indeed, she argues that it is precisely because we have failed, in the past, to characterize pregnancy in this way (as a bilateral relationship between a woman and a fetus) that policy-makers and judges have allowed external interests (e.g., the interest of the state in the continuation of fetal life) to limit the right of a woman to terminate an unwanted – or to use McDonagh's term, "nonconsensual" – pregnancy. By re-characterizing pregnancy as a bilateral relationship, according to McDonagh, we are able to resist such limits on this right.
>
> "There is another, less welcome consequence of this bilateralism, however. As discussed above, in order to regard pregnancy as an attack to which consent may be given or withheld (an understanding pivotal to McDonagh's argument as a whole), it is necessary to first sever the connection, both in cultural iconography and in the law, between an act of sexual intercourse and any subsequent ("resulting") pregnancy. Unless we abandon the notion that sex causes pregnancy, we cannot embrace the proposition that the cause of pregnancy is the fetus, exercising its coercive influence to change a woman's body from a nonpregnant to a pregnant state in pursuit of its own self-interest. I have already identified some ontological and epistemological problems with the notion that the fetus can plausibly be regarded as causing pregnancy, but this element of McDonagh's theory also encounters a more practical problem, namely that treating pregnancy as anything other than a consequence of sexual intercourse impairs (perhaps fatally) the ability of the law to attribute responsibility for the pregnancy, and even more importantly, for the resulting child, to the genetic father…"

In other words, Ford fears that McDonagh is letting men off the hook in terms of their obligation to support the mother they have impregnated, and the child who is the result of that act.

What is the libertarian view of this matter? Let us separate it into three parts, as the answer will vary in each of these cases. First, take the example of rape. What does the father owe to the mother, and child? It would take us too far afield to discuss libertarian punishment theory. Suffice it to say that this is very Draconian. If not executed, the rapist would spend a goodly part of the rest of his life at hard labor, the proceeds of which would go to the victim and her baby. So, yes, the rapist is indeed a debtor.

Second, there is voluntary sexual intercourse. Here, the father owes the mother not a single solitary cent, not a sou. Why not? Under libertarianism, there are no positive obligations. Not a one. All rights imply duties. In the case of negative rights, if A has a right not to be murdered, raped, kidnapped, stolen from, then B and everyone else is required to refrain from such nefarious activities. In the case of positive rights, if A has a right to food, clothing, shelter, then, again, B, and everyone else has an obligation to supply these aspects of wealth to A. But, libertarianism is limited to the NAP and private property rights based on homesteading. Requiring anyone to give anything to anyone else is this incompatible with this philosophy.

Third, contract. There could be two types of such commercial interactions: surrogacy, and an agreement between the two consenting adults who engage in sexual intercourse. If and to the extent that the male parent is contractually obligated to support the female parent and their offspring, that would be a justification for the father's fiscal responsibility as set out in the contract. But nothing else would suffice. Thus, while McDonagh's letting the father off the hook, so to speak, is incompatible with Ford's notion of feminism, it is not at all inconsistent with libertarianism. However, the way Ford sees matters, McDonagh's position constitutes an overpowering reductio ad absurdum.

According to the former (p. 651):

> "If having sex should not lead to legal obligations for a woman, why should it for a man? Why should a man be obliged by law to provide financial or other support for a child that, on McDonagh's analysis, he did not 'cause' or 'create '? Why should a woman, by consenting to a pregnancy relationship with a fetus, be able thus to impose legal obligations on a man, regardless of his consent to parenthood? McDonagh responds to this objection rather weakly: 'The flaw here is the failure to recognize that the [US] Constitution allows the state to intrude upon a person's economic assets with greater latitude than upon a person's bodily integrity and liberty.'
>
> "This is wholly unsatisfactory as an answer, however, since state intrusion must always have some form of justification in a liberal democracy. McDonagh's insistence that the fetus is the only legal cause of pregnancy divorces the father's sexual act from any subsequent pregnancy and child, thereby denying the state any justification for impinging on his finances, since no legal link exists between the man and the pregnancy, or between the man and any child that may eventually be born."

Ford argues as if it is a foregone conclusion, a veritable philosophical axiom, that a woman should have legal obligations to care for her baby. But, this, too, amounts to positive rights for the child, of which there are none, at least not for the libertarian. This legal theorist's position is problematic not only because it violates the freedom philosophy, but due to the fact that she blithely assumes the doctrine of positive rights to be true. She offers no justification for this contention of hers. Ford thinks it a fatal flaw in McDonagh's position that the state has no justification for "impinging" on the finances of the father. But this is mere black letter law according to libertarianism. No one, of either gender, should be "impinged." The only time someone's property may be properly taken away from him is if he is a criminal, or, is contractually obligated to make a payment.

Our author launches yet another critique of her target for unfairness to men (p. 652):

> "Following an act of consensual sexual intercourse, on McDonagh's model, women have the ongoing ability to withdraw their consent, and avoid the responsibilities of parenthood; men, by contrast, have no corresponding opportunity to consent, or refuse to consent, to become a parent. As such, McDonagh's model is discriminatory and endows women with the power to decide, for men, whether or not they will become parents. This power incorporates both the right to prevent a man from developing a relationship with a child he wants, and the right to force parenthood on a man who does not wish to be a father.
>
> "Returning to McDonagh's claim that the law 'elevates' genetic parenthood above gestational and social parenthood, it is now possible to respond that, at least for the purposes of attaching parental responsibility, genetic parenthood is the only stage at which both men

> and women can be held to have consented to become parents, without discriminating unfairly between the genders by endowing women with power over men's parental identity."

In olden times, on the basis of which modern law is often predicated, in the case of a dispute the judge could be absolutely sure of the identity of the mother of the child. Paternity was not at all so clear. Nowadays, with genetic testing, matters have changed to a great degree. Even so, if we apply a Lockean-Rothbardian libertarian spin to the matter, the female parent still comes up way ahead of the father. For, while both spend an equal amount and let us postulate an equal amount of effort in coitus, the mother then spends some nine months, subsequently, "mixing her labor with" the fertilized egg as it develops. Of course, the mother cannot "own" the baby, outright. However, she can indeed be the proprietor of the guardianship rights over him. Thus, vis-a-vis the father, she has a far better claim than he does, in cases of conflict. But just because her prerogative is stronger than his does not mean, as Ford would have it, that the father has no rights whatsoever. To the contrary, he has the second best claim to rear the child on the entire planet, second, only, to the mother. Of course "McDonagh's model is discriminatory." It must be so, based on elemental notions of justice. We are here discussing who has a better claim to be the guardian of the baby, mother or father? Any decision, apart from a dead-even tie, will be "discriminatory" in favor of the winner of this dispute and against the loser. As for "prevent(ing) a man from developing a relationship with a child he wants," no strict deduction from McDonagh's correct theory does this, at least not when interpreted through libertarian lenses. For, while his contribution to the creation of this new human being is certainly less than hers, it is not zero; it is far greater than anyone else's infinitely more so, since no other person was biologically involved. Modern courts lean in the direction of taking into account the best interests of the child, and, unless it can be demonstrated that the male parent is unfit, this, plus libertarian homesteading theory, would move us in the direction of partial guardianship for him, but greatly less so than for the mother.

In like manner, Ford's next sally against McDonagh fails. The former states (p. 652):

> "One consequence of McDonagh's approach is that the current grounds for wrongful pregnancy actions would be undermined, or even disappear; neither a man nor a surgeon can be held responsible, legally, for a pregnancy that occurs subsequent to rape or incompetent sterilization if the fetus alone 'causes the pregnancy in the legal sense … Indeed, no one can be held liable for any instance of wrongful, nonconsensual pregnancy on McDonagh's account since the agent that causes every pregnancy, the fetus, lacks mental competence."

One would have to travel some distance to unearth a less sympathetic interpretation of a target's verbiage. Yes, it is true that McDonagh sees the fetus as solely responsible for the pregnancy, or the invasion, or the trespass. But, this is true only in the sense of proximate cause. Regarding the ultimate cause, as a devotee of the McDonagh thesis as I am, I can easily deduce that the rapist, or the ineffectual medico, is indeed responsible for the woman's plight. It is decidedly untrue that "no one can be held liable" for this incursion since the baby, of course, lacks even a vestige of blameworthiness. Yes, the pre-born child is the interloper, but those ultimately responsible for this state of affairs are the guilty parties. It is only regarding voluntary sexual intercourse, where the woman later changes her mind about carrying the baby for nine months, that there is no guilty party. But this causes no discomfort to McDonagh's theory. Why need there be a criminal in every case of victimization? There is not in cases of storm, earthquake, etc., nor in this example either.

Any half-way sympathetic reading of McDonagh would interpret her as seeing unwanted "pregnancy as analogous to assault, rape or slavery. Instead, Ford (p. 653) leaves out the word "unwanted." Ford doubles down on this attribution by writing (ibid.):

> "If, as I will suggest, it is possible to treat all pregnancies, at least initially, as nonconsensual and therefore 'wrongful', on McDonagh's model, then it follows that all fetuses are inescapably 'rapists', albeit without mens rea."
>
> Ford continues (ibid.) Can an attack analogous to rape really be validated by ex post facto consent? If pregnancy begins as an uninvited, intrusive 'rape', how can the addition of consent transform it into something benign, even wonderful? These are the questions to which I turn now."

I acknowledge that this is a fascinating philosophical issue that Ford has set herself. I shall follow her down this garden path, even though I think the entire enterprise, while to be sure of great intrinsic importance, lies too far afield from the issue of abortion, my main interest. Why? I want to leave no stone unturned in my defense of McDonagh against what I see as Ford's unwarranted criticisms. In any case, the entire enterprise can be obviated by realizing that McDonagh does not consider the welcome fetus as a(n innocent) criminal, despite the fact that "pregnancy is even more invasive than intercourse in a number of ways: the physical impact is much more prolonged; the physical changes effected upon the body of the woman are extensive; and the woman is potentially placed in a health- or life-threatening situation" (Ford, p. 653).

It seems almost grotesque, a philosophical howler, to consider the longed for pre-born child as a rapist.

In her effort to refute McDonagh on this matter, Ford opines (p. 654):

> "Nevertheless, since pregnancy is characterized in her model as a massive intrusion, it is pertinent to ask whether it is the type of intrusion that could be rendered benign by the presence of consent. McDonagh certainly does not consider her model to be incompatible with benign, 'good Samaritan' pregnancy, or with the moral ideals of nurturing, caring, and relationships generally. She attempts to demonstrate this possibility of 'consensual pregnancy' by way of yet another analogy, between pregnancy and live organ donation…
>
> "Certainly, if the law permits us, under certain circumstances, to consent to having our bodies massively invaded and permanently depleted or endangered in order to provide sustenance to another, it seems likely that the law will also permit women to consent to donate their bodies to fetuses temporarily. However, this is where the analogy begins to break down. The law allows one person to consent to an invasion or harm chiefly for the benefit of another person; but, as has already been shown, McDonagh has failed to establish that the fetus is really a 'legal person' in the relevant sense of having the status, rights, and dignity of a person under law. Her characterization of the legal personality of the fetus undermines her argument because she has concentrated only on the neutral aspects of fetal

personality (how the personhood of the fetus does not negate the right of the woman to defend herself) and its negative aspects (how the fetus may plausibly be regarded as an 'attacker', an agent of harm). Ultimately, her treatment of fetal personality has not been authentic, since the legal personhood of the fetus is not central to her thesis, and is not necessary for the application of the two main premises of her model: the fetus as the cause of pregnancy; and the right of the woman to refuse her consent to a relationship with the fetus and to exercise her refusal by the use of deadly force."

There are problems here. First of all, Ford's critique of McDonagh on the ground that the latter has not established the fetus as a "legal person" comes with particular ill grace from the former. So as to not create a straw man, all three of us, the present writer, and these two authors, may stipulate that the preborn child is indeed a human being with all the rights thereto. Second, Ford's rejection of the analogy stems from what she perceives the law to be. However, as is well known in law circles, "the law is an ass." Just because a group of people with black robes have come to a certain finding, does not confer any magical benefit on their opinions.

In both pregnancy and live organ donation one person, A, confers a benefit on another, B. Neither should be required by law. Both are supererogatory; over and above the call of duty.

Ford rejects this insight on the ground that (p. 655):

"A woman may undoubtedly give her consent to surgery to remove one of her kidneys for donation to her daughter; however, could a childless woman with a family history of hereditary kidney disease opt to have a healthy kidney removed and kept in storage in case a future child required a transplant? It seems highly unlikely that such a procedure would be countenanced by medical practitioners, or that the woman's informed consent would be sufficient to establish its permissibility. Why? It could be argued that in the former case, there is a known need for the organ, and compatibility has been established, while this is not the case in the latter scenario. However, even if we expand the example of the childless woman such that she knows for certain that (1) she is fertile and intending to become pregnant, (2) any child she bears will definitely be affected by the hereditary disease, and (3) she would be a compatible donor, it is still difficult to imagine the law supporting her desire to have her healthy kidney removed, thereby debilitating herself and placing her life in danger."

One is sorely tempted to say Who gives a rat's rear end about what a "medical practitioner" has to say about anything? As far as just law is concerned, a physician plays roughly the role of a carpenter, a seamstress or a plumber. Doctors, merely, cut and splice, and sew things together afterward. Their opinions on ethics and law be damned. And we have already established the part of the human anatomy "the law" most resembles. We can see that McDonagh's position very closely resembles that of libertarianism, where consent, based on the premise of private property rights emanating from homesteading, is crucially important. In contrast, for Ford, consent should be taken into account, to be sure, but only if the choice made is approved by outsiders such as sawbones, of all people, politicians, and judges, forsooth.

Nothing daunted, Ford expresses herself as follows (p. 655):

"My claim here, then, is that although the law will occasionally allow one person to volunteer to be endangered in order that another person may benefit, this permission is based on assumptions about the equal value of human lives and the social valuing of samaritanism when practised between persons. If persons attempt to engage in purported acts of

> samaritanism by endangering or disadvantaging themselves for the benefit of a creature that the law does not regard as the moral equivalent of a person, then it is doubtful whether this would be regarded as authentic samaritanism at all. The law cannot, of course, always intervene to prevent people from risking their lives to save a pet; however, we can be reasonably sure that such behaviour would not be encouraged. It is likely that people wishing to donate their kidneys to animals (were that biologically viable), or to children not yet in existence, would be dissuaded and ultimately thwarted by the refusal of the medical profession or the courts to support such a sacrifice, despite the presence of clear and authentic consent. In short, samaritanism must benefit someone, and it is doubtful whether the fetus would count as "someone" on McDonagh's model, given the emptiness and negativity of the "personality" she ascribes to it."

Here, Ford aligns herself with the evil[2] Coase (1960), in thinking that the law should jettison all notions of justice and instead promulgate whatever increases wealth ("value of human lives"). I say, in contrast, damn the "medical profession" and the "courts" if they will not allow people to voluntarily donate their organs to pets, or, act in other way to promote "capitalist acts between consenting adults" in the felicitous phrase of Nozick (1974, p. 163).

Consider the following scenario. It is 1925, in the midst of the Jim Crow era. A white sheriff is holding in prison for trial an innocent black man falsely charged with rape. Outside the jail a white mob is demanding that the inmate be turned over to them for "justice," with a rope. If the sheriff releases his prisoner to the tender mercies of the mob, only one person will die: the innocent African-American. If he does not, both he, the sheriff, along with the prisoner, and half the mob, along with hundreds of townsfolk, will perish in the ensuing melee. Should the sheriff send the prisoner to his certain and unjustified death? One can be sure that the "medical profession" and the "courts" relied upon by Ford, along with Coase, would "encourage" him to do exactly that. However, elemental, basic, justice clearly requires the very opposite.

The utilitarian could reply, not unreasonably, that if the law is trashed in any such way, many more people will perish in the future, as this becomes a precedent for mob rule. However, suppose, the world was to end one minute after all the shooting stopped, so that there would be no precedent for the future for the pragmatist to rely upon. Letting the innocent black man leave the safety of the prison would still be unjust, Ford, Coase, doctors, judges, experts, to the contrary notwithstanding. Yes, just law tends to promote GDP, but to base the former on the latter is to place the cart before the horse.

Ford (p. 657) charges that "it is finally possible to refute the objection that McDonagh's model, in characterizing pregnancy as an attack, leaves no scope for consensual, benign instances of pregnancy." How, pray tell, does the former arrive at this dismissal of the latter? Ford (p. 656) takes an excursion through several law

---

[2] Barnett and Block 2007, 2009a, b; Block 1977, 1995, 1996, 2000, 2003a, b, c, d, e, f, g, 2006a, b, c, 2010a, c, d, 2011; Block et al. 2005; Bylund 2014; Cordato 1989, 1992a, b, 1997, 1998, 2000; DiLorenzo 2014; Fox 2007; Hoppe 2004; Krause 1999; Krecke 1996; Lewin 1982; North 1990, 1992, 2002; Rothbard 1982, 1997a, b; Stringham 2001; Stringham and White 2004; Terrell 1999; Wysocki 2017.

cases such as R. v. Brown which found "it is not in the public interest that people should try to cause, or should cause, each other actual bodily harm for no good reason" and that voluntary sadomasochism between consenting adults did not pass muster. True, Ford positively mentions Bix (1997) who rejects this analysis, but then undermines his own libertarian tendencies by stating that "the moral value or public value of the activity in question" should be determinative in such findings. No, no, no, if an act is mutually agreed upon, it should be lawful, whether or not is has any "moral value or public value." It may readily be argued that pornographic films and prostitution have little or no "moral value or public value." This hardly demonstrates that they should be prohibited by law.

In making her case against McDonagh, Ford (p. 657) also relies on the equally non-libertarian (Pa 2001) who avers:

> "[I]f actual bodily injury occurs, no consent defense is [normally] available because a breach of the peace occurred, and the State has a compelling interest in punishing this behavior. The individual cannot consent to an injury inflicted against the community."

The libertarian in me sides with McDonagh's emphasis on consent. Community schamunity. The injury in question was not imposed upon the "community." Rather, the non-victim of this victimless crime was the individual who consented to what would otherwise be considered an invasion. Boxers do not "breach the peace" even though the manly sport is hardly a peaceful one.

We should also give the back of the hand to Ford's (p. 657) contention that

> "consensual pregnancy would undeniably be regarded as 'conducive to the enhancement or enjoyment of family life' and 'conducive to the welfare of society', in Lord Lowry's words. Second, it would certainly be considered to be 'in the public interest' for women to consent to pregnancy at least some of the time."

Ford, here, reckons by ignoring the over-populationists. Let her ask Malthus (1798), or Ehrlich (1968) if they regard even voluntary pregnancy as "conducive to the welfare of society." The point is, the very concept "public interest" is highly problematic. The "public" simply has no interests. Only individuals do. And, they diverge. In contrast, consent is pellucidly clear.

In my view, McDonagh is entire correct in maintaining that unwelcome pregnancy indeed constitutes an "attack." Ford never demonstrates that this author takes the position what welcome pregnancy is also an "attack," although she quotes her repeatedly. The difficulty with Ford's analysis at this point is that it engages, once again, in legal positivism. Her major premise is founded on legal decisions. But, they are not necessarily correct, as legal positivism would have it. This premise, moreover, is an aspect of positive economics: the judge said X, therefore it must be correct.

The next issue to arise concerns the distinction between consent and mere submission. According to Ford (p. 657):

> "With this distinction between consent and mere submission in mind, it is clear that, on McDonagh's model, pregnancy cannot, at least initially, be consensual. Since, on that model, the woman can do nothing to prevent the fetus from attacking her by implanting

> itself in her uterus, consent to pregnancy is only possible retrospectively, once the woman is already pregnant; she cannot consent to become pregnant, only to remaining pregnant."

Forget, for the moment, whether McDonagh herself can, without self-contradiction, make sense of consent. Instead, ask whether anyone, for example a libertarian such as myself who broadly supports this author, can maintain that the unwanted fetus is a trespasser. This seems to be the core of the controversy. And, it is fully coherent that this can indeed be done. Assume, arguendo, that Ford's censuring of McDonagh is correct. Ford has no cogent reply to the stance, possibly made by others, that while the desired fetus is not an invader, the undesired one certainly is. We need only contrast the baby who is a product of rape with the one who is welcomed, via consensual intercourse. If the former is not an interloper, then that word has no references.

Ford plows ahead against McDonagh (p. 658): "… in the context of pregnancy as McDonagh construes it, the pregnant woman has never had the option to give prior consent – she cannot prevent the fetal 'attack' and the resulting pregnancy by refusing to consent to it." But yes, she most certainly can. All she need do is refuse coitus, or any other means of becoming pregnant, such as in vitro fertilization. Similarly, Ford (p. 658) claims that "McDonagh describes pregnancy as an attack" when she should have said "McDonagh describes unwanted pregnancy as an attack" which would be eminently reasonable. One source of the lack of "want" is of course rape. But, consider a woman who voluntarily engages in intercourse, with the express purpose of becoming pregnant. She succeeds in attaining this goal. But later on, some days, weeks or months afterward, she changes her mind, and no longer wishes to maintain her present situation. Namely, the fetus is now unwanted. How, then, other than an (of course innocent) attacker, an interloper, an invader, a trespasser, can we describe this very young person now growing inside of her body? If the shoe fits… If it walks like a duck, quacks like a duck…

Our author now enters the treacherous waters of voluntary slavery. It seems she is willing to throw everything she can at McDonagh, including the (philosophical) kitchen sink. Ford opines (p. 659):

> "How apt, then, is the slavery analogy? Could the willingness of a slave to be a slave render the "slavery relationship" legally benign on account of its consensuality? If not, and if the analogy between pregnancy and slavery is a fair one, then why is it that the consent of a woman to be pregnant can render the pregnancy relationship benign? In fact, the analogy with slavery threatens to undermine the power of consent in McDonagh's model by casting doubt on the notion of 'benign, consensual pregnancy' altogether. In Western legal systems, slavery would never be recognized as a legitimate relationship between consenting parties. We are not permitted to 'contract out' of our fundamental human rights. If pregnancy were to involve a similar alienation of personhood – even a temporary one–, the law would struggle to recognize the possibility of benign pregnancy."

The issue of voluntary slavery is an important one in the philosophical literature. There are good arguments made on both sides of this debate. But Ford's is a rather weak one. Again, she resorts to legal positivism: whatever the court or legislature opines, must necessarily be correct. It is a logical contradiction to say that the court found X, but X is false. Nonsense, on stilts. Just because something would never be accepted as legitimate by "Western Legal Systems" no matter how consensual they were, amounts to no argument at all. For "Western Legal Systems" might be wrong on this or any other matter.

Consider the following case. Alan's child, Arthur, has a dread disease. It will cost $5 million to cure him. Alan is a poor man, and could never raise any such amount of money. Robert, a very wealthy individual, has long wanted Alan as a slave. So, they make a deal. Robert pays Alan these funds. Alan turns the money over to Arthur's doctors, and then repairs to Robert's plantation, there to serve out the remainder of his days as the latter's slave. Both Alan and Robert gain from this exchange, in the ex-ante sense of anticipations. Alan values his son's life more than his freedom. Robert rates Alan's servitude to him more highly than the money he spent to obtain it. If "Western Legal Systems" disallow such voluntary contracts, Alan will not be a happy camper; Arthur will perish. Yes, ex post, Alan might regret his decision, as he is being beaten by Robert, but the same can be said of any sale or purchase. Sometimes, there is regret after the fact, but that hardly justifies forbidding all commercial transactions. Nor this one, either.

Ford's next error comes about in her defense of West and McKee (1983). She first mentions that "West is keen to show that consensual relationships can be damaging, too" and then quotes the latter as follows (p. 660):

> "Women consent to events and transactions and arrangements all the time – day in and day out – that do us considerable harm: from marriages, to love affairs, to one-night stands, to unequal pay for comparable work, to sexually harassing work and school environments, to second shifts in the home, and to mommy tracks at work."

Ford (660) continues:

> "We must therefore look beneath the consensual surface of relationships to discover whether the voluntariness they embody is authentic or not. West argues that caregiving such as that undertaken in pregnancy must be authentically consensual in order to be "good" and not harmful; McDonagh's model, she claims, is guilty of overemphasizing the superficialities of consent, at the expense of this need for real voluntariness in the giving of care."

Sorry, but this is really dreadful on West's and Ford's part. Consent only holds true, is only "authentic," if, in retrospect, the choice was a wise one? A marriage that ends in divorce was not really "authentically" agreed upon? A bad love affair was necessarily a non-consensual, non "authentic" one? There is no such thing as a one-night stand to which both partners "authentically" arranged? A job where women are paid less than men is one where the former were kidnapped, and compelled to work for lower pay? Consent is only "superficial" if it turns out to be satisfactory after the event? To say that this analysis is sophomoric is to unjustly compliment it.

We now move to another topic, on in which Ford acquits herself well, in contrast to McDonagh, a rarity. Ford (p. 660–661) cites Scully (1997) as follows:

> "[Another] problem with McDonagh's theory, is that it would permit abortions even in the final weeks of pregnancy – a result that the majority of the American public probably would not support… McDonagh appears to argue that a woman's right to withdraw her consent to pregnancy can be exercised at any time, even in the ninth month of pregnancy. This conclusion seems extreme, and it fails to adequately address the fact that, at some point in time, a fetus becomes viable and no longer needs to rely on a woman's body for survival. If a fetus

> is a person and it has a right to life, then, at the point at which it becomes viable, it would seem appropriate to weigh its right to life against the continuing intrusion upon the woman's bodily integrity … Thus, at the point of viability, it seems reasonable to limit a pregnant woman's ability to decide to terminate a pregnancy because she no longer consents to being pregnant."

There are problems here, grave ones. First, what the American public supports is very much beside the point. Philosophical analysis is not a nose-counting operation. Second, just because a solution is "extreme" does not mean it is incorrect. Third, it talks of "weighing" one right against another. However, at least in the libertarian lexicography, there is no, there can be no, conflict in rights. If there seems to be, then one or the other or both of these "rights" are mis-specified. Thus, there is never any reason to "weigh" one right against another. In the present case, there is no "right to life" since that would be a positive right, anathema to libertarians. All rights imply obligations. Thus, only negative rights pass muster in this regard. If I have a right not to be murdered, you have an obligation not to murder me. No problem there. But, if I have a right to life, you have an obligation to feed me, house me, clothe me, etc., and the difficulty comes about specifying why one stranger has any such obligation to support another. Further, we are all murderers, since there are always people dying unjustly somewhere on the planet, and if they have a right to life, and we all have an obligation to defend it, we have all failed. We are all almost necessarily rights violators.

However, we must acknowledge that Scully, with Ford's support, comes so close to a correct analysis. They are within inches of the goal line, but have not been able to push the football past this stripe. Allow me to repeat the last line of the above quote, since it so nearly attains the correct analysis, the thesis of the present book: "Thus, at the point of viability, it seems reasonable to limit a pregnant woman's ability to decide to terminate a pregnancy because she no longer consents to being pregnant."

No, no, no. The woman has a right to terminate her pregnancy at any time she wishes. Remember, the unwanted pre-born baby is a trespasser, an interloper, a squatter – on the property of someone else, the mother in this case. So, the woman has a right to terminate her pregnancy. But, she has not the slightest right in all of God's creation to have an abortion, which means, eviction plus killing. Rather, she has only the right to engage in the former, eviction. Given the baby's viability at this point, we legal philosophers can have our cake and eat it too: our theory can save the precious pre-born infant's life, and, also, allow the mother to rid herself of an unwanted intruder. Thus, there is absolutely no need to "weigh" anything against anything else. They have come so very, very, close, but no cigar to either Ford or Scully.

Ford again offers her legal positivistic perspective, and more with the "balancing" (p. 661):

> "A potential counter-argument is that, in the United States, the fetus is emerging as a 'second patient' in medical law, raising the issue of balancing the woman's refusal to consent to a Caesarean against the fetus's right to life as a serious possibility. In the UK, this problem does not arise because several important cases have clarified the area, securing the right of

the competent pregnant woman to consent or refuse consent to medical treatment, meaning that a competent patient cannot be compelled to undergo a Caesarean section against her will."

Yes, of course, it cannot be denied, judicial findings can indeed establish legal rights. But we are not at all interested in mere legal rights. Instead, we are concerned, herein, with what the law ought to be. Ford fails to distinguish between what economists characterize as a normative versus a positive examination. She adopts the latter: what is the law? In contrast, I am interested, only, in the normative issue of the legitimacy of the law.

Ford, however, does not always adopt this stance. In her eminently reasonable criticism of Scully's (1997) paternalism, our author opines as follows (p. 662):

"When legislatures decide what abortion laws to have, or when judges decide how to dispose of a particular case involving maternal-fetal issues, it would be paternalistic of them to concern themselves with these factors in the same way. Public policy considerations are likely to play a part in their deliberations, but it would be inappropriate for a judge to decide a case on the basis that he thought a woman was simply wrong to choose an abortion in her circumstances. Because the issues and responsibilities of judges and the issues and responsibilities that pregnant women must contend with are quite different, it is perfectly possible to endorse a legal model that permits late abortions and repeated abortions so long as those educating and counselling women warn them of the dangers of taking full advantage of these legal rights."

Yes, judges can indeed be paternalistic; at least according to libertarian doctrine, it should be no part of their brief to act in a parental role with regard to adult women. Ford is entirely correct in opposing such effronteries. However, she takes it all back, or at least a goodly part of it, when she calls for "educating and counselling women" who are adults. If they are so stupid that they need uncalled for "educating and counselling," then the right to vote should be taken away from them, a manifest ludicrous position. But, if females are smart enough to be given the vote, then, it is thereby demonstrated that they do not at all need what Ford proffers them, to wit, "educating and counselling."

To conclude. McDonagh makes a few errors, the most serious of them is to fail to see eviction as an alternative to abortion. Ford lambastes McDonagh from soup to nuts, but rarely lays a glove on her. And, in her attempt to undermine the semi-libertarian McDonagh, Ford makes numerous mistakes of her own.

References

Barnett, William II, and Walter E. Block. 2007. Coase and Van Zandt on Lighthouses. *Public Finance Review* 35 (6, November): 710–733. http://pfr.sagepub.com/content/35/6/710

———. 2009a. Coase and Bertrand on Lighthouses. *Public Choice* 140 (1–2): 1–13. https://doi.org/10.1007/s11127-008-9375-x.

———. 2009b. Financial Intermediaries, the Intertemporal-Carry Trade, and Austrian Business Cycles; Or; Crash and Carry: Can Fraudulent Time deposits lead to an Austrian Business Cycle? Yes. *Journal Etica e Politica/Ethics & Politics* XI (1): 455–469. http://www2.units.it/~etica/2009_1/BARNETT_BLOCK.pdf

Block, Walter E. 1977. Coase and Demsetz on Private Property Rights. *The Journal of Libertarian Studies: An Interdisciplinary Review* I (2, Spring): 111–115. http://www.mises.org/journals/jls/1_2/1_2_4.pdf

———. 1995. Ethics, Efficiency, Coasean Property Rights and Psychic Income: A Reply to Demsetz. *The Review of Austrian Economics* 8 (2): 61–125.

———. 1996. O.J.'s Defense: A Reductio Ad Absurdum of the Economics of Ronald Coase and Richard Posner. *European Journal of Law and Economics* 3: 265–286.

———. 2000. Private Property Rights, Erroneous Interpretations, Morality and Economics: Reply to Demsetz. *Quarterly Journal of Austrian Economics* 3 (1, Spring): 63–78.

———. 2003a. *The Death Penalty*, November 11. http://www.lewrockwell.com/block/block34.html

———. 2003b. *Death Penalty Essential for Social Justice*. Loyola University New Orleans Loyola University New Orleans The Maroon, October 10.

———. 2003c. Libertarianism vs. Objectivism; A Response to Peter Schwartz. *Reason Papers* 26 (Summer): 39–62.

———. 2003d. Private Property Rights, Economic Freedom, and Professor Coase: A Critique of Friedman, McCloskey, Medema and Zorn. *Harvard Journal of Law and Public Policy* 26 (3, Summer): 923–951.

———. 2003e. Toward a Libertarian Theory of Inalienability: A Critique of Rothbard, Barnett, Gordon, Smith, Kinsella and Epstein. *Journal of Libertarian Studies* 17 (2, Spring): 39–85.

———. 2003f. Socialized Medicine Is the Problem. *Surgical Neurology* 60 (5, November): 467–446.

———. 2003g. *The Non-aggression Axiom of Libertarianism*, February 17. http://archive.lewrockwell.com/block/block26.html

———. 2006a. Epstein on Alienation: A Rejoinder. *International Journal of Social Economics* 33 (3-4): 241–260.

———. 2006b. Coase and Kelo: Ominous Parallels and Reply to Lott on Rothbard on Coase. *Whittier Law Review* 27 (4): 997–1022.

———. 2006c. Radical Libertarianism: Applying Libertarian Principles to Dealing with the Unjust Government, Part II. *Reason Papers* 28 (Spring): 85–109.

———. 2010a. A Response to Brooks' Support of Demsetz on the Coase Theorem. *Dialogue* 2.

———. 2010b. Rejoinder to Brooks on Coase and Demsetz. *Quarterly Journal of Austrian Economics* 13 (4, Winter): 56–73.

———. 2010c. Rejoinder to Boettke on Coasean Economics and Communism. *Romanian Economic and Business Review* 5 (3, Fall): 9–90.

———. 2011. Rejoinder to Bertrand on Lighthouses. *Romanian Economic and Business Review* 6 (3, Fall): 49–67.

———. 2013a. *Legalize Blackmail*. New Orleans: Straylight Publishing.

———. 2013b. *More Than Passing Curious: George Jonas and Libertarianism*, January 20. http://www.lewrockwell.com/blog/lewrw/archives/130927.html

Block, Walter E., William Barnett II, and Gene Callahan. 2005. The Paradox of Coase as a Defender of Free Markets. *NYU Journal of Law & Liberty* 1 (3): 1075–1095. http://tinyurl.com/2hbzd4

Bylund, Per L. 2014. Ronald Coase's 'Nature of the Firm' and the Argument for Economic Planning. *Journal of the History of Economic Thought* 36 (3, September). ISSN 1053-8372 print; ISSN 1469-9656 online/14/03000 305 - 329 © The History of Economics Society. https://doi.org/10.1017/S1053837214000352

Coase, Ronald H. 1960. The Problem of Social Cost. *Journal of Law and Economics* 3: 1–44. http://www.sfu.ca/~allen/CoaseJLE1960.pdf

Cordato, Roy E. 1989. Subjective Value, Time Passage, and the Economics of Harmful Effects. *Hamline Law Review* 12 (2, Spring): 229–244.

———. 1992a. Knowledge Problems and the Problem of Social Cost. *Journal of the History of Economic Thought* 14 (Fall): 209–224.

———. 1992b. *Welfare Economics and Externalities in an Open-Ended Universe: A Modern Austrian Perspective*. Boston: Kluwer.
———. 1997. Market-Based Environmentalism and the Free Market: They're Not the Same. *The Independent Review* 1 (3, Winter): 371–386.
———. 1998. Time Passage and the Economics of Coming to the Nuisance: Reassessing the Coasean Perspective. *Campbell Law Review* 20 (2, Spring): 273–292.
———. 2000. Chasing Phantoms in a Hollow Defense of Coase. *The Review of Austrian Economics* 13 (2, September): 193–208.
DiLorenzo, Thomas J. 2014. *When Did Ronald Coase Become the Ayatollah of Economic Theory?*, January 2. http://www.lewrockwell.com/2014/01/thomas-dilorenzo/the-beltarian-cult/
Fox, Glenn. 2007. The Real Coase Theorems. *The Cato Journal: An Interdisciplinary Journal of Public Policy Analysis* 27 (3, Fall): 373–396. http://www.cato.org/pubs/journal/cj27n3/cj27n3-5.pdf
Hoppe, Hans-Hermann. 2004. *The Ethics and Economics of Private Property*, October 11. http://www.lewrockwell.com/hoppe/hoppe11.html
Krauss, Michael. 1999. Tort Law, Moral Accountability, and Efficiency: Reflections on the Current Crisis. *Markets and Morality* 2 (1, Spring). http://www.acton.org/publicat/m_and_m/1999_spr/krauss.html
Krecke, Elisabeth. 1996. Law and the Market Order: An Austrian Critique of the Economic Analysis of Law. *Journal des Economistes et des Etudes Humaines* 7 (1, March): 19–37. Commentaries on Law & Economics, 1997 Yearbook, ed. Robert W. McGee, 86–109.
Lewin, Peter. 1982. Pollution Externalities: Social Cost and Strict Liability. *Cato Journal* 2 (1, Spring): 205–229.
McDonagh, E.L. 1996. *Breaking the Abortion Deadlock: From Choice to Consent*. New York: Oxford University Press.
North, Gary. 1990. *Tools of Dominion: The Case Laws of Exodus*. Tyler: Institute for Christian Economics.
———. 1992. *The Coase Theorem*. Tyler: The Institute for Christian Economics.
———. 2002. Undermining Property Rights: Coase and Becker. *The Journal of Libertarian Studies: An Interdisciplinary Review* 16 (4, Fall): 75–100. http://www.mises.org/journals/jls/16_4/16_4_5.pdf
Nozick, Robert. 1974. *Anarchy, State and Utopia*. New York: Basic Books. http://www.amazon.com/Anarchy-State-Utopia-Robert-Nozick/dp/0465097200
Rothbard, Murray N. 1982. Law, Property Rights, and Air Pollution. *Cato Journal* 2 (1, Spring); Reprinted in Economics and the Environment: A Reconciliation, ed. Walter E. Block, 233–279. Vancouver: The Fraser Institute, 1990. http://www.mises.org/rothbard/lawproperty.pdf; http://mises.org/story/2120
———. 1997a. Value Implications of Economic Theory. In *Logic of Action I*, 255–265. Cheltenham: Edward Elgar.
———. 1997b. Toward a Reconstruction of Utility and Welfare Economics. In *The Logic of Action: Method, Money and the Austrian School*, vol. I, 211–254. Cheltenham: Edward Elgar.
Stringham, Edward. 2001. Kaldor-Hicks Efficiency and the Problem of Central Planning. *Quarterly Journal of Austrian Economics* 4 (2, Summer): 41–50. http://www.mises.org/journals/qjae/pdf/qjae4_2_3.pdf.
Stringham, Edward Peter, and Mark White. 2004. Economic Analysis of Tort Law: Austrian and Kantian Perspectives. In *Law and Economics: Alternative Economic Approaches to Legal and Regulatory Issues*, ed. Margaret Oppenheimer and Nicholas Mercuro, 374–392. New York: M.E. Sharpe. http://www.sjsu.edu/stringham/docs/Stringham.and.White2005.pdf.
Terrell, Timothy D. 1999. Property Rights and Externality: The Ethics of the Austrian School. *Journal of Markets and Morality* 2 (2, Fall). www.acton.org/publications/mandm/mandm_article_114.php
Thomson, Judith Jarvis. 1971a. A Defense of Abortion. *Philosophy and Public Affairs* I: 47–66.

———. 1971b. *A Defense of Abortion*. University of Colorado at Boulder, Fall, 2007, March 4. http://spot.colorado.edu/~heathwoo/Phil160,Fall02/thomson.htm

———. 1971c. A Defense of Abortion. *Philosophy & Public Affairs* 1 (1, Fall); Reprinted in Intervention and Reflection: Basic Issues in Medical Ethics, 5th ed., ed. Ronald Munson (Belmont; Wadsworth 1996), 69–80.

West, Edwin, and Michael McKee. 1983. De Gustibus Est Disputandum: The Phenomenon of "Merit Wants" Revisited. *The American Economic Review* 73 (5, December): 1110–1121.

Wysocki, Igor. 2017. Justice and Pareto-Efficiency (The Case Against Coase). *Dialogi Polityczne/ Political Dialogues*, 33–46.

Chapter 10
Response to Lee's "A Christian Philosopher's View of Recent Directions in the Abortion Debate"

Lee is an attempt to promote the pro-life perspective from a Christian point of view. He

> "argue(s) that a distinct, whole (though immature) human individual comes to be at conception, that he or she is a person, with full moral worth, from the moment he or she comes to be, and the mothers and fathers have a special responsibility to their children which entails (at least) that they ought not to choose to abort them."

So far, so good, at least insofar as an introduction is concerned. My own view is 100% in accord with this statement. Abortion is an abomination. It is the murder of an innocent very young person. Human life begins with the fertilized egg. That now single cell bears all the right not to be murdered borne by an adult member of our species.

However, this author gets started on the wrong foot with his citation of Pope Paul:

> "As far as the right to life is concerned, every innocent human being is absolutely equal to all others. This equality is the basis of all authentic social relationships which, to be truly such, can only be founded on truth and justice, recognizing and protecting every man and woman as a person and not as an object to be used. Before the moral norm which prohibits the direct taking of the life of an innocent human being there are no privileges or exceptions for anyone. It makes no difference whether one is the master of the world or 'the poorest of the poor' on the face of the earth. Before the demands of morality we are all absolutely equal."

What are the difficulties here? I skip past the "right to life." I interpret this positive right, instead, in the format of a negative one: the right not to have violence initiated against the baby. I arrive at the claim that it is impermissible for civilized persons to use each other as "objects." Of course we may do so. We do so all the time. When we purchase something on Amazon for example, we are using the people who man that operation totally as a means. We do not so much as know who they are. It is only the rare customer who even thinks about this. And, for most of these few who do, even only a distinct minority of them bestir themselves to inquire as to the health and well-being of the vendors. The overwhelming majority of us are instead focused on that which we are purchasing, its quality, delivery, price, etc. And, there is nothing untoward about this perfectly understandable reaction. Human

W. E. Block, *Evictionism*, https://doi.org/10.1007/978-981-16-5014-7_10

beneficence is in limited supply. It would do no one any good to refrain from using such people as means to an end, or "objects." The libertarian point, of course, is that we may do anything to other people, anything, as long as it is with their permission. Smith orders a cup of coffee. He barely glances at the waitress, let alone treats her as anything other than a coffee-dispensing machine. She, for her part, returns the favor, and deals with him as a money creating spigot. Both people violate the pope's strictures, and good for them, say I.

After this false start, Lee (pp. 8–9) returns to the straight and narrow. He maintains, quite properly, and, very eloquently,

> "... in normal reproduction a new organism of the relevant mammalian species is generated with the completion of the fertilization process ... this new human embryo is a whole, though obviously immature, human being."

He brilliantly refutes the criticism of this position to the effect that the fertilized egg is no different, from a legal point of view, than any other cell in the body. They all contain the entire DNA code.

Lee's refutation of this thesis is superlative (p. 11):

> "... in the human embryo, even at the one-cell stage, the program is totally active; in the somatic cell most of this information is 'switched off.' The argument simply ignores the profound and decisive differences between the two. No somatic cell has the active disposition to become a mature human being. No somatic cell will actively develop itself to a mature stage of a human being, requiring only a suitable environment for its natural development... Somatic cells, in the context of cloning, are analogous, then, not to embryos, but to gametes (spermatozoon and oocyte) ... Moreover, the argument comparing human embryos to somatic cells ignores the most obvious difference between any of our cells and a living human embryo. Each of our cells is a mere part of a larger organism; but the embryo himself or herself is a complete, though immature, human organism (human being). Somatic cells are not, and embryonic human beings are, distinct, self-integrating living beings actively disposed to direct their own maturation as members of the human species. Thus, if a skin cell dies, the human being does not; the human being lives on. If a human embryo dies, the entire human organism is dead, and cannot be replaced."

Lee (pp. 13–14) is also right on the money when it comes to lambasting Thomson for her equation of the right not to be murdered, with the right to vote. His criticism of her is nothing less than superlative:

> "We can begin to see that this view is mistaken by considering Thomson's comparison of the right to life with the right to vote. Thomson fails to advert to the fact that some rights vary with respect to place, circumstances, talents and other factors, while other rights do not. We recognize that one's right to life does not vary with place, as does one's right to vote. One may have the right to vote in Switzerland, but not in Mexico. Moreover, some rights and entitlements accrue to individuals only at certain times, or in certain places or situations, and others do not. But to have the right to life is to have moral status at all; to have the right to life, in other words, is to be the sort of entity that can have rights or entitlements to begin with. And so it is to be expected that this right would differ in some fundamental ways from other rights, such as a right to vote.

"In particular, it is reasonable to suppose ... that having moral status at all, as opposed to having a right to perform a specific action in a specific situation, follows from an entity's being the type of thing (or substantial entity) it is. And so, just as one's right to life does not come and go with one's location or situation, so it does not accrue to someone in virtue of an acquired (i.e., accidental) property, capacity, skill or disposition. Rather, this right belongs to a person, a substantial entity, at all times that he or she exists, not just during certain stages of his or her existence, or in certain circumstances, or in virtue of additional, accidental attributes."

It is time, now, to stop throwing bouquets in the direction of this author. After all, he supports the pro-life position, and, as I have taken pains to demonstrate, this is not the perspective compatible with libertarianism. Therefore, it is incorrect (☺).

Let me begin by saying that I agree, enthusiastically, with everything he writes in criticism of the pro-choice position. It is too bad that he is totally unaware that there is actually a third position, evictionism.

Let us now consider where his viewpoint and mine diverge. First, some minor points. States this author (p. 15):

"If abortion were morally acceptable on the grounds that the human embryo or fetus lacks such a capacity for characteristically human mental functions, then one would be logically committed to the view that, subject to parental approval, human infants could be disposed of as well" (emphasis added).

But why is parental approval necessary? According to the "logic" of the abortion supporters, baby humans would be fair game for anyone, whether parents approved or not. After all, even up to the toddler age, and sometimes beyond, the very young "lack ... characteristically human mental functions." Therefore, it should be open season on them, as it is for fish or chickens. If Jones kills a cow owed by Smith, the former is not guilty of murder, only property damage. If Jones kills Smith's child, there should be even less of a penalty, according to this "logic," since while Smith can own his cow, he cannot own his child. All he has is guardianship rights over his progeny.

Another minor disagreement arises with Lee's statement (p. 16) characterizing as "the most basic canon of justice: (that) similars should be treated similarly." This is of course true in a court of law. But, it opens up a whole can of worms were it to be employed elsewhere. Alice and Betty might be "similar" in every respect seen by an outsider, but Charlie wants to marry the one, not the other. May he propose to the one he loves, even though he would not thereby be treating these "similars" similarly? Of course he may.

Lee writes as follows on this matter (pp. 17–18):

"A ... major development in the recent abortion debate has been significant refinements of an argument first presented by Judith Jarvis Thomson in 1971. Following Thomson, these philosophers have attempted to justify abortion by denying (in effect) that all abortions are intentional killing. They have granted (at least for the sake of argument) that an unborn human being has a right to life, but have then argued that this right does not entail that the child in the womb is morally entitled to the use of the mother's body for life support. In effect, their argument is that, at least in many cases, abortion is not a case of intentionally killing the child, but a choice not to provide the child with assistance, that is, a choice to expel (or 'evict') the child from the womb, despite the likelihood or certainty that expulsion (or 'eviction') will result in his or her death (Thomson 1971a, b, c; McDonagh 1996.)"

Sorry, I cannot help it. I must toss yet another compliment in the direction of this author. Well, a critical compliment: he is far too generous to Thomson and Little. Neither so much as mentions the words "evict" or "eviction." As to McDonagh, the same applies. No, Lee, and Lee alone, in this group of non-libertarian commentators on this subject, deserves rare credit for mentioning this crucially important concept. In fact, I go so far as to claim, even in the absence of reading the entire non-libertarian literature on the pro-life, pro-choice debate, that Lee is the only analyst to have ever mentioned this perspective. However, unhappily, he deals with it rather superficially, and erroneously, as we shall see.

Lee (p. 18) continues, describing the views of his intellectual opponents:

> "Various analogies have been proposed by people making this argument. Famously, Thomson compared the mother's gestating a child to allowing someone the use of one's kidneys, and others have compared gestation to donating an organ. We are not required (morally or as a matter of law) to allow someone to use our kidneys, or to donate organs to others, even when they would die without this assistance (and we could survive in good health despite rendering it). Analogously, the argument continues, a woman is not morally required to allow the embryo or fetus the use of her body. Let us call this "the bodily rights argument" (Beckwith 1993). It may (be) objected that a woman has a special responsibility to the child she is carrying, whereas in the cases of withholding assistance to which abortion is compared there is no such special responsibility. Proponents of the bodily rights argument have replied, however, that the mother has not voluntarily assumed responsibility for the child, or a personal relationship with the child, and we have strong responsibilities to others only if we have voluntarily assumed such responsibilities (Thomson 1971a, b, c) or only if we have consented to a personal relationship which generates such responsibilities. True – say proponents of this argument – the mother may have voluntarily performed an act which she knew may result in a child's conception, but that is distinct from consenting to gestate the child if a child is conceived. And so (according to this position) it is not until the woman consents to pregnancy, or perhaps not until the parents consent to care for the child by taking the baby home from the hospital or birthing center, that the full duties of parenthood accrue to the mother (and perhaps the father)."

And how does Lee attempt to refute this argument? He opines (p. 18):

> "In reply to this argument I wish to make several points. It seems to me true that in some few cases abortion is not intentional killing, but a choice to expel the child, the child's death being an unintended, albeit foreseen and (rightly or wrongly) accepted, side effect. However, these constitute a small minority of abortions. In the vast majority of cases, the death of the child in the womb is precisely the object of the abortion. In most cases the end sought is to avoid being a parent; but abortion brings that about only by bringing about the death of the child. Indeed, the attempted abortion would be considered by the woman requesting it and the abortionist performing it to have been unsuccessful if the child survived. In most cases abortion is intentional killing. Thus, even if the bodily rights argument succeeded, it would justify only a small percentage of abortions."

But this will not do.

The first problem: where oh where has the concept of eviction gone? After having mentioned this in passing, our author has no more truck with this notion. But as the entirety of the present book is intent upon demonstrating, without making the distinction between abortion and eviction, no sense can be made of this challenge. Second, the number of abortions which take place is almost entirely irrelevant to what should be our concern in this matter. We are embarked upon a mission to shed philosophical light on this issue. If even one abortion as opposed to eviction occurs, then it constitutes plain old first degree murder. To dismiss the importance of abortion on this ground as Lee does, is to deprecate a rare form of murder. Just because something occurs only rarely is no reason not to focus our spotlight on it. Third, there is the question of the motivation of the abortionist. Whether the purpose is to "avoid being a parent" or not is entirely irrelevant to the question of whether or not it is a crime in the first place. In my view, it is difficult to avoid that conclusion; it most certainly is criminal behavior. Fourth, I must take issue with Lee's concession to the abortion supporters to the effect that if the bodily rights argument succeeded, it would justify only a small percentage of abortions. No, no, no, the bodily rights argument does indeed succeed. The unwanted fetus is a trespasser, and has no right to avail himself of the property of another person, the mother in this case. However, no small percentage of abortions is ever justified as a result of this consideration, or, indeed, of any other.

Another difficulty with this response of Lee's to the "bodily rights argument" is that it contradicts what he says elsewhere. Here, he supports a continuum stance. He relies on there being only degrees of difference, not in-kind ones. For example, he speaks of "small minority of abortions," "in most cases," "a small percentage," etc.

However, elsewhere in his otherwise splendid essay of his he takes the very opposite, and correct, point of view. For example:

> "Death is not just worse in degree than the difficulties involved in pregnancy, it is worse in kind."

As well as here (pp. 15–16):

> "Between the ovum and the approaching thousands of sperm, on the one hand, and the embryonic human being, on the other hand, there is a clear difference in kind. But between the embryonic human being and that same human being at any later stage of its maturation, there is only a difference in degree. One might object to this that sometimes one must draw a line at some arbitrary point: if there are no more than quantitative differences among infants, fetuses, embryos, and sperm and ova, then one simply must pick a dividing line somewhere along that continuum. However, there is a fundamental difference (as shown above) between the gametes (the sperm and the ovum) on the one hand, and the human embryo and fetus, on the other. When a human being comes to be, then a substantial entity that is identical with the entity that will later reason, make free choices, and so on, begins to exist. So, those who propose an accidental characteristic as qualifying an entity as a bearer of the right to life (or as a "person" or being of "moral worth") are ignoring a radical difference among groups of beings (a difference in kind, not a mere difference in degree), and instead fastening onto a mere quantitative difference as the basis for treating different groups in radically different ways. In other words, there are beings a, b, c, d, e, etc. And between a's and b's on the one hand, and c's, d's and e's on the other hand, there is a fundamental difference, a difference in kind not just in degree. But proponents of the position that being a person is an accidental characteristic ignore that difference and pick out a mere difference in degree between, say, d's and e's, and make that the basis for radically different types of treatment (emphasis added by present author)."

Could Lee defend himself against this charge? He might say that for some quandaries an all or none (in kind) analysis is apropos; while for others, a more gradual perspective must be taken. This, indeed, is true, in general. It is unlikely in the extreme that one analytic tool would suffice for all challenges. But the specifics of these two cases suggest otherwise. Both cases reek of an all or none essence, not one of marginalism, or gradualism, or continuumism, if I may be permitted to coin a word. In the first case, Lee is incorrect in focusing on the number of babies slaughtered. Any one murder of a preborn infant is one way too many. In the second case, he is entirely correct. When we view the sperm and the egg, in isolation from one another, there is no human being; however, when they merge, at that point and thereafter there most certainly is one. There is no intermediate ground. There never is in this entire process, any such thing as a partial person.

Lee (p. 19) writes as follows: "Of course, in many abortions there may be mixed motives: the parties making the choice may intend both ending the condition of pregnancy and the death of the child."

This is true. However, in all abortions, without any exception whatsoever, the baby perishes. If the young human being does not die, then it is not an abortion. Rather, it is an eviction, or an ejection, call it what you will. True, this is only a verbal matter, but it is of the utmost importance, as important as life or death, for that is what hangs in the balance for the youngster.

Let us consider yet another instance wherein Lee (p. 19) and I diverge:

> "... while it is true that in some cases abortion is not intentional killing, it is misleading to describe it simply as choosing not to provide bodily life support. Rather, it is actively expelling the human embryo or fetus from the womb. There is a significant moral difference between not doing something that would assist someone, and doing something that causes someone harm, even if that harm is an unintended (but foreseen) side effect. It is more difficult morally to justify the latter than it is the former. Abortion is the act of extracting the unborn human being from the womb – an extraction that usually rips him or her to pieces or does him or her violence in some other way.
>
> "It is true that in some cases causing death as a side effect is morally permissible. For example, in some cases it is morally right to use force to stop a potentially lethal attack on one's family or country, even if one foresees that the force used will also result in the assailant's death. Similarly, there are instances in which it is permissible to perform an act that one knows or believes will, as a side effect, cause the death of a child in the womb. For example, if a pregnant woman is discovered to have a cancerous uterus, and this is a proximate danger to the mother's life, it can be morally right to remove the cancerous uterus with the baby in it, even if the child will die as a result."

Here, Lee comes so close, so very close, to embracing, or, at the very least, taking cognizance of, my evictionism theory. He says that "Abortion is the act of extracting the unborn human being from the womb – an extraction that usually rips him or her to pieces or does him or her violence in some other way." Usually? This means sometimes yes, sometimes no. Specifically, sometimes the baby is ripped to shreds but at other times this is not the case. And, when this is not what happens, what does occur? Why, an eviction! The mother rids herself of the unwanted fetus while the latter lives! If that is not close to seeing the point, then nothing is. Unfortunately, this is a near miss. I cannot award the proverbial cigar to this author.

Lee (p. 20) next considers the case of a man with a child who suffers from a respiratory problem, and opines that he certainly should not smoke at home, and, should even move his family to another city with less pollution, despite the fact that he then must take a less satisfactory job as a result.

Even from a common sense point of view, there are complications here. Suppose the lesser paying job in the other city puts at risk his other children. Or, possibly, the less satisfactory job is far less satisfactory, so much so that the father is depressed, and the child ends up being hurt even the more. The point is that these considerations are all marginal ones, and it is difficult, in the absence of specifics, to make any such determination in all possible cases.

Our author continues (p. 20):

> "... a) the parent has a special responsibility to his child, but (b) the act that would cause the child's death would avoid a harm to the parent but cause a significantly worse harm to his child. And so, although the harm done would be a side effect, in both cases the act that caused the death would be an unjust act, and morally wrongful as such. The special responsibility of parents to their children requires that they at least refrain from performing acts that cause terrible harms to their children in order to avoid significantly lesser harms to themselves. But (a) and (b) also obtain in intentional abortions (that is, those in which the removal of the child is directly sought, rather than the correction of a life-threatening pathology) even though they are not, strictly speaking, intentional killing. First, the mother has a special responsibility to her child, in virtue of being her biological mother (as does the father in virtue of his paternal relationship). The parental relationship itself – not just the voluntary acceptance of that relationship – gives rise to a special responsibility to a child."

The heart of all men of good will cries out in support of these thoughts. Of course, it is estimable for parents to place the welfare of their children above their own. Such behavior is eminently virtuous. Most of us would not be here at all, or, in very worse circumstances, did our own parents not do things of this sort for us.

However, let us look at this from the libertarian perspective. Remember, this philosophy is solely and only an analysis of criminality. Its lone focus is to distinguish between actions (or non-actions) that should be legal from those that should not pass muster under this criterion. Murder, rape and theft? Clearly, criminal behavior. But failing to be a good parent, even a decent one? That is a horse of an entirely different color. One of the building blocks of libertarianism is that there are no positive obligations. We are only required to live up to our contractual agreements, for, if we do not, that amounts to theft, a rights violation. For example, I borrow money from you, and then fail to repay my debt to you. It is as if I have stolen these funds. But, there is simply no contract between the parent and child, which should legally require the former to care for the latter, no matter how righteous that would be. In this view, the parent has no "special responsibility to his child." If he does not want to be its guardian, all he need do is bring it to someone else who will do so: the orphanage, the church, the hospital, etc.

But Lee is not finished imposing obligations on parents, not quite yet. He avers (pp. 20–21):

> "... parents have special responsibilities to their children from conception on ... (because) ... their voluntary action has caused the child to be in an especially imperiled condition. The point is that one is, in general, responsible for the foreseen consequences of one's actions, even if one has also tried to prevent them."

I engage in risky behavior. I break my leg as a result. I must assume responsibility for my plight. Does this mean I may not pay a doctor to set my broken bone? Of course I may do exactly that. Yes, one is indeed "responsible for the foreseen consequences of one's actions." But my "responsibility" does not mean I cannot legitimately act so as to ward off the harm to me of my impetuous action with a physician's help. Similarly, there is no legal requirement that parents be "responsible" for caring for their children.

What about the charge of the parents placing the baby in "... an especially imperiled condition?" Compared to what? Let us contrast this to not being conceived in the first place. It seems clear that the parents, in connecting their egg and sperm, have improved the condition of the baby; they have reduced the "peril" that previously beset this infant; that is, the "peril" of non-existence. They have done more for this very young child than any other two people on the entire planet. To then blame them, and call upon them to do even more for him, appears somewhat of an unfair imposition.

Lee (p. 22) asks a very important question:

> "Clearly, whatever the precise explanation of why it is so, parents do have a responsibility to make sacrifices for their children, even if they have not voluntarily assumed such responsibilities, or given their consent to the personal relationship with the child. What is the source of this special responsibility?"

He answers this query as follows (pp. 23–24):

> "... we are by nature members of communities. Our moral goodness or character consists to a large extent (though not solely) in contributing to the communities of which we are members. We ought to act for our genuine good or flourishing (I take that as a basic ethical principle), but our flourishing involves being in communion with others. And communion with others of itself – even if we find ourselves united with others because of a physical or social relationship which precedes our consent – entails duties or responsibilities. Moreover, the contribution we are morally required to make to others will likely bring each of us some discomfort and pain. This is not to say that we should simply ignore our own good, for the sake of others. Rather, since what I am, who I am, is in part constituted by various relationships with others, not all of which are initiated by my will, my genuine good includes the contributions I make to the relationships in which I participate. Thus, the life we constitute by our free choices should be in large part a life of mutual reciprocity with others. For example, I may wish to cultivate my talent to write and so I may want to spend hours each day reading and writing. Or I may wish to develop my athletic abilities and so I may want to spend hours every day on the baseball field. But if I am a father of minor children, and have an adequate paying job working (say) in a coal mine, then my clear duty is to keep that job. Similarly, if one's girlfriend finds she is pregnant and one is the father, then one might also be morally required to continue one's work in the coal mine (or steel mill, factory, warehouse, etc.). In other words, I have a duty to do something with my life that contributes to the good of the human community, but that general duty becomes specified by my particular situation. It becomes specified by the connection or closeness to me of those who are in need. We acquire special responsibilities toward people, not only by consenting to contracts or relationships with them, but also by having various types of unions with them. So, we have special responsibilities to those people with whom we are closely united. For example, we have special responsibilities to our parents, and brothers and sisters, even though we did not choose them. The physical unity or continuity of children to their parents is unique. The child is brought into being out of the bodily unity and bodies of the mother

> and the father. The mother and the father are in a certain sense prolonged or continued in their offspring. So, there is a natural unity of the mother with her child, and a natural unity of the father with his child. Since we have special responsibilities to those with whom we are closely united, it follows that we in fact do have a special responsibility to our children anterior to our having voluntarily assumed such responsibility or consented to the relationship."

There are grave problems with the foregoing, at least for the libertarian. First of all, this philosophy is not at all concerned with morality, only with an aspect of it, namely, what is just law. A man might be morally obligated to do, and refrain from doing, certain actions, but this does not necessarily imply that the law ought to compel him to act in such a manner. For example, it might be moral to pray, or to study, but a law requiring such behavior would be an immoral one. Or, it might well be immoral to drink alcohol, but that hardly justifies prohibition.

Secondly, hermits are not "in communion with others." But, it would be unjust to have separate laws for such people. Therefore, being "in communion with others" cannot establish legal duties.

Third, slaves were indeed "in communion with others." But this was decidedly against their will. When Lee says this, it is all too easy to interpret this as support for the "curious institution": "Rather, since what I am, who I am, is in part constituted by various relationships with others, not all of which are initiated by my will, my genuine good includes the contributions I make to the relationships in which I participate." But the slaves "participated" in slavery. It is difficult to deny this. Thus, if Lee wants to ward off the charge that he favors slavery, which I have no reason to assume otherwise, he is logically required to acknowledge that "consent" is all important; that without it, his entire edifice falls to the ground. And, yet, he is attempting to disparage the importance of accord. He cannot be allowed to do so.

Fourth, this author is attempting to impose positive obligations on all people. This is certainly incompatible with libertarianism, the philosophy that rejects all such notions, root and branch.

Fifth, just how far does this Christian philosopher intend to extend his claim? To people in other cities, other states, other countries? He talks of the "human community," but why only members of our own species. Surely, we are "in communion with" our brothers and sisters of field and stream. Are we not obliged not only not to kill and eat them, but to call forth succor on their behalf? It seems that vegetarianism is a "special responsibility" of ours.

Next, consider this statement (p. 24):

> "... we have received benefits from our parents and society and therefore have a duty to help others who are in need in similar ways that we have been."

But to say this is to trash the concept of charity, something, surely, that a "Christian philosopher" should be loath to do. For donations to the poor, or others, cannot imply any obligation to anyone else, otherwise it ceases to be philanthropy, and becomes, rather, a contractual arrangement, such as barter. I will give you some money provided you do something for me is a sale, not an act of altruism. Yes, it would be "nice" to give back something to those, including "society" who have given to us. But, libertarianism, qua libertarianism, is not concerned with being agreeable, being responsible, being a good citizen, being a good neighbor, etc. It is focused, solely, on legal requirements, and there are none here.

Our author now engages in a bit of utilitarianism (p. 25):

> "... in the types of cases we are considering, the harm caused (death) is much worse than the harms avoided (the difficulties in pregnancy). Pregnancy can involve severe impositions, but it is not nearly as bad as death – which is total and irreversible."

This constitutes a foundation of quicksand upon which to build a legal system. Yes, of course, most people would vastly prefer a serious inconvenience to being done away with. That is why, apart from Jack Benny, when a holdup man threatens us with "Your money or your life," we quickly give up the former. But this is of no help in determining just law. Suppose the victim gets the drop on this criminal; would it be wrong for the former to shoot the latter, even though he may well die, and at the very least be in danger of losing a limb or spending months in hospital? Hardly. Suppose the victim only has a few dollars in his possession, and the robber will be satisfied with that small amount of money. According to Lee, the victim would be proscribed from shooting the perpetrator on these utilitarian grounds he sets forth. Yet this will not only appear unjust to most people, it will certainly contravene libertarian theory. The victim has every right to plug the mugger, even apart from the fact that he can never be sure that the latter will be satisfied with the lean pickings afforded him. And, suppose instead, that the victim has his life savings in his pocket. May he then be entitled to shoot the attacker. No, no, no, I will not follow Lee down this garden path of utilitarianism. The prey is entitled to protect his property with deadly force no matter how valuable it is. Thieves beware!

Nor can I see my way clear to agreeing with this sally of Lee's (p. 25):

> "Where the pregnancy is unwanted, the baby's 'occupying' the mother's womb may involve a harm; but the child is committing no injustice against her. The baby is not forcing himself or herself on the woman, but is simply growing and developing in a way quite natural to him or her. The baby is not performing any action that could in any way be construed as aimed at violating the mother."

Of course, the infant is not purposefully intending to "force himself" on his mother; he is not "aiming at violating" her. We do not properly attribute purposeful behavior to fetuses. But he is indeed "occupying" property that does not belong to him. The mother, not the young child, is the proper owner of her body, particularly, her womb. She was "there" first, long before this conception occurred. She might have beat him by as much as two or even three dozen years. He is not aiming at "violating the mother" but that is precisely what he is doing. Consider the fertilized egg who is a product of rape. He no more intends to "force himself" or to "violate" the mother any more than members of his age cohort who are created from voluntary sexual intercourse. But he, too, is "occupying" territory that he simply does not own.

I started out this commentary of Lee on a very positive note, and I again congratulate him for those initial pro human life statements of his. I am especially grateful to him for at least coming close to taking evictionism seriously. But, I am an evictionist, not a pro-lifer, so I have had many critical things to say about this very important essay of Lee's.

References

Beckwith, F.J. 1993. *Politically Correct Death: Answering Arguments for Abortion Rights*. Grand Rapids: Baker Books.

McDonagh, E.L. 1996. *Breaking the Abortion Deadlock: From Choice to Consent*. New York: Oxford University Press.

Thomson, Judith Jarvis. 1971a. A Defense of Abortion. *Philosophy and Public Affairs* I: 47–66.

———. 1971b. *A Defense of Abortion*. University of Colorado at Boulder, Fall, 2007, March 4. http://spot.colorado.edu/~heathwoo/Phil160,Fall02/thomson.htm

———. 1971c. A Defense of Abortion. *Philosophy & Public Affairs* 1 (1, Fall); Reprinted in Intervention and Reflection: Basic Issues in Medical Ethics, 5th ed., ed. Ronald Munson (Belmont; Wadsworth 1996), 69–80.

Chapter 11
Marquis on Abortion

This is a two part chapter, both elements devoted to a libertarian commentary on the views of Marquis on abortion. The first will deal with Marquis (1989) and the second with Marquis (2007).

I. Marquis (1989)

Our author sets out for himself an exceedingly modest goal. He eschews discussion of the "hard cases" such as abortion after rape or to save the woman's life or health, and contents himself by writing that "The purpose of this essay is to develop a general argument for the claim that the overwhelming majority of deliberate abortions are seriously immoral."

One might at this point seriously question why I am including my commentary on his essay in this section of the present book, given that I am intent upon comparing and contrasting the libertarian perspective on abortion, e.g., evictionism, with non-libertarian scholars such as Marquis. All I can see this point is, Gentle reader, keep reading. There will indeed be philosophical space between his and my perspective on these issues.

Marquis first sets himself the task of what makes killing of anyone wrong, whether fetus, child or adult. In his view

> "What primarily makes killing wrong is neither its effect on the murderer nor its effect on the victim's friends and relatives, but its effect on the victim. The loss of one's life is one of the greatest losses one can suffer. The loss of one's life deprives one of all the experiences, activities, projects, and enjoyments which would otherwise have constituted one's future. Therefore, killing someone is wrong, primarily because the killing inflicts (one of) the greatest possible losses on the victim."

But this is the rankest of utilitarianism. The libertarian view, in sharp contrast, is that we each own our own bodies, and, for anyone to murder us is a violation of the libertarian non-aggression principle (NAP) and an infringement of our private

W. E. Block, *Evictionism*, https://doi.org/10.1007/978-981-16-5014-7_11

property rights, two of the basic foundational building blocks of this philosophy. Suppose the following. Jones is dying of a dread and painful disease. He is on his last legs. He will soon, in two minutes, be "deprive(d) … of all the experiences, activities, projects, and enjoyments which would otherwise have constituted (his) future." Whereupon Smith comes along and delivers a fatal bullet to Jones. Was Smith a murderer even though he didn't "deprive" Smith of more than two minutes' worth of "future"? Of course Smith is guilty of this crime. Murder is incompatible with the libertarian philosophy, albeit not necessarily for utilitarianism, as this scenario demonstrates. In sharp contrast, had Jones' doctor delivered a mercy killing to him, at Jones' request, our conclusion would be far different.

But Marquis is having none of this. He avers:

> "Persons who are severely and incurably ill, who face a future of pain and despair, and who wish to die will not have suffered a loss if they are killed. It is, strictly speaking, the value of a human's future which makes killing wrong in this theory. This being so, killing does not necessarily wrong some persons who are sick and dying." (emphasis added by present author)

Forget about that "who wish to die" business. Posit that, stubbornly, unreasonably, obstinately, unwisely, stupidly, they refuse to die. They cling to life, perhaps in the hope that a miracle cure will soon appear; perhaps out of sheer bloody mindedness. If the wrongness of murdering them stems from people like Marquis determining that they will not "suffer a loss" if they are shot or poisoned, then it would be justified to do exactly that, at least on his utilitarian grounds. However, contrary to Marquis, on the basis of libertarianism they still have a right not to be murdered, no matter what loss they may or may not suffer.

This author separates himself from libertarianism when it comes to inflicting pain. He asserts:

> "The structure of this anti-abortion argument can be both illuminated and defended by comparing it to what appears to be the best argument for the wrongness of the wanton infliction of pain on animals. This latter argument is based on the assumption that it is prima facie wrong to inflict pain on me (or you, reader). What is the natural property associated with the infliction of pain which makes such infliction wrong? The obvious answer seems to be that the infliction of pain causes suffering and that suffering is a misfortune. The suffering caused by the infliction of pain is what makes the wanton infliction of pain on me wrong. The wanton infliction of pain on other adult humans causes suffering. The wanton infliction of pain on animals causes suffering. Since causing suffering is what makes the wanton infliction of pain wrong and since the wanton infliction of pain on animals causes suffering, it follows that the wanton infliction of pain on animals is wrong."

To be sure, part of the explanation of why this author and I part company is that he is concerned with what is "wrong," while I as a libertarian focus, only, on whether a given act should be declared illegal. But this is only a part of our disagreement. For the record, I join Marquis in condemning the infliction of pain on any creature, human or not, as "wrong." However, what about the people who cannot feel pain? Their nerve receptors do not deliver such messages to their brains. If we take Marquis' analysis literally, then it would be open season on such unfortunate people. We predators should be able to legally, and not "wrongfully," smack them around, hit them, maybe even murder them. But this is surely a reductio ad absurdum of his thesis. From a libertarian point of view it is impermissible to do any such thing to such individuals, even though they will not feel pain from our depredations. Rather, the "wrongness," or better yet, the illegality, stems from the fact that they are rights bearing creatures, and to molest them in this or any other such manner is to violate these rights of theirs. Moreover, if avoidance of "pain" is the only consideration, then it would be quite alright for the doctor to murder the patient while he is on the operating table, unconscious from the drugs given to him by the anesthesiologist. Pain is to be avoided, surely, but it cannot be the be-all and end-all of legal analysis.

Nor can I see my way clear to agreeing with this statement of our author's:

> "Presumably abortion could be justified in some circumstances, only if the loss consequent on failing to abort would be at least as great. Accordingly, morally permissible abortions will be rare indeed unless, perhaps, they occur so early in pregnancy that a fetus is not yet definitely an individual. Hence, this argument should be taken as showing that abortion is presumptively very seriously wrong, where the presumption is very strong – as strong as the presumption that kilting (sic) another adult human being is wrong."

Again, we have a profoundly disparate way of looking at these matters. In what I take to be the libertarian point of view, abortion, that is, killing the fetus while still inside of the mother, and then evicting him, rather than eviction with no killing, is justified only in the mother's self-defense: if and only if the unborn baby will kill or injure the mother unless that is done; but it would be the truly rare case when this would be necessary, and mere eviction would not suffice to protect the pregnant woman. In contrast, Marquis sees this as sort of "balancing act": which "loss" is greater, and the goal is to reduce overall "losses." I disagree, also, with the claim that at any stage of its development "a fetus is not yet definitely an individual." As far as I am concerned, the tiny infant is a human individual, with equal rights as any other person, from the fertilized egg stage and onward. Marquis thinks "abortion is immoral" but his claim that the fetus becomes "an individual" only later on is a weak foundation upon which to make that claim.

Perhaps I have been misinterpreting Marquis, or, maybe he is a bit inconsistent, when he writes:

> "… we do regard it as seriously wrong to kill persons who have little desire to live or who have no desire to live or, indeed, have a desire not to live. We believe it is seriously wrong to kill the unconscious, the sleeping, those who are tired of life, and those who are suicidal."

I could not have said this better myself. I am now ready to issue a libertarian card to this author. This is exactly on point. But, how, then, to interpret his statements above, for example, to the effect that pain is so important? This is somewhat of a mystery.

And what are we to say about this view of our authors?

> "It is also worth noting that, if future desires have moral force in a modified desire account of the wrongness of killing, one can find support for an anti-abortion ethic even in the absence of a value of a future-like-ours account. If one decides that a morally relevant property, the possession of which is sufficient to make it wrong to kill some individual, is the

> desire at some future time to live – one might decide to justify one's refusal to kill suicidal teenagers on these grounds, for example – then, since typical fetuses will have the desire in the future to live, it is wrong to kill typical fetuses. Accordingly, it does not seem that a desire account of the wrongness of killing can provide a justification of a pro-choice ethic of abortion which is nearly as adequate as the value of a human-future justification of an anti-abortion ethic."

The major difficulty here is that it is difficult to attribute to the fetus: "the desire at some future time to live." It is not easy to deny this, nor to affirm it, since none of us can recollect what it was like when we ourselves occupied this category. My best surmise is that the fetus has no "desires" whatsoever. That he is just sort of lying there, merely existing, as if the most powerful coma that an adult can experience. This being the case, Marquis' example cannot suffice to oppose abortion since, if this is the only criteria, it would indeed be justified to kill the preborn infant, since, by stipulation if for no other reason, he does not, at least at present "desire at some future time to live."

Marquis continues:

> "Is the discontinuation account just as good an account as the value of a future-like-ours account? The discontinuation account will not be adequate at all, if it does not refer to the value of the experience that may be discontinued. One does not want the discontinuation account to make it wrong to kill a patient who begs for death and who is in severe pain that cannot be relieved short of killing... Accordingly, the discontinuation account must be more than a bare discontinuation account. It must make some reference to the positive value of the patient's experiences. But, by the same token, the value of a future-like-ours account cannot be a bare future account either. Just having a future surely does not itself rule out killing the above patient. This account must make some reference to the value of the patient's future experiences and projects also. Hence, both accounts involve the value of experiences, projects, and activities. So far we still have symmetry between the accounts."

I contend it is improper for this author to hark to mercy killing, which would be fully compatible with libertarian law. What if this sufferer does not want to have someone murder him? He is still in as much pain as his counterpart who asks for death. And, yet, according to the criterion of "the value of the patient's future experiences" he is not more a candidate to be protected from killing than is the person who requests death. Yet, surely, it should be illegal to murder the masochist who wants to continue to live despite great agony. So, I say to Marquis, value schmvalue. The reason is it wrong to murder someone has nothing to do with the "value" of his life; it is because he is a human being, and, according to libertarian law, it is a rights violation to kill a member of our species, no matter how young or old, in pain or pain free.

References

Marquis, Don B. 1989. Why Abortion Is Immoral. *Journal of Philosophy* 86: 183–202.

———. 2007. An Argument That Abortion Is Wrong. In *Ethical Theory: An Anthology*, ed. Russ Shafer-Landau, 439–450. Blackwell.

Chapter 12
Tooley on Abortion: A Rejoinder

Tooley (1972) sets an important question for himself:

> "The basic issue to be discussed, then, is what properties a thing must possess in order to have a serious right to life." He defends the position that "this condition is not satisfied by human fetuses and infants, and thus that they do not have a right to life."

He maintains:

> "In contrast, it may turn out that our treatment of adult members of other species-cats, dogs, polar bears-is morally indefensible. For it is quite possible that such animals do possess properties that endow them with a right to life."

So, human babies are not rights bearing entities, while our brothers and sisters of field and stream may properly be characterized in this manner. This author has a lot of "splaining" to do.

He starts out on the wrong foot with this passage:

> "The problem the liberal encounters is essentially that of specifying a cutoff point which is not arbitrary: at what stage in the development of a human being does it cease to be morally permissible to destroy *it*?" (emphasis added by present author).

What is my objection? Tooley uses the word "it" to refer to a preborn child. It is my contention that "it" properly refers to his "cats, dogs, polar bears" but not to human beings, at whatever stage, including the fertilized egg. Yes, this is a minor point, not to say a mere verbal one, but it sets the stage for what comes later. This scholar and I view the fetus very differently.

Consider this bit of philosophical analysis of his:

> "How is the term 'person' to be interpreted? I shall treat the concept of a person as a purely moral concept, free of all descriptive content. Specifically, in my usage the sentence 'X is a person' will be synonymous with the sentence 'X has a (serious) moral right to life.' This usage diverges slightly from what is perhaps the more common way of interpreting the term 'person' when it is employed as a purely moral term, where to say that X is a person is to say that X has rights. If everything that had rights had a right to life, these interpretations would be extensionally equivalent. But I am inclined to think that it does not follow from acceptable moral principles that whatever has any rights at all has a right to life. My reason is this. Given the choice between being killed and being tortured for an hour, most adult humans would surely choose the latter. So it seems plausible to say it is worse to kill an adult human being than it is to torture him for an hour. In contrast, it seems to me that while

W. E. Block, *Evictionism*, https://doi.org/10.1007/978-981-16-5014-7_12

> it is not seriously wrong to kill a newborn kitten, it is seriously wrong to torture one for an hour. This suggests that newborn kittens may have a right not to be tortured without having a serious right to life."

A difficulty with the foregoing concerns the distinction between the normative and the positive. He slips, almost imperceptibly from an "is" to an "ought" ignoring Hume's (1739) warnings to the contrary.

Stated Hume (1739):

> "In every system of morality, which I have hitherto met with, I have always remark'd, that the author proceeds for some time in the ordinary way of reasoning, and establishes the being of a God, or makes observations concerning human affairs; when of a sudden I am surpriz'd to find, that instead of the usual copulations of propositions, is, and is not, I meet with no proposition that is not connected with an ought, or an ought not. This change is imperceptible; but is, however, of the last consequence. For as this ought, or ought not, expresses some new relation or affirmation, 'tis necessary that it shou'd be observ'd and explain'd; and at the same time that a reason should be given, for what seems altogether inconceivable, how this new relation can be a deduction from others, which are entirely different from it ... [I] am persuaded, that a small attention [to this point] wou'd subvert all the vulgar systems of morality, and let us see, that the distinction of vice and virtue is not founded merely on the relations of objects, nor is perceiv'd by reason."

And how, pray tell, does Tooley run afoul of the brilliant insight that you may not deduce an "ought" from an "is"? What is his "is?" It is that "Given the choice between being killed and being tortured for an hour, most adult humans would surely choose the latter." Well, maybe so; no, probably so. I know I would make that decision. But this is, surely, merely an "is." It is part and parcel of what economists call "positive economics." It is a statement of fact, not values. Yet, from this basic premise, Tooley draws all sorts of "oughts," which are characterized in the dismal science as "normative economics." For example, "So it seems plausible to say it is worse to kill an adult human being than it is to torture him for an hour." Plausible? Yes, perhaps. But valid? No, because this constitutes deducing an "ought" from an "is."

On the basis of this philosophical excursion, this author arrives at the following conclusion: "while it is not seriously wrong to kill a newborn kitten, it is seriously wrong to torture one for an hour. This suggests that newborn kittens may have a right not to be tortured without having a serious right to life." Those considerations may indeed suggest this to Tooley, but they by no means logically follow. Just because it is rather disgusting to torture a kitten does not at all mean it is a rights violation. This philosopher, here, argues in a circle, assuming the truth of the very point at issue: do animals such as cats have rights? If they do, then, when a dog kills a cat, the former is a murderer and the latter a murder victim. This "suggests" to me that Tooley is in error, here. Just because, admittedly, it is far more despicable[1] to torture than to cleanly kill a kitten does not at all lead to the conclusion that this creature has any rights at all humans are legally obliged to respect.

---

[1] In my subjective tastes, which I share with Tooley.

But Tooley is not without a response, and a powerful one at that. He might reply that he is only trying to show that "X has rights" does not imply "X has a right to life." He takes it to be intuitively obvious that it is wrong to torture a cat but not intuitively obvious that it is wrong to kill a newborn kitten. If it is wrong to torture the cat, then, in his usage, the cat has a right not to be tortured. But the cat does not have a right not to be killed in this interpretation. Tooley is here not deducing an "ought" from an "is." He is starting with the "ought" principle, "If it is wrong to do some act to X, it is wrong to do some worse act to X." He concludes that for humans, "if it is wrong to torture X, it is wrong to kill X" based on this principle. But he holds that for cats, it is false that killing them is worse than torturing them, so the principle "If it is wrong to do some act to X, it is wrong to do some worse act to X" cannot be used to show that it is wrong to kill cats. In other words, Tooley is not deducing an "ought" from an "is"; rather, he is deducing one "ought" from another "ought."

But this response is problematic, since, as stated above, Tooley arrives at his first "ought" from an "is": which setback people would likely prefer, an hour's torture or death? This quandary surely falls into the "is" category, not the "ought" one. But some people might prefer to be murdered rather than tortured. Ditto for those seriously considering suicide. These preferences also lie in the realm of the "is" not the "ought." So, it is difficult to avoid the conclusion that our author is indeed still committing the is-ought fallacy regarding humans. As to cats, if they were asked, "which would you prefer, to be tortured for one minute, or killed outright?" I presume they would favor the former, assuming they were capable of answering any such question. True, I reduced the torture time from 60 to one minute, but why quibble about aspects of the "is?" If I were the "God" of cats, charged with promoting their well-being, I would certainly choose torture for one minute in their behalf, even for one hour, rather than death.

Tooley might respond that only those capable of recognizing obligations have them. Thus, dogs, wolves, lions, cannot be murderers. But he may also maintain that this does not preclude animals from having moral claims, i.e., rights, against those who can recognize them, namely, human beings.

Consider the following retort to him: There is a shortcoming with this possible riposte. Forget about the dog for the moment, focus on the cat. Tooley claims that the latter has rights. If so, when a dog kills it, its rights have been violated. This author might then reply, yes, the cat has rights, but only against humans, who can "recognize obligations." But rights inhere to the victim. They are "located," if we can be permitted a bit of geographical poetry here, within the victim, not between the victim and the victimizer.

But this will not suffice. If it did my rights would be violated by an earthquake or a storm or a flood or a volcano. Ditto for a lion. If I have a right, you have an obligation to respect it; but, only if "you" are not a volcano or a tiger, that is, if you are a sentient being, who recognizes obligations.

Storms, volcanos have no rights. If we cloud seed against the former, and plug up the latter, they cannot complain of a rights violation. Given that storms and volcanoes have no rights, and, of course they do not, they are not blameworthy, then this applies to lions that attack zebras, dogs that kill cats and cats that dispatch rats.

However, consider these two claims. First, only those capable of recognizing obligations have moral obligations. Thus, lions and tigers have no moral obligations. They may "have at" zebras and cows to their heart's content, without being branded as murderers. However, here is a second claim: only "those capable of recognizing obligations have" rights. Neither cats nor dogs, nor lions, tigers, cows and zebras are so capable. Therefore, none of them have rights.

What of the following argument? Animals recognize obligations. They urinate so as to demonstrate property rights, by marking their turf. The dog that pees when not supposed to takes on a guilty "hang-dog" expression.

I reject this criticism. It seems a bit too anthropomorphic. Does the wolf really have a sense of property rights? Why, then, does he attack the farmer's sheep? If the response is that he recognizes only his own rights to property, that hardly rises to the level of respect for this institution. As to the countenance of the ill-behaved canine, are we really sure we correctly interpret his facial expression? And that this is due to guilt, as opposed to the opprobrium he usually encounters when urinating out of turn?

Tooley now asks the $64 thousand dollar question:

> "What properties must something have in order to be a person, i.e., to have a serious right to life? The claim I wish to defend is this: An organism possesses a serious right to life only if it possesses the concept of a self as a continuing subject of experiences and other mental states, and believes that it is itself such a continuing entity."

The obvious objection to this is that while, yes, a fetus, even a one-year-old child would not pass muster under this requirement, something that this author might view with a certain equanimity, neither would a sleeping, or unconscious adult, and this might well perturb him. But, this is only a first approximation of his theory, so we wait with bated breath to see how he deals with this objection. He is not long in satisfying us in this regard.

Tooley attempts to obviate this obvious objection to his theory regarding the sleeping or comatose person who fails the "self-consciousness requirement." He is very thorough in attempting to do so. He mentions three cases which fail this requirement, but, nevertheless, he avers, it would be wrong to kill such a person. They are:

> "(i) situations in which an individual's desires reflect a state of emotional disturbance; (ii) situations in which a previously conscious individual is temporarily unconscious; (iii) situations in which an individual's desires have been distorted by conditioning or by indoctrination."

This is all well and good. The issue is, do these attempted obviations succeed in preserving his thesis against the charge of being a logical howler. I cannot think that they do. Consider the fetus, or the one-year-old baby. His desires, if they exist at all, may be fairly characterized as "disturbed." Second, both the pre-born and the post-born baby can be construed as "temporarily unconscious." The point is, Tooley is trying to drive a philosophical wedge between the out-of-sorts adult, who certainly has the right not to be murdered, and the young baby, who, he thinks, lacks this saving grace. But, he has not done so. Both, not only the former, can be interpreted as "disturbed," or "temporarily unconscious." Adults can be in comas for as long as nine months. It is difficult to see why a fertilized egg, which will be "out of sorts" for an equal amount of time, should have fewer rights than an adult afflicted in an all but identical manner.

Tooley at this point summarizes his position as follows:

> "To sum up, my argument has been that having a right to life presupposes that one is capable of desiring to continue existing as a subject of experiences and other mental states. This in turn presupposes both that one has the concept of such a continuing entity and that one believes that one is oneself such an entity. So an entity that lacks such a consciousness of itself as a continuing subject of mental states does not have a right to life."

It would appear from this that the commentator, me in this case, is entitled to conclude that it is murder to do away with an adult, since they are capable of fulfilling these criteria, but not a fetus, and not even a very young child. For the latter, if they are killed in cold blood, it simply is not murder. What is it, then, pray tell, if it is not murder? We are left wondering how Tooley would characterize such events. All I can say is that Tooley had better keep his hands off of 6 month old babies, who are not "capable of desiring to continue existing as a subject of experiences and other mental states." In his view, if he killed one of them, this would not be murder since they are not yet human rights bearers. Happily, the law will very strongly take an alternative viewpoint.

It is time to offer a different theory, as a counterweight to Tooleyism. People have a right not to be murdered simply because they are human beings. Fetuses are very young human beings. Babies are intermediately aged human beings. Adults are well-developed human beings. It does not matter one iota of what thoughts, actions, they are capable. Consider the case of Terri Schiavo (Block 2011). She was a member of our species, but had no brain function. She, presumably, had no "consciousness of (her)self as a continuing subject of mental states." Forget about pulling the plug on her. Suppose someone, the proverbial Jones, went up to her hospitable bed and slit her throat, killing her. According to Tooley, Jones would not have been guilty of committing murder. Rather, his act would have been akin, one supposes, to a meat-cutter butchering a cow for steaks. No, desire is not all but irrelevant to being a rights-bearing entity, it is entirely irrelevant, as this example dramatically illustrates. I no longer desire this pair of socks of mine. But if you steal it from me before I can throw it out, you are still a thief. Terri Schiavo has no desires nor any potential for achieving them. It is still murder to kill her. If the fetus, or the small child has no rights – they may all be violated with impunity – then who bears the rights over such human beings? There is only one answer emanating from the libertarian philosophy: the guardian. But the guardian loses rights to be the guardian of the helpless infant the moment he does not protect him.

Tooley next moves to a refutation of the conservative position, and a defense of the liberal one. He proceeds as follows:

> "Many have felt that the conservative's position is more defensible than the liberal's because the conservative can point to the gradual and continuous development of an organism as it changes from a zygote to an adult human being. He is then in a position to argue that it is morally arbitrary for the liberal to draw a line at some point in this continuous process and to say that abortion is permissible before, but not after, that particular point. The liberal's reply would presumably be that the emphasis upon the continuity of the process is misleading. What the conservative is really doing is simply challenging the liberal to specify the properties a thing must have in order to be a person, and to show that the developing organism does acquire the properties at the point selected by the liberal. The liberal may then reply that the difficulty he has meeting this challenge should not be taken as grounds for rejecting his position. For the conservative cannot meet this challenge either; the conservative is equally unable to say what properties something must have if it is to have a right to life."

As a libertarian, I am no conservative. I have no brief for them, any more than I have for liberals.[2] However, fairness requires that I acknowledge they have by far the better position in this debate set up by our author. For it is by no means true that "the conservative is equally unable to say what properties something must have if it is to have a right to life." Au contraire, he has a perfectly good answer: all human beings have a right not to be murdered, and this applies to no member of any other species but ours. This can easily be demonstrated by the fact that when the lion kills the zebra, no one, not even the most impassioned vegetarian, nor animal rights advocate, accuses the former of being a murderer, and considers the latter to be a victim of this "crime." Were animals to have rights, this could hardly be the case.

Tooley continues his case against the conservative position:

> "... defenders of the view that abortion is always wrong have failed to face up to the question of the basic moral principles on which their position rests. They have been content to assert the wrongness of killing any organism, from a zygote on, if that organism is a member of the species Homo sapiens. But they have over- looked the point that this cannot be an acceptable basic moral principle, since difference in species is not in itself a morally relevant difference."

A "difference in species is not in itself a morally relevant difference"? This is problematic. If so, why does Tooley speak with equanimity about "it is not seriously wrong to kill a newborn kitten," from which, I deduce, that he himself would undertake such an action were there no home for these young cats. I do not know this man, but I doubt he has ever done away with any year-old baby. Why ever not, assuming he could get away with such an evil act?

But this author is not yet quite finished lambasting his conservative target. He avers, not unreasonably, that this position stands or falls on the basis of what he calls the "potentiality principle": yes the infant, or fetus, does not yet have quintessentially human characteristics, but, potentially he does, whereas the ape fetus does not. This is not totally unreasonable, but, it still falls on the rock of the Terri Schiavo case: she has no potential to lead a normal human life, and, yet, it would be plain and simple murder to shoot her to death while she is lying in her hospital bed.

---

[2] The position of the former aligns more with libertarianism in economic issues; with the latter on personal liberties. Neither, very much, on the third leg of political economy, foreign policy.

Nothing daunted, Tooley launches yet another powerful criticism of this potentiality principle:

"Suppose at some future time a chemical were to be discovered which when injected into the brain of a kitten would cause the kitten to develop into a cat possessing a brain of the sort possessed by humans, and consequently into a cat having all the psychological capabilities characteristic of adult humans. Such cats would be able to think, to use language, and so on. Now it would surely be morally indefensible in such a situation to ascribe a serious right to life to members of the species Homo sapiens without also ascribing it to cats that have undergone such a process of development: there would be no morally significant differences."

So far, so good. This cat is a potential Einstein, or Mozart, or Mises. All hats off to the inventor of this chemical. To Mr. Cat: welcome to the human race. You now have all the privileges and responsibilities of our species. Go thou and multiply. This "cat" would be akin to the cat-like human beings who play a role in movies such as Star Trek.

Continues our author:

"Secondly, it would not be seriously wrong to refain (sic) from injecting a newborn kitten with the special chemical, and to kill it instead. The fact that one could initiate a causal process that would transform a kitten into an entity that would eventually possess properties such that anything possessing them ipso facto has a serious right to life does not mean that the kitten has a serious right to life even before it has been subjected to the process of injection and transformation. The possibility of transforming kittens into persons will not make it any more wrong to kill newborn kittens than it is now."

Here Tooley and I part company. Think of these ordinary house-cats as young members of the Star Trek cat species. They would be miffed, they would take serious umbrage, at this philosopher murdering their progeny. These cats would have as many rights as any other person, for they would now be (potential) adult people, just like our human 2-year-olds. The possibility of transforming kittens into persons will indeed make it very much "more wrong to kill newborn kittens than it is now."

Now for our author's attempt to place a stake in the heart of the potentiality principle:

"… if it is not seriously wrong to destroy an injected kitten which will naturally develop the properties that bestow a right to life, neither can it be seriously wrong to destroy a member of Homo sapiens which lacks such properties, but will naturally come to have them. The potentialities are the same in both cases. The only difference is that in the case of a human fetus the potentialities have been present from the beginning of the organism's development, while in the case of the kitten they have been present only from the time it was injected with the special chemical. This difference in the time at which the potentialities were acquired is a morally irrelevant difference."

Tooley proves too much, far too much. Yes, as is his goal, he demonstrates, at least to his own satisfaction, that it is perfectly alright to kill the human fetus. It only has potentiality, not actuality. He also catches in his net the human infant. Infanticide, too, would be legally justified. But more. Consider the 10-year-old, or maybe even the 14-year-old. They, too, are not quite yet adult human beings. They, too, only have a potential to achieve that exalted status. They, too, should not be protected from murder, on Toolian grounds. If this is not a devastating reductio ad absurdum, then nothing is. This very creative "cat" example breaks up on the shoals of the sleeping, or comatose adult, who, also, has only the potential to "develop the properties that bestow a right to life." This author strives mightily to obviate this objection, but fails. If it is legally acceptable to kill the kitten, and the fetus and the infant and the very old person, then this applies, also, to the adult. Have we left anyone out? Hardly. I urge Professor Tooley never to go to sleep again. If he does, according to his own theory, he would be fair game to be killed. For while he is asleep, he only has the potential to be a thinking, acting, human being.

Consider the following reductio: I have just developed a magic "gun." It enables me to "shoot" any pregnant woman I want, and her fetus will immediately perish. There will be no physical harm to this adult person herself. According to Tooley, I should be allowed to employ my weapon in this evil, criminal, manner. But that would be anathema to any decent, just law.

States our author:

> "The point is merely that if it is seriously wrong to kill something, the reason cannot be that the thing will later acquire properties that in themselves provide something with a right to life."

This is an accurate summary of his position. But it is fatally undermined by the Terri Schiavo case, by my anti-pregnancy weapon, by the supposed justified murdering of young teenagers, by human adults who are asleep, and by the Star Trek (human) cat species.

Here is another attempt of Tooley's to make his case:

> "… a newborn baby does not possess the concept of a continuing self, any more than a newborn kitten possesses such a concept. If so, infanticide during a time interval shortly after birth must be morally acceptable."

Well, maybe it is "morally acceptable" at least insofar as some interpretations of this universe of discourse is concerned. But from a libertarian point of view, anyone acting on it would be breaking the law against murder, and should be prosecuted to the full extent of that law. Infanticide, indeed. Tooley had better stay away from the children of most parents. They might well take umbrage at this man. All I can say at this point is that I admire Tooley's courage and sense of logic. He does not shrink from even one of the most powerful reductios ad absurdum of his position. On the other hand, I strongly feel like shaking him by the shoulders, and thus pounding some sense into him. Perhaps I should refrain from doing so until I can catch him asleep.

He writes as follows:

> "… in the vast majority of cases in which infanticide is desirable, its desirability will be apparent within a short time after birth. Since it is virtually certain that an infant at such a stage of its development does not possess the concept of a continuing self, and thus does not possess a serious right to life, there is excellent reason to believe that infanticide is morally permissible in most cases where it is otherwise desirable. The practical moral problem can thus be satisfactorily handled by choosing some period of time, such as a week after birth, as the interval during which infanticide will be permitted. This interval could then be modified once psychologists have established the point at which a human organism comes to believe that it is a continuing subject of experiences and other mental states."

Why, ever, one week after birth? Surely, the two-year-old baby also does not "believe that (he) is a continuing subject of experiences and other mental states." He is too busy drooling and being incontinent. Tooley must have been a very precocious and mentally developed child, but as far as my own recollection is concerned, I didn't believe I was a continuing subject of experiences and other mental states until much later on in my life. Maybe, this sort of thing kicked in when I was eleven years old. If so, I would have been fair game for Tooley and his murderous minions up until that time.

Tooley ends on this note of animal liberation, or animal rights:

> "The troubling worry is whether adult animals belonging to species other than Homo sapiens may not also possess a serious right to life. For once one says that an organism can possess the concept of a continuing self, together with the belief that it is itself such an entity, without having any way of expressing that concept and that belief linguistically, one has to face up to the question of whether animals may not possess properties that bestow a serious right to life upon them. The suggestion itself is a familiar one, and one that most of us are accustomed to dismiss very casually. The line of thought advanced here suggests that this attitude may turn out to be tragically mistaken. Once one reflects upon the question of the basic moral principles involved in the ascription of a right to life to organisms, one may find himself driven to conclude that our everyday treatment of animals is morally indefensible, and that we are in fact murdering innocent persons."

This is more than highly troubling. Tooley faces with a certain equanimity the murder of young human beings, but is deeply concerned that we may possibly be committing an injustice to our animal colleagues. It is indeed logically possible, it is not a blatant self-contradiction, to suppose that pigs, porpoises, chimpanzees, "possess the concept of a continuing self, together with the belief that it is itself such an entity, without having any way of expressing that concept and that belief linguistically." But there is simply no evidence for this claim. Indeed, what indication we do have mitigates, heavily, against any such supposition. This philosopher's concern for the welfare of animals does him credit. His lack of concern for human beings leads in the very opposite direction.

A baby is born with no brain. He has not the slightest hope of attaining "... the concept of a self as a continuing subject of experiences and other mental states, and believes that it is itself such a continuing entity." So, when I shoot that brainless baby, I am not a murderer? I am not even any kind of a criminal? If I shot a tumor (someone else's), or a corpse (hopefully not mine, at least not yet), I would be a criminal, although not a murderer, but I cannot reconcile that with his viewpoint. Someone owns that tumor, someone owns that corpse. But if I shoot the baby to death, I'm an out and out murderer. I do not think Tooley's view can accommodate this conclusion. A human baby is born. He has no brain. He's kept alive by machines at his parent's, his guardian's, insistence. I go and shoot this baby to death, right there in his (not its) crib. Am I a murderer? According to Tooley, I am not. But of course I am. The determinations are made by the species, not by potential. The table in my office is not a human being, even though, who knows, it might one day wake up and become a rights bearing creature, thanks to Toolian table-drugs. It is not a logical contradiction to suppose that this is so. But that is irrelevant. That table is not human, the baby is.

Consider the following. A is in the act of injecting the cat-drug into a cat which will turn this feline into a human being with full rights. B stops A from doing so. We abstract from who owns the kitten. Maybe, we assume B is the owner of the cat? Is B justified in stopping A.? Suppose it is an unowned cat. This scenario is so far not determinative.

Instead, assume the cat has already been injected with this human-creating drug, but it will take nine months for it to do 100% of its work. However, the cat has been injected yesterday, and, already, he is slowly turning into a human being, much more than any other cat, in all of history. Would it now be alright for Tooley to do away with this "animal?" It is not at all as clear that it would, certainly not as clear as this author makes it out to be.

Why the difference? Perhaps it rests with the divergence between doing something, and refraining from doing something? Between killing and letting die. We are all, right now, allowing people to die in India, Africa, other poor areas. But we are not unjustifiably killing them, so we are not murderers. In like manner, there is a disanalogy in Tooley's very creative and otherwise brilliant example. All we need do with the human fetus is leave him alone; he will soon enough become a fully functioning human being. Whereas with the cat, we have to do something in order to render it into human form: we must inject it with this drug.

One tack to take is to grasp the bull by the horns and acquiesce in the notion that yes, henceforth, after the invention of Tooley's cat drug, every member of this species is now strictly off-limits. No more killing them at all, humanely or not. After all, they all have the potential to be functioning human beings. And the same can be said not only for fetuses, but also for very young post-born children. They cannot think, have purposes either, as can adult human beings. What is sauce for the cat is sauce for the 3-month old baby: hands off!

With the invention of Tooley's drug, we can now define two types of human beings: the plain, old, ordinary kind, of the sort that now reads essays of this type. And second, wait for it, cats. We now have the wherewithal to turn our furry friends into fellow creatures, and must therefore respect their rights.

Another response is to maintain that the criterion for bearing rights is not the ability to think, plan, engage in dialogue. No adult who is asleep, or in a coma, or senile, or severely mentally damaged can pass muster under that criterion, and, yet, it would be wildly inappropriate to excuse murder of such individuals. Rather, the benchmark should be bearing human DNA, which people have at all stages of their development right from the stage of the fertilized egg.

Then, there is the claim available to the evictionist that Tooley sets up a false analogy. His attempt at a reductio ad absurdum is that with the advent of the drug, the kitten is just as human as the fetus: they each have the same potential to become a functioning human being. But they do not. The analogy breaks down in that nothing more need be done to the zygote to allow it to develop into a rights bearing human being, except of course, the usual: food, oxygen, warmth, etc. The feline needs this too to survive, but it requires one more thing in addition: the magic drug. Of course, this is not a morally tinged requirement. For all we know, the baby might also need a drug to survive, albeit a different one, for example, penicillin. Here we must introduce the distinction between killing and letting die; between acting and failing to act. All of us are guilty of allowing people to die. There are starving people in the poorest areas of the globe. Some of us do something to stop this, but the demises continue. We, thus, even those who donate to this worthy cause, engage in the letting die process. Such people could have done even more to alleviate this scourge. But, clearly, we are not all murderers. Similarly, there is all the world of difference between the fertilized human egg and the cat: the former need not be acted upon in the manner necessary for the latter.

Reductio: newborn babies do not, either, satisfy Tooley's criterion for being a human being. They are totally dependent upon the help of others to stay alive. There is not even that much difference between them and a not-yet born fetus, aged one hour before delivery. Yes, the latter is totally dependent upon his mother for oxygen, food, blood circulation. But, a just-born baby, in difficulty, can avail himself of this support in a modern hospital.

One way to deal with Toomey's vivid cat example is to admit defeat and say, ok, I give up, all cats henceforth have rights, inoculated with the chemical or not. After all, every last one of them now has the potential to be coherent, to have all human facilities.

But we need not give into this argument. For the reason the baby, the sleeping, the comatose person has rights is not due merely and only to their potential. The latter might never wake up, after all. Yet, it would still be murder most foul to kill him. No, the reason we all have rights is because right now, whatever their present state, they are human beings, thus rights bearing entities. This is something that cats, even under Tooley's example, entirely lack. When and if he wakes them up, and their situation becomes human-like, then and only then will we be required to respect their rights.

I have been very critical of Tooley in this chapter. I must end by congratulating him, yet again, for his courage, for his creativity, for his brilliance. A lesser writer than myself[3] would have accused this great philosopher of "triggering him," demanded that his voice be shut down, that this essay of his be cancelled, would have claimed to have felt "unsafe," demanded that Tooley be fired from his academic post. Not I, not I. The very opposite. I know full well when I've been in an intellectual tussle with a first rate mind. Thanks to him, I shall never look at a cat in the same way that I had done before.

---

[3] Ahem, excuse me while I sprain my elbow patting myself on the back

References

Block, Walter E. 2011. Terri Schiavo: A Libertarian Analysis. *Journal of Libertarian Studies* 22: 527–536.

Hume, David. 1739. *A Treatise of Human Nature: Being an Attempt to Introduce the Experimental Method of Reasoning into Moral Subjects*. http://www.gutenberg.org/ebooks/4705; http://oll.libertyfund.org/?option=com_staticxt&staticfile=show.php%3Ftitle=342&Itemid=27

Tooley, Michael. 1972. Abortion and Infanticide. *Philosophy and Public Affairs* 2 (1): 37–65. https://eclass.uoa.gr/modules/document/file.php/PPP504/Michael%20Tooley%2C%20Abortion%20and%20infanticide.pdf

Correction to: Evictionism

Correction to:
W. E. Block, Evictionism,
https://doi.org/10.1007/978-981-16-5014-7

The book was inadvertently published with a typo error in the title that read "Evicitionism" whereas it should be "Evictionism". The title has been updated in the book.

The updated version of the book can be found at
https://doi.org/10.1007/978-981-16-5014-7

W. E. Block, *Evictionism*, https://doi.org/10.1007/978-981-16-5014-7_13

Bibliography

Anderson, Terry L., and Peter J. Hill. 1979. An American Experiment in Anarcho-Capitalism: The Not So Wild, Wild West. *Journal of Libertarian Studies* 3: 9–29.

———, eds. 1996. *The Privatization Process: A Worldwide Perspective*. Lanham: Rowman & Littlefield Publishers.

Bagus, Philipp. 2003. *The Commons and the Tragedy of Banking*, November 12. http://mises.org/story/1373

Bagus, Philipp, David Howden, and Walter E. Block. 2013. Deposits, Loans and Banking: Clarifying the Debate. *American Journal of Economics and Sociology* 72 (3): 627–644. http://onlinelibrary.wiley.com/doi/10.1111/ajes.12023/abstract; http://bastiat.mises.org/2013/07/fractional-reserve-banking-paper/

Barnett, Randy E. 1986. Contract Remedies and Inalienable Rights. *Social Philosophy and Policy* 4 (1, Autumn): 179–202.

———. 1988. *The Structure of Liberty: Justice and the Rule of Law*. Oxford: Clarendon Press.

———. 2007. *Libertarians and the War*, July 17. http://online.wsj.com/news/articles/SB118463507387568429

Barnett, Randy E., and John Hagel III, eds. 1977. *Assessing the Criminal*. Cambridge, MA: Ballinger.

Barnett, William II, and Walter E. Block. 2005a. In Defense of Fiduciary Media – A Comment; Or, What's Wrong with "Clown" Or Play Money?" *Quarterly Journal of Austrian Economics* 8(2, Summer): 55–69.

———. 2005b. Professor Tullock on Austrian Business Cycle Theory. *Advances in Austrian Economics* 8: 431–443

———. 2008. Time Deposits, Dimensions and Fraud. *Journal of Business Ethics* 88 (4, September): 711–716. http://www.walterblock.com/wp-content/uploads/2009/06/barnett-block_time-deposits-fraud-2009-1.pdf; http://www.springerlink.com/content/a881166702524r55/; http://blog.mises.org/archives/011398.asp; http://www.springerlink.com/content/a881166702524r55/fulltext.pdf?page=1; https://www.researchgate.net/publication/225634696_Time_Deposits_Dimensions_and_Fraud?ev=prf_pub; http://link.springer.com/article/10.1007%2Fs10551-008-9976-9

Baxendale, Tony. 2010. *Free Banking, the Balance Sheet and Contract Law Approach*, March 15. www.cobdencentre.org/2010/03/freebanking-the-balance-sheet-and-contract-law-approach/

Benn, S. 1973. Abortion, Infanticide, and Respect for Persons. In *The Problem of Abortion*, ed. J. Feinberg, 92–104. Belmont: Wadsworth.

Benson, Bruce L. 1989. Enforcement of Private Property Rights in Primitive Societies: Law Without Government. *The Journal of Libertarian Studies* IX (1, Winter): 1–26.

W. E. Block, *Evictionism*, https://doi.org/10.1007/978-981-16-5014-7

———. 1990. *The Enterprise of Law: Justice Without the State*. San Francisco: Pacific Research Institute for Public Policy.
———. 2002. *Justice Without Government: The Merchant Courts of Medieval Europe and Their Modern Counterparts*. Printed in ed. Beito, Gordon and Tabarrok, 127–150. The Voluntary City/Oakland: Choice, Community and Civil Society/The Independent Institute.
Beutler, B. 2011. *Rand Paul: I Have Less Choice in Toilets Than Women Have in Abortions*, March 10. http://tpmdc.talkingpointsmemo.com/2011/03/rand-paul-i-have-less-choice-in-toilets-than-women-have-in-abortions-video.phpble.html
Block, Walter E. 1969. Voluntary Slavery. *The Libertarian Connection* I (3, April): 9–11.
———. 1976. *Defending the Undefendable*. Auburn: Mises Institute.
———. 1977. Toward a Libertarian Theory of Abortion. *The Libertarian Forum* 10 (9, September): 6–8.
———. 1988. Rent-a-Womb Market. *Thunder Bay Ontario Daily*, June 26.
———. 1993. Drug Prohibition: A Legal and Economic Analysis. *Journal of Business Ethics* 12: 107–118.
———. 1994. Libertarianism vs. Libertinism. *The Journal of Libertarian Studies: An Interdisciplinary Review* 11 (1): 117–128.
———. 1998a. A Libertarian Case for Free Immigration. *Journal of Libertarian Studies: An Interdisciplinary Review* 13 (2, Summer): 167–186.
———. 1998b. Roads, Bridges, Sunlight and Private Property: Reply to Gordon Tullock. *Journal des Economistes et des Etudes Humaines* 8 (2/3, June–September): 315–326.
———. 2002–2003. Berman on Blackmail: Taking Motives Fervently. *Florida State University Business Review* 3 (1): 57–114.
———. 2004. Reply to Frank van Dun's 'Natural Law and the Jurisprudence of Freedom'. *Journal of Libertarian Studies* 18 (2, Spring): 65–72.
———. 2007. Secession. *Dialogue* 4: 1–14.
———. 2010. Van Dun on Freedom and Property: A Critique. *Libertarian Papers* 2 (4): 11.
———. 2015. The Trolley: A Libertarian Analysis. *Journal Etica e Politica/Ethics & Politics* XVII (2): 237–251.
Block, Walter E., and Matthew Block. 1996. Roads, Bridges, Sunlight and Private Property Rights. *Journal Des Economistes Et Des Etudes Humaines* VII (2/3, June–September): 351–362.
Block, Walter E., and Gene Callahan. 2003. Is There a Right to Immigration? A Libertarian Perspective. *Human Rights Review* 5 (1, October–December): 46–71.
Block, Walter E., and Bryan Caplan. 2008. *Walter E. Block versus Bryan Caplan on Fractional Reserve Banking*, November 1. www.lewrockwell.com/block/block110.html
Block, Walter E., and Kenneth M. Garschina. 1996. Hayek, Business Cycles and Fractional Reserve Banking: Continuing the De-Homoginization Process. *The Review of Austrian Economics* 9 (1, 1995): 77–94.
Block, Walter E., and John Humphries. 2008. *Humphries vs Block on Fractional Reserve Banking*, November 17. http://alsblog.wordpress.com/2008/11/17/fractional-reservebanking/
Block, Walter E., and Eric Posner. 2008. *Posner vs. Block on Fractional Reserve Banking*, November 29. www.lewrockwell.com/block/block114.html
Block, Walter E., Stephan Kinsella, and Roy Whitehead. 2006. The Duty to Defend Advertising Injuries Caused by Junk Faxes: An Analysis of Privacy, Spam, Detection and Blackmail. *Whittier Law Review* 27 (4): 925–949.
Boldrin, Michele, and David K. Levine. 2008. *Against Intellectual Monopoly*. Cambridge: Cambridge University Press. http://www.dklevine.com/general/intellectual/against.htm
Boonin-Vail, David. 1997. A Defense of 'A Defense of Abortion': On the Responsibility Objection to Thomson's Argument. *Ethics* 107 (2, January): 286–313.
Calabresi, Guido, and Douglas Melamed. 1972. Property Rules, Liability Rules, and Inalienability: One View of the Cathedral. *Harvard Law Review* 85 (6, April): 1089–1128.
Callahan, Gene. 2001. *De Gustibus Non Est Disputandum*, April 27. http://mises.org/daily/666

Chomsky, Noam. 2011. *Noam Chomsky on US Libertarian Party*, November 24. http://www.youtube.com/watch?v=gbL3zRgZUBo

Cobin, J. 1998. Abortion Policy and the Market. *Journal of Interdisciplinary Studies* 15: 79–98.

Copple, Roger. 2010. *Noam Chomsky, Libertarians, Intentional Communities, and the Venus Project*, June 11. http://disinfo.com/2010/06/noam-chomsky-libertariansintentional-communities-and-the-venus-project/

Correa, Felipe. 2007. *Des mêmes auteurs The Libertarian Socialist Thought of Noam Chomsky*. http://www.fondation-besnard.org/article.php3?id_article=581

Cuzan, Alfred G. 1979. Do We Ever Really Get Out of Anarchy? *The Journal of Libertarian Studies* 3 (2, Summer): 151–158.

Davidson, Laura. 2008. *Fractional Reserve Banking Is Indeed Fraudulent*, November 17. www.lewrockwell.com/orig9/davidson-l1.html

Davidson, Laura, and Walter E. Block. 2011. The Case Against Fiduciary Media: Ethics Is the Key. *The Journal of Business Ethics*. 98 (3): 505–511.

Dawkins, R. 1976/1989. *The Selfish Gene*. New York: Oxford University Press.

Delkeskamp, Corinna. 1977. Medicine, Science, and Moral Philosophy: David Hartley's Attempt at Reconciliation. *Journal of Medicine and Philosophy* 2 (2): 162–176.

DeMarco, D. 2003. Peter Singer: Architect of the Culture of Death. *Social Justice Review* 94 (9–10): 154–157.

Demsetz, Harold. 1979. Ethics and Efficiency in Property Rights Systems. In: *Time, Uncertainty and Disequilibrium: Explorations of Austrian Themes*, ed. Mario Rizzo. Lexington: D.C.Heath and Co. http://tinyurl.com/lypvgl

DiLorenzo, Thomas J., and Walter E. Block. 2017. *An Austro-Libertarian Critique of Public Choice*. Addleton: Academic Publishers.

Dyke, Jeremiah. 2009. No Compromise: A Rejoinder to Block and Whiteheads' (sic) Compromising the Uncompromisable: A Private Property Rights Approach to Resolving the Abortion Controversy. *Libertarian Papers* 1: 1–17.

———. 2010. *Property Rights and Whale Wars*, March 18. http://mises.org/daily/4175

Ehrlich, Isaac. 1975. The Deterrent Effect of Capital Punishment – A Question of Life and Death. *American Economic Review* 65 (3, June): 397–417.

Engelhardt, H. Tristram, Jr. 1977. Splitting the Brain, Dividing the Soul, Being of Two Minds: An Editorial Concerning Mind-Body Quandaries in Medicine. *The Journal of Medicine and Philosophy* 2 (2): 89–100.

———. 1995. *The Foundations of Bioethics*. 2nd ed. Oxford: Oxford University Press.

Epstein, Richard. 1985. Why Restrain Alienation. *Columbia Law Review* 85: 970.

Epstein, Richard, and Walter E. Block. 2005. Debate on Eminent Domain. *NYU Journal of Law & Liberty* 1 (3): 1144–1169. www.nyujll.org/articles/Vol.%201%20No.%203/Vol.%201%20No.%2

Erde, Edmund L. 1977. Mind-Body and Malady. *Journal of Medicine and Philosophy* 2: 177–190.

Evers, Williamson. 1977. Toward a Reformulation of the Law of Contracts. *Journal of Libertarian Studies* 1 (Winter): 3–13. http://mises.org/journals/jls/1_1/1_1_2.pdf

———. 1978a. The Law of Omissions and Neglect of Children. *The Journal of Libertarian Studies* 2 (1, Winter): 1–10.

———. 1978b. Rawls and Children. *The Journal of Libertarian Studies* 2 (2, Summer): 109–114.

Feinberg, J. 1986. Abortion. In *Matters of Life and Death: New Introductory Essays in Moral Philosophy*, ed. T. Regan. New York: Random House.

Feldman, F. 1992. *Confrontations with the Reaper: A Philosophical Study of the Nature and Value of Death*. New York: Oxford University Press.

Fielding, Karl T. 1978. The Role of Personal Justice in Anarcho-Capitalism. *The Journal of Libertarian Studies* 2 (3, Fall): 239–242.

Fleming, Thomas. 2002. Perspective: Abuse Your Illusions. *Chronicles*, January. www.chroniclesmagazine.org/Chronicles/January2002/0102Fleming.htm; http://tinyurl.com/dh79a

Friedman, David. 1979. *Private Creation and Enforcement of Law: A Historical*. www.daviddfriedman.com/Academic/Iceland/Iceland.html

———. 1989. *The Machinery of Freedom: Guide to a Radical Capitalism*. 2nd ed. La Salle: Open Court.

Gordon, David. 1999. Private Property's Philosopher. *The Mises Review* 5 (1, Spring): 1–7.

Gwartney, James, Robert W. Lawson, and Walter E. Block. 1996. *Economic Freedom of the World, 1975-1995*. Vancouver: Tthe Fraser Institute.

Hanke, Steve H., ed. 1987. *Privatization and Development*. San Francisco: Institute for Contemporary Studies.

———. 2008. Banking Crises: Plus Ça Change… *GlobeAsia*, November, 168–169. www.freemarketfoundation.com/Hanke%5CBanking%20Crises--

Hayek, Friedrich A. 1979. *The Counter-Revolution of Science*. 2nd ed. Indianapolis: Liberty Press.

Hentoff, Nat. 1986. *The Indivisible Fight for Life*. http://groups.csail.mit.edu/mac/users/rauch/nvp/consistent/indivisible.html

Hoppe, Hans-Hermann. 1989. *A Theory of Socialism and Capitalism: Economics, Politics and Ethics*. Boston: Kluwer.

———. 1994. How Is Fiat Money Possible? Or, The Devolution of Money and Credit. *The Review of Austrian Economics* 7 (2): 49–74.

———. 1998. The Case for Free Trade and Restricted Immigration. *The Journal of Libertarian Studies* 13 (2, Summer): 221–233.

———. 2001. *Democracy – The God That Failed: The Economics and Politics of Monarchy, Democracy, and Natural Order*. Rutgers University: Transaction Publishers.

———. 2003. National Defense and the Theory of Externalities, Public Goods and Clubs. In *The Myth of National Defense: Essays on the Theory and History of Security Production*, ed. Hans-Hermann Hoppe. Auburn: Mises Institute.

———. 2006. *The Economics and Ethics of Private Property: Studies in Political Economy and Philosophy*, 2nd ed. Auburn: Ludwig von Mises Institute. http://mises.org/books/economics-ethics.pdf

Hoppe, Hans-Hermann, and Walter E. Block. 2002. Property and Exploitation. *International Journal of Value-Based Management* 15 (3): 225–236. http://www.mises.org/etexts/property-exploitation.pdf

Hoppe, Hans-Hermann, Guido Hulsmann, and Walter E. Block. 1998. Against Fiduciary Media. *Quarterly Journal of Austrian Economics* 1 (1): 19–50. www.mises.org/journals/qjae/pdf/qjae1_1_2.pdf

Huebert, J. 2010. *Libertarianism Today*. Santa Barbara: Praeger.

Huerta de Soto, Jesús. 1995. A Critical Analysis of Central Banks and Fractional-Reserve Free Banking from the Austrian Perspective. *The Review of Austrian Economics* 8 (2): 25–38.

———. 1998. A Critical Note on Fractional-Reserve Free Banking. *The Quarterly Journal of Austrian Economics* 1 (4): 25–49.

———. 2001. A Critical Note on Fractional Reserve Free Banking. *The Quarterly Journal of Austrian Economics* 1 (4, Fall): 34–35.

———. 2006. *Money, Bank Credit and Economic Cycles*. Auburn: Ludwig von Mises Institute.

———. 2010. *Economic Recessions, Banking Reform, and the Future of Capitalism*. http://mises.org/daily/4817

Hülsmann, Jorg Guido. 1996. Free Banking and the Free Bankers. *The Review of Austrian Economics* 9 (1): 3–53.

———. 2000. Banks Cannot Create Money. *The Independent Review: A Journal of Political Economy* 5 (1, Summer): 101–110. www.independent.org/pdf/tir/tir_05_1_hulsman.pdf

———. 2002a. Free Banking and the Free Bankers. *Review of Austrian Economics* 9 (1): 3–53. www.mises.org/journals/rae/pdf/rae9_1_1.pdf

———. 2002b. Free Banking Fractional Reserves: Reply to Pascal Salin. *Review of Austrian Economics* 1 (3). www.mises.org/journals/qjae/pdf/qjae1_3_8.pdf

———. 2003. Has Fractional-Reserve Banking Really Passed the Market Test? *Independent Review* 7/3 (Winter): 399–422. www.independent.org/publications/tir/article.asp?a=90

———. 2008. *The Ethics of Money Production*. Auburn: Ludwig von Mises Institute.
Kant, Immanuel. 1963. *Lectures on Ethics*. Trans. L. Infeld. New York: Harper.
Kaufman, Bill. 1992. The Child Labor Amendment Debate of the 1920's; Or, Catholics and Mugwumps and Farmers. *The Journal of Libertarian Studies* 10 (2, Fall): 139–170.
Keeler, D.E. 1981. Bearing Witness: Should You Be Forced? *Reason* 22: 42–43.
Kinsella, N. Stephan. 1992. Estoppel: A New Justification for Individual Rights. *Reason Papers* (17, Fall): 61.
———. 1994. The Undeniable Morality of Capitalism. *St. Mary's Law Journal* 25: 1419.
———. 1996a. Punishment and Proportionality: The Estoppel Approach. *The Journal of Libertarian Studies* 12 (1, Spring): 51–74. http://www.mises.org/journals/jls/12_1/12_1_3.pdf
———. 1996b. New Rationalist Directions in Libertarian Rights Theory. *Journal of Libertarian Studies* 12 (2): 313–326.
———. 1997. A Libertarian Theory of Punishment and Rights. *30 Loy. L.A. L. Rev*, 607–645.
———. 1998–1999. Reply to George Smith: A Victim's Right to Punish. *Journal of Libertarian Studies* 14 (1, Winter): 79–93.
———. 2001. Against Intellectual Property. *Journal of Libertarian Studies* 15 (2, Winter): 1–53. http://www.mises.org/journals/jls/15_2/15_2_1.pdf
Kirzner, Israel M. 1973. *Competition and Entrepreneurship*. Chicago: University of Chicago Press.
Kors, A., and H. Silverglate. 1998. *The Shadow University: The Betrayal of Liberty on America's Campuses*. New York: The Free Press.
Krawiec, Kimberly D. 2009. *Price and Pretense in the Baby Market. Baby Markets: Money, Morals, and the Neopolitics of Choice*. Cambridge University Press. https://scholarship.law.duke.edu/cgi/viewcontent.cgi?referer=&httpsredir=1&article=5507&context=faculty_scholarship&preview_mode=1&z=1360332415
Kronman, Anthony. 1983. Paternalism and the Law of Contracts. *92 Yale Law Journal*. http://www.lewrockwell.com/blog/lewrw/archives/58459.html
Kuflik, Arthur. 1984. The Inalienability of Autonomy. *Philosophy and Public Affairs* 13 (4, Fall): 271–298.
———. 1986. The Utilitarian Logic of Inalienable Rights. *Ethics* 97 (October): 75–87.
Landes, Elizabeth, and Richard A. Posner. 1978. The Economics of the Baby Shortage. *7 Journal of Legal Studies* 323.
Locke, John. 1955. *Second Treatise of Civil Government*. Chicago: Henry Regnery.
Long, Roderick. 1994–1995. Slavery Contracts and Inalienable Rights: A Formulation. *Formulations* (Winter). http://libertariannation.org/a/f22l1.html
Long, R.T. 2003. Austro-libertarian Themes in Early Confucianism. *The Journal of Libertarian Studies* 17: 35–62.
Long, Roderick. 2004. *Libertarian Anarchism: Responses to Ten Objections*. http://www.lewrockwell.com/long/long11.html
Machan, Tibor R. 2010. Rights May Never Be in Conflict. *The Daily Bell*. www.thedailybell.com/1088/TiborMachan-Rights-May-Never-Be-In-Conflict.html
Mack, Eric. 1995. The Self-Ownership Proviso: A New and Improved Lockean Proviso. *Social Philosophy and Policy* 12 (1, Winter).
MacQueen, Ken. 2010. A Piece of Their Mind. *Maclean's Magazine*.
Marquis, Don B. 1994. A Future Like Ours and the Concept of Person: A Reply to Mcinerney and Paske. In *The Abortion Controversy: A Reader*, ed. L.P. Pojman and F.J. Beck, 354–368. Boston: Jones and Bartlett.
———. 1995. Fetuses, Futures and Values: A Reply to Shirley. *Southwest Philosophy Review* II: 263–265.
May 31. http://szatyor2693.wordpress.com/2010/05/29/column-onwhy-basic-rights-cannot-conflict/
McClarey, D.R. 2011. Rand Paul, Abortion and Toilets. *The American Catholic*, March 10. Retrieved from http://the-american-catholic.com/2011/03/11/rand-paul-abortion-and-toilets/
McConnell, Terrance. 1984. The Nature and Basis of Inalienable Rights. *Law and Philosophy* 3 (1): 25–59.

———. 1996. The Inalienable Right of Conscience: A Madisonian Argument. *Social Theory and Practice* 22 (3, Fall): 397–416.

McElroy, W. 2005. *Will Science Trump Politics in Resolving Abortion Debate?* [Online]. Available: http://lewrockwell.com/mcelroy/mcelroy91.html. Accessed 12 Mar 2014.

McInerney, P. 1990. Does a Fetus Already Have a Future like Ours? *Journal of Philosophy* 87: 264–268.

Mill, John Stuart. 1947 [1859]. *On Liberty*, 36. Northbrook: Ahm Publishing. www.bartleby.com/130/

Moore, Stephen, and Stuart Butler, eds. 1987. *Privatization*. Washington, DC: Heritage Foundation.

Morris, Herbert. 1968. Persons and Punishment. *The Monist* 52 (4, October): 475–501. http://www.law-lib.utoronto.ca/bclc/crimweb/bboard/personsandpunishment.pdf

Murphy, Robert P. 2002. *Chaos Theory: Two Essays on Market Anarchy*. New York: RJ Communications LLC.

———. 2005. *But Wouldn't Warlords Take Over?* July 7. http://www.mises.org/story/1855

———. 2011. *The Fractional-Reserve Banking Question*, June 14. http://mises.org/daily/4499

Noonan, J. 1970. An Almost Absolute Value in History. In *The Morality of Abortion*, ed. J. Noonan. Cambridge, MA: Harvard University Press.

Norcross, A. 1990. Killing, Abortion, and Contraception: A Reply to Marquis. *Journal of Philosophy* 87: 268–277.

North, Gary. 2009. *What Is Money? Part 5: Fractional Reserve Banking*, November 8. http://www2.macleans.ca/2010/11/02/a-piece-oftheir-mind/; http://www.lewrockwell.com/north/north769.html

Nozick, Robert. 1981. *Philosophical Explanations*. Cambridge, MA: Harvard University Press.

Olson, Charles B. 1979. Law in Anarchy. *Libertarian Forum* XII (6, November-December): 4. http://64.233.167.104/u/Mises?q=cache:gFT18_ZusWoJ:www.mises.org/journals/lf/1979/1979_11-12.pdf+two+teeth+for+a+tooth&hl=en&ie=UTF-8; p. 4; http://64.233.167.104/u/Mises?q=cache:gFT18_ZusWoJ:www.mises. Papers 3 (article no. 6).

Osterfeld, David. 1989. Anarchism and the Public Goods Issue: Law, Courts and the Police. *The Journal of Libertarian Studies* 9 (1, Winter): 47–68. www.mises.org/journals/jls/9_1/9_1_3.pdf

Parish, R. 1996. Killing People: Peter Singer on Life and Death. *Agenda* 3 (3): 359–366.

Paske, G. 1994. Abortion and the Neo-natal Right to Life: A Critique of Marquis's Futurist Argument. In *The Abortion Controversy: A Reader*, ed. L.P. Pojman and F.J. Beck, 343–353. Boston: Jones and Bartlett.

Peden, Joseph R. 1977. Property Rights in Celtic Irish Law. *The Journal of Libertarian Studies* 1 (2, Spring): 81–96.

Philmore J. 1982. The Libertarian Case for Slavery: A Note on Nozick. *Philosophical Forum* 14: 43–58. http://cog.kent.edu/lib/Philmore1/Philmore1.htm. Accessed 12 Mar 2014.

Pirie, Madson. 1986. *Privatization in Theory and Practice*. London: Adam Smith Institute. https://www.adamsmith.org/research/privatization-in-theory-and-practice

Polleit, Thorsten. 2010. *The Faults of Fractional-Reserve Banking*, December 23. http://mises.org/daily/4880

Poole, Robert. 1976. *Cutting Back City Hall*. New York: Reason Press.

Posner, Richard A. 1987. *The Regulation of the Market in Adoptions*. 67 B.U. L. Rev. 60. https://chicagounbound.uchicago.edu/cgi/viewcontent.cgi?article=2903&context=journal_articles

Presley, Sharon, and Robert, Cooke (aka Morgan Edwards). 1979. *The Right to Abortion: A Libertarian Defense*. Association of Libertarian Feminists Discussion Paper. http://www.alf.org/abortion.php

Puccetti, R. 1997. Sperry on Consciousness: A Critical Appreciation. *Journal of Medicine and Philosophy* 2 (2): 127–144.

Radin, Margaret Jane. 1986a. Time, Possession and Alienation. *64 Washington University Law Quarterly* 64 (3): 739.

———. 1986b. Residential Rent Control. *Philosophy and Public Affairs* 15: 350–380.

———. 1987. Market-Inalienability. *Harvard Law Review* 100 (8, June): 1849–1937.

Rawls, John. 1971. *A Theory of Justice*. Oxford: Oxford University Press.
Reinach, Adolf. 1913. *The Apriori Foundations of the Civil Law*. Trans. John F. Crosby.
———. 1998. On the Concept of Causality in the Criminal Code. *Criminal Law*. Trans. Berit Brogaard.
Reisman, George. 1996. *Capitalism*, 954–963. Ottawa: Jameson Books.
———. 2009. *A Pro-Free-Market Program for Economic Recovery*, November 20. http://mises.org/daily/3870
Richman, Sheldon. 1978. Slaves Contracts and the Inalienable Will. *The Libertarian Forum*, July–August, 4–5. http://mises.org/journals/lf/1978/1978_07-08.pdf
Rizzo, Mario J., and G. Whitman. 2003. The Camel's Nose Is in the Tent: Rules, Theories and Slippery Slopes. *UCLA Law Review* 51: 539–592.
Rothbard, Murray N. 1956. *Toward a Reconstruction of Utility and Welfare Economics*. Reprinted in The Logic of Action, vol. I, 225–227. Lyme: Edward Elgar.
———. [1963] 1975. *America's Great Depression*. Kansas City: Sheed and Ward.
———. 1977a. Punishment and Proportionality. In *Assessing the Criminal: Restitution, Retribution, and the Legal Process*, ed. R.E. Barnett and J. Hagel III, 259–270. Cambridge, MA: Ballinger Publishing Co.
———. 1977b. Should Abortion Be a Crime? The Abortion Question Once More. *Libertarian Forum* 10: 2–3.
———. 1990. *What Has Government Done to Our Money?* Auburn: Ludwig von Mises Institute. www.mises.org/rothbard/rothmoney.pdf
———. 1991a. On Denationalizing the Courts. Rothbard-Rockwell Report. Burlingame: Center for Libertarian Studies 2 (10, October).
———. 1991b. The Case for a 100 Percent Gold Dollar. In *Search of a Monetary Constitution*, ed. Leland B. Yeager, 94–136. Cambridge, MA/Auburn: Harvard University Press/Ludwig von Mises Institute.
———. 1993. *Man, Economy, and State*. Auburn: Ludwig von Mises Institute.
———. 2005. *The Heresy of Prudence*. http://www.lewrockwell.com/rothbard/rothbard65.html
Sacred Congregation for the Propagation of the Faith, Declaration on Euthanasia (Vatican City, 1980).
Salerno, Joseph T. 2010. *White Contra Mises on Fiduciary Media*, May 14. http://mises.org/daily/4389
Salter, J. 2014. Premature Babies: How 24 Week-Old Babies Are Now Able. *Telegaraph*.
Sanger, Carol. 2007. *Developing Markets in Baby-Making: In the Matter of Baby M*. 30 Harv. J. L. & Gender 67. http://www.telegraph.co.uk/women/womenshealth/11121592/Premature-babies-How-24-week-old-babies-are-nowable-to-survive.html
Savas, E.S. 1987. *Privatization*. Chatham: Chatham House Publishers.
———. 2000. *Privatization and Public – Private Partnerships*. Chatham: Chatham House Publishers.
Sechrest, Larry J. 1999. Rand, Anarchy, and Taxes. *The Journal of Ayn Rand Studies* 1 (1, Fall): 87–105.
Shaffer, Jerome A. 1977. Personal Identity: The Implications of Brain Bisection and Brain Transplants. *Journal of Medicine and Philosophy* 2 (2): 147–161.
Shaub, William E. 2011. Revisiting Chomsky's Views on Ron Paul. *The Firebrand Magazine*, June 11. http://thefbm.com/2011/06/10/revisiting-noam-chomskys-views-onron-paul/
Shirley, E.S. 1995. Marquis' Argument Against Abortion: A Critique. *Southwest Philosophy Review* II: 79–89.
Singer, P. 1996. *Rethinking Life and Death: The Collapse of Our Traditional Ethics*. St. Martin's Griffin.
Smith, George. 1996. A Killer's Right to Life. *Liberty* 10 (2, November): 46–54.
———. 1997. Inalienable Rights? *Liberty* 10 (6, July): 51.
Sneed, John D. 1977. Order Without Law: Where Will Anarchists Keep the Madmen? *The Journal of Libertarian Studies* 1 (2, Spring): 117–124.

Sperry, R.W. 1977. Forebrain Commissurotomy and Conscious Awareness. *Journal of Medicine and Philosophy* 2 (2): 101–126.

———. 1997. Reply to Professor Puccetti. *Journal of Medicine and Philosophy* 2 (2): 145–146.

Spinelli, M.G. 2004. Maternal Infanticide Associated with Mental Illness: Prevention and the Promise of Saved Lives. *American Journal of Psychiatry* 161 (9): 1548–1557.

Spooner, Lysander. (1870) 1966. *No Treason*. Larkspur: Ralph Myles. http://www.lysanderspooner.org/notreason.htm

Staib, Eric M. 2010. *Economics of Adoption: A Libertarian Approach*, February 24. http://mises.org/daily/4106

Steinbock, B. 1992. *Life Before Birth: The Moral and Legal Status of Embryos and Fetuses*. New York: Oxford University Press.

Steiner, Hillel. 2013. Directed Duties and Inalienable Rights. *Ethics* 123 (January): 230–244.

Stigler, George J., and Gary S. Becker. 1977. De Gustibus Non Est Disputandum. *American Economic Review* 67: 76–90.

Stringham, Edward. 1998–1999. Justice Without Government. *Journal of Libertarian Studies* 14 (1, Winter): 53–77.

Stroup, Richard. 1988. Buying Misery with Federal Land. *Public Choice* 57: 69–77.

Szasz, Thomas Stephen. 1961. *The Myth of Mental Illness; Foundations of a Theory of Personal Conduct*. New York: Hoeber-Harper.

———. 1963. *Law, Liberty, and Psychiatry; An Inquiry into the Social Uses of Mental Health Practices*. New York: Macmillan.

———. 1979. The Lying Truths of Psychiatry. *The Journal of Libertarian Studies* 3 (2, Summer): 121–139.

Tannehill, Morris, and Linda. 1984. *The Market for Liberty*. New York: Laissez Faire Books.

Thomson, Judith Jarvis. 1986. *Rights, Restitution and Risk*. Cambridge: Harvard University Press.

———. 1991. Self-Defense. *Philosophy and Public Affairs* 20 (4, Autumn): 283–310.

Tinsley, Patrick. 1998–1999. With Liberty and Justice for All: A Case for Private Police. *Journal of Libertarian Studies* 14(1, Winter): 95–100. http://www.mises.org/journals/jls/14_1/14_1_5.pdf

Touchstone, Kathleen. 2010. Rand, Rothbard, and Rights Reconsidered. *Libertarian Papers* 2: Art. No. 18. http://libertarianpapers.org/articles/2010/lp-2-18.pdf

Tribe, L.H. 1990. *Abortion: The Clash of Absolutes*. New York: Norton.

Tullock, Gordon. 1996. Comment on 'Roads, Bridges, Sunlight and Private Property', by Walter E. Block and Matthew Block. *Journal des Economistes et des Etudes Humaines* 7 (4, December): 589–592. University Press, 17–18.

Warren, M.A. 1973. On the Moral and Legal Status of Abortion. *The Monist* 57: 43–61.

Watkins, Michael. 2006. Re-reading Thomson: Thomson's Unanswered Challenge. Journal of Libertarian Studies 20 (4, Fall): 41–59. https://mises.org/journals/jls/20_4/20_4_3.pdf

Wells, H.G. 1895. *The Time Machine*. http://www.marxists.org/reference/archive/hgwells/works/1890s/time/

White, Lawrence H. 1978. Privatization of Municipally-Provided Services. *The Journal of Libertarian Studies* 2 (2, Summer): 187–197.

Whitman, G., and Mario J. Rizzo. 2007. Paternalist Slopes. *NYU Journal of Law & Liberty* 2 (3): 411–443.

Williams, M.E. 2011. Rand Paul Is Pro-choice for Toilets: The Senator Gives a Stunning Rant Against Energy Efficiency – And Reproductive Choice. *Salon*, March 11. http://www.salon.com/entertainment/tv/feature/2011/03/11/rand_paul_anti_choice_pro_toilet

Wittman, D. 1980. 1st Come, 1st Served – An Economic Analysis of Coming to the Nuisance. *The Journal of Legal Studies* 9 (3): 557–568.

Woolridge, William C. 1970. *Uncle Sam the Monopoly Man*. New Rochelle: Arlington House.

Zwolinski, M. 2017. Book Review: Loren Lomasky, Rights Angles. *Notre Dame Philosophical Review*. Available at: http://ndpr.nd.edu/news/rights-angles/

The manufacturer's authorised representative in the EU is Springer Nature Customer Service Centre GmbH, Europaplatz 3, 69115 Heidelberg, Germany. If you have any concerns regarding our products, please contact ProductSafety@springernature.com

Printed and bound by CPI Group (UK) Ltd, Croydon, CR0 4YY
30/09/2026
02225234-0019